WANDERING

AND

HOME

Eyal Amiran

WANDERING
AND
HOME

Beckett's Metaphysical Narrative

for Steve and
peris,
these leaves by your grace —
love, Eyal

The Pennsylvania State University Press
University Park, Pennsylvania

Excerpts from *Collected Poems in English and French* (1977) by Samuel Beckett are reproduced with permission by Grove Press, Inc.

Library of Congress Cataloging-in-Publication Data

Amiran, Eyal.
    Wandering and home : Beckett's metaphysical narrative / Eyal Amiran.
        p.   cm.
    Includes bibliographical references (p.   ) and index.
    ISBN 0-271-00860-1
    1. Beckett, Samuel, 1906–89—Knowledge—Literature. 2. Beckett,
Samuel, 1906–89—Philosophy. 3. Influence (Literary, artistic,
etc.) 4. Neoplatonism in literature. 5. Metaphysics in literature.
6. Philosophy in literature. I. Title.
PR6003.E282Z5632   1993
848'.91409—dc20   91-47504
                                                                    CIP

This book is composed in Bembo.

Published by The Pennsylvania State University Press,
Suite C, Barbara Building, University Park, PA 16802-1003

It is the policy of The Pennsylvania State University Press to use acid-free paper for the first printing of all clothbound books. Publications on uncoated stock satisfy the minimum requirements of American National Standard for Information Sciences—Permanence of Paper for Printed Library Materials, ANSI Z39.48–1984.

Contents

Acknowledgments

I thank Michael Levenson and Robert Langbaum for their careful reading and encouragement. Daniel Albright stimulated first ideas. H. Porter Abbott, Gordon Braden, Daniel Kinney, Keith Monley, James Nohrnberg, Charles Rossman, Nathan Scott, Jr., and Rei Terada helped with all or part of the book. My thanks to the Departments of English at the University of Virginia, the College of William and Mary, and North Carolina State University for financial support; a Forstmann fellowship from the UVA Society of Fellows allowed me to study at the Reading University Library and to meet Beckett in Paris. At Reading, James Knowlson and Michael Bott helped with matters archival. John Unsworth provided electronic know-how. My family supported the enterprise from the start. Edoh read *Watt*. Susan Schultz read the manuscript and helped in countless ways.

Part of Chapter 2 appeared as an essay in the *Journal of Beckett Studies*.

Introduction

Samuel Beckett has written an epic in pieces, abstract and lyrical without compromise. Beckett belongs in the modern romantic tradition of self-projection and self-reconstruction; he also appropriates through his vision a reading of the past, looking back through and not beyond his tradition. Not a Penelope-writer, one whose thread unravels its own fabric, he uses the particular failures of phenomenological thinking to build a larger argument. Frustration and failure are important in Beckett, though it is not my purpose in this study to make that point again; these frustrations, after all, have been the focus of much critical work. Frustration and failure in Beckett, I argue, are made to serve a larger, sustained argument. Beckett's fiction is consistently organized and ordered in its development: it does not subvert the Western metaphysical tradition but participates in it, appropriating in particular the Neoplatonic tradition, its interpretations in Augustine and Dante (among others), and its descent in the cosmological worldview of his immediate precursors, Yeats and Joyce. His work strives for a governing and lyrical unity, for simplification through intensity, as Yeats puts it, by rejecting the world/mind division; it tests and reaffirms this reconciliation of the All to itself, its many parts embraced in a unity of being worthy of Beckett's collected works. Figure and ground, self and other, wandering and home, converse inextricably with each other to form the whole. It is a work governed through and through by rules of reconciliation and continuity, synthesis and differentiation. These paired terms are not interchangeable; rather, they express consistently different aspects of Beckett's vision of a whole made of particulars. Beckett's fiction not only portrays these ideas but is ruled by them and develops according to them. As it develops, it reenacts the subject's metaphysical journey in the life cycle, forming a long philosophical narrative. Beckett's narrative, which I follow here, argues by its unfolding as it unfolds its argument.

Beckett's fiction is systematic in that it depends on coherent abstraction—a consistent logic—to organize it, and because it develops, with some looseness in the late, short fiction, as a single encompassing narrative. It portrays life as a double cycle much like Yeats's chiasmic gyres: Beckett's subjects travel this course in their ascent to unity and in their descent back to the particular world. If there were an adequate image of this cycle, it might be the 8/∞ Beckett uses in *The Way*. Beckett pursues this modern neoclassical quest first from the subject's narrow, agonized perspective and then from that of a detached, anthropological understanding of the whole. Abstract transpersonality characterizes his system. As it unfolds, and as it assimilates his early proto-Proustian formulations about perception and desire to the larger interpretative framework of Neoplatonic metaphysics, his traveling subjects lose their human particularity: the system uses its servants indifferently and interchangeably.

This study alternates between chapters which consider the intertextual construction of Beckett's fiction and those which consider the fiction closely as a narrative that unfolds a larger story. These depend on each other and, I hope, help make the overall argument more compelling.

How much of this argument did Mr. Beckett see? Or was he blind like Milton, and working, as he once said, like a mole in a molehill? It is hard to call him ignorant of his work's unfolding narrative, in light of the evidence—quotations, allusions, consistency, dialogues with the living and the dead, lecture and production notes. And while he often protests his ignorance, he also protests his knowledge, in his fiction: "And if I were to tell you," he writes in *Molloy* about the bees' dance, "what these levels were, and what the relations between them, for I had measured them with care, you would not believe me. And this is not the moment to jeopardize my credit" (169). Elsewhere he suggests how the artist can dream up the bees' dance and still blame it on the bees: "The art of combining is not my fault. It's a curse from above. For the rest I would suggest not guilty" (*Enough* 54). On the other hand, the Beckett I allude to in these pages personifies an agency in the text, unless specified otherwise, and the interest I find in this Beckett lies most in the way his fiction works. Allusions and quotations are one thing; the logic and development of the narrative is a related, but other, matter. It is good to have both in Beckett's text. Beckett's art is moving not because of its clearsighted sense of the immediate scandal but because it imagines a world that is subject to the iron rule of abstraction. Vladimir and Estragon in *Waiting for Godot*, some say, are spared metaphysical desire (Girard 257–58, Robbe-Grillet), but what *else* do they desire? Beckett's work is in many ways about desire, about the enormous gaps in our understanding—gaps like the infinite cold spaces evoked in the "Ithaca" chapter of *Ulysses*—which one can see but cannot bridge. Beckett's metaphysical narrative has made something lyrical and precise of that desire.

A note about citation in the text:

It is often difficult to tell about a work of Beckett's fiction whether it is a novel, a short story, a "short," or something else. I also find these works hard to separate on a textual level, and so would not like to insist on their generic differences. So I have chosen to italicize all fiction titles, regardless of other conventions.

1

Beckett's Positive Logic

Beckett's fiction does not represent life as a process of utter disintegration but just the opposite, as a process that cannot end, that can never reach nothing; nor is his art itself a self-deconstructing art of failure. Beckett's work, instead, is serial and formal, as Beckett has said; it depends on virtual semblance, on the image, and is governed by a notion of temporal periodicity and by literalized metaphors.

Positive Relativism

It is easy to see why Beckett is not generally considered a system maker. He constantly writes about failure, and his work appears disjunctive; he has rejected romantic excess for abstraction. But this is only one part of him: his writing is also extremely lyrical and appropriates elaborate imaginative traditions. He does not presuppose the everyday world as a base for irony, as do moderns from Mann to Robbe-Grillet, but builds an abstract and timeless universe of mud and shade—and world building is romantic work. By disavowing "occasion" for art Beckett does not declare his own death but his immense presence, taking up himself the entire stage, the power that makes and divides, names and orders. "What am I doing," asks the narrator of *Texts for Nothing 4*, imitating the authorial voice, "talking, having my figments talk, it can only be me" (93). That Beckett discovers the inefficacy of naming matters little in the context of the logic of his undertaking. His interest in Descartes (his most noted philosophical influence) exemplifies this power to name and order. Descartes reacted against the skeptical philosophers of the sixteenth century, who derided the vanity of human knowledge (Agrippa), claimed that nothing is or can be known (Sánchez), and rejected the self as too unreliable to judge the world (Montaigne). Descartes answered radical skepticism neither with faith, as Pierre Charron arguably did, nor with empiricism, as Bacon did, but with assertion *ex nihilo*, rational fiat. In *Ulysses* Stephen argues similarly that the church is "founded irremovably because founded, like the world, macro- and microcosm, upon the void" (207). Such a foundation may be fictional, but it is rock solid. Beckett, like Descartes, founds his system on the void; and like Descartes he assumes with this act a surpassing authority. This affinity emphasizes not Beckett's skepticism, which does exist, but his implicit affirmation of logical process, of the mind.

It is curious that the *Three Dialogues*, which are so explicitly dramatized, and in which Beckett acts a part, have been generally considered to represent the unqualified views of Samuel Beckett, man and author. The *Three Dialogues* (1949), which proclaim failure as the inevitable goal of art, should be considered first of all as a dramatic production in which the figure of the author acts. Beckett's admission of failure ("Yes, yes, I am mistaken") at the end of the third dialogue successfully substantiates his thesis. He would have failed, not to fail; here he demonstrates Stephen's dictum in *Ulysses*—really Coleridge's comment on Shakespeare—that genius makes no mistakes. The *Dialogues*, furthermore, far from being true to life, are all Beckett's own invention; Georges Duthuit, for whom Beckett wrote them, was not well pleased with the role Beckett had assigned to him.[1] That the *Dialogues* can be derived, up to a point, from Beckett works that precede them also helps to put them on a fictional footing. Watt had already discovered the failure to give an example of failure, of failure as an event, while being obliged to do so (78–79). "Not to want to say," says Molloy, "not to know what you want to say, not to be able to say what you think you want to say, and never to stop saying, or hardly ever, that is the thing to keep in mind, even in the heat of composition" (28). In act 3 of *Éleuthéria*, an unpublished play (1947), Beckett anticipates the closing lines of the *Three Dialogues*. When Victor, the protagonist, says that he has nothing more to say—Beckett's words at the end of the *Dialogues*—the "Spectator," a character in the play, insists that he explain how he would "abandon himself"; Victor claims he would be free of himself by not

---

1. As Beckett told me in August 1987.

moving, thinking, speaking, listening, perceiving, and so on, but then, as in the *Dialogues*, admits defeat: "J'abandonne. . . . Je renonce à être libre. Je me suis trompé" (115–18). Beckett's *Dialogues* are modeled at least in part after these earlier sources. What I am looking for in reading Beckett is not confirmation from this or that corner of his universe, but a logic that underwrites the work.

In his aesthetic writings and in his literary work Beckett repeatedly asserts the failure of art, and some have accepted these assertions *in toto*. There is something odd about accepting, after 125 pages, the Unnamable's word that he cannot go on. Beckett appears to establish a ground of failure against which any possibility of advance or success is astonishing, but the logic of his undertaking is not a poetics of failure.[2] It is also essential to remember that for Beckett failure and futility are by no means the same: there is for him a positive failure, just as he believes in "positive nothingness" (Büttner 30 n. 57) or in a silence that has "nothing negative about it" (*Malone Dies* 221). For him absence is a condition for being, in a classical sense that I address in later chapters.[3] Beckett has complained that he cannot understand why some call him a nihilist: "There is no basis for that" (Büttner 30 n. 57). Some critics do point out that he is not so helpless as his *Three Dialogues* (and other affirmations of loss) suggest (Abbott 13, Booth 259). H. Porter Abbott calls him "a cunning literary strategist" (1), and Wayne Booth, citing Harold Pinter's praise for Beckett (260–63), enumerates the qualities of his work that do us good: "Honesty, courage, generosity, prophetic wisdom, a bitter passion for a justice that is denied us, and compassion" (263). One Beckett narrator acknowledges the issue:

> Ah yes, I hear I have a kind of conscience, and on top of that a kind of sensibility, I trust the orator is not forgetting anything,

2. See, for example, Robinson, "The Poetics of Failure," in *The Long Sonata of the Dead*, 33–61, and Jenkins, "A Lifelong Fidelity to Failure." "This omni-present sense of failure," writes Calder, "lies at the heart of what I feel to be, personally speaking, Samuel Beckett's greatest gift to his public"; Beckett derives his own aesthetic from his "undoing" of modernism (Gontarski, "Molloy and the Reiterated Novel" 59). Beckett "has accustomed us to paralysis, senile drivelling, voices from ashcans, and general thwart" (Ellmann, *Golden Codgers* 41). Henning, who sees Beckett's interest in the Western metaphysical tradition, argues in *Beckett's Critical Complicity* that Beckett invokes the tradition to undermine and carnivalize it.

3. For now, consider the following from Tommaso Campanella's *The City of the Sun* (which is mentioned in *Murphy*): "Their metaphysical principles are being, which is God, and nothingness, which is absence of being, the condition without which a thing cannot come into existence" (115).

and without ceasing to listen or drive the old quill I'm afflicted by
them, I heard, it's noted. (*Texts for Nothing 5* 96)

"And thus," Booth continues, using the kind of logic I elaborate here,
though I do not follow his ethical call, "all the debates about what he
'means' are peripheral to the genuine communication of this 'good' that
takes place regardless of whether our metaphysics is cold like his or
warm" (263). Thomas Trezise cautions that Beckett's "so-called despair
[has been] (mis)construed as the pathos of an existential humanist" (33);
and it is not the case that Beckett's meaning is irrelevant. My point,
simply, is that there is another level of signification on which Beckett
work draws heavily. As one of his narrators says, "there is reasoning
somewhere, moments of reasoning, that is to say the same things recur,
they drive one another out, they draw one another back, no need to
know what things" (*Texts for Nothing 9* 117). I will be arguing, furthermore, that the fiction signifies by working according to systems of logic
that are both constructed intertextually and argued consistently within
the fiction.

Beckett's work often shows a positive logic, especially an inclination
to reconcile and solve basic epistemological problems. The most
significant of these is the hostile alterity of the physical world. Physical
reality, something like Yeats's "Body of Fate," is not only exterior to
mind but also essentially foreign to it, "that residue of execrable frippery
known as the non-self and even the world, for short" (*First Love* 18). For
Murphy, "there was the mental fact and there was the physical fact,
equally real if not equally pleasant" (*Murphy* 108). This "physical fact"
includes the body; Beckett does not see it as neutral (as Bacon would)
but, with Nietzsche (in *The Birth of Tragedy*), as monstrous and
antagonistic to the mind, and calls it "anti-mind." Beckett inherits this
battle with nature in part from those romantics who find nature
antagonistic to the imagination.[4] He sides with the Wordsworth who
finds the mind in nature—the imposing Forms of the first book of *The
Prelude,* for instance—and against the purported prophet of "heart-
warming ecology" (Leighton). This is one of Beckett's neglected
affinities with romanticism: he privileges and preserves the power of the

4. See Bloom, *Romanticism and Consciousness* 9–12; the romantic self, far from trying to
dissolve itself in nature, seeks objectivity (Langbaum, *The Poetry of Experience* 31ff.).
Beckett finds precursors here also because the romantics found the final enemy not in
nature but in "a recalcitrance in the self" (Bloom 11).

imagination with Blake, Shelley, and Keats—and does not "surrender the imagination's autonomy," as Harold Bloom puts it (6), with Eliot. When in *Waiting for Godot* Estragon and Vladimir consider nature as an alternative, testing a quasi-romantic vision, they decide it does not work:

> ESTRAGON: We should turn resolutely toward Nature.
> VLADIMIR: We've tried that.
> ESTRAGON: True. (41)

The world "out there," like the auditorium and backstage in *Godot* (47), is an impossible alternative; in *Endgame* the "whole universe," all of anti-mind, body included, is "corpsed" (30, and see 46).

In a production notebook for *Krapp's Last Tape* Beckett has written that Krapp "turns from fact of anti-mind alien to mind to thought of anti-mind constituent of mind" (Pilling, "Beckett's 'Proust'" 61). Beckett can overcome the antagonism of anti-mind by dealing not with the world itself but with thoughts of the world, which may still be frightening but are a part of the mind. Watt also understands this principle:

> Then, as Watt still waited for the figure to draw very near indeed, he realised that it was not necessary . . . but that a moderate proximity would be more than sufficient. For Watt's concern, deep as it appeared, was not after all with what the figure was, in reality, but with what the figure appeared to be, in reality. (*Watt* 227)

Watt cannot always keep himself from desiring to know what alterior things are "in reality," but he knows the beneficial aspect of appearance, of mental image. This is a mystical approach to difficulty, in the tradition of Pascal: "It is not from space that I must seek my dignity, but from the government of my thought. I shall have no more if I possess worlds. By space the universe encompasses and swallows me up like an atom; by thought I comprehend the world" ("A Thinking Reed," *Pensées* VI, no. 348, 97). The alterity of the physical can be overcome *because* it is foreign to the mind: Murphy, though he recognizes a "partial congruence" of world and mind, "neither thought a kick because he felt one nor felt a kick because he thought one" (109). Had Beckett imagined a more harmonious world, he would not have been able to give the mind the powers it has in his work. "To compose," Ruskin said, "is to arrange unequal things"; where all things are equal, composition is impossible. Beckett's dualism allows the mind its full powers of composition. "I could say it easily, because it wouldn't be true," says Molloy (19).[5] The most potent human action, in Beckett's fiction, is translation or reconstitution, restating *physis* as *psyche*, rebuilding the world in mental terms, making headway.

More celebrated is Beckett's solution to the problem of art: art inevitably fails to express anything genuine, it only displays itself, its own generic and historical conventions. Language can only speak itself. Beckett realizes this as few artists do, but claims that "to be an artist is to fail, as no other dare fail" (*Disjecta* 145). That is, the failure of art is not a problem at all because the only true art is failure. He insists—as he must—that this failure is not itself an occasion for the artist, though he does not explain how this can be. It remains a knotty issue, but the problem of the failure of art is solved: the artist is meant to fail. Sartre tries to solve this puzzle when he explains that Genet wants his life to be a failure. "If failure is achieved as failure," he worries, "it is a success, since that is what Genet wanted." He claims to find an answer in a dubious distinction between Genet's will and his desire: Genet does want to succeed—otherwise he could not fail—but wills his failure. "Wanting a certain result, Genet fails, and willing his failure, succeeds. He wills what he does not want and does not will what he wants" (*Saint Genet* 335). Sartre cleverly sees here that the artist succeeds when he fails, and that success is his failure. But implicit in his rhetoric is the assumption that the artist creates with a will toward a certain end. Beckett does not say that. To create, to will art and to produce it, is that not success? Beckett imagines in the *Dialogues* an artist who wills neither success nor failure, who works not to achieve an end but from compulsion, under duress. The true artist does not "want" to fail; the artist "dares" fail, dares acknowledge failure. But implicit in Beckett's rhetoric too is some positive verb, if not "to will" then "to dare."

A better solution to the artist's predicament (that failure becomes a new goal), and one furthermore that is compatible with Beckett's logic, may lie in the familiar distinction between telling and showing. The

5. "Beckett's comedy," says Kenner, "if it can deal with everything it touches because it operates solely with the laws of thought, by the same token can really deal with nothing, because thought is not prior to things, and things escape" (*The Stoic Comedians* 106).

artist can tell about failure, but cannot show failure. This failure to show cannot itself be shown, and so on, creating a Zenovian regressive series of potential failures that can never yield an artistic occasion. If one should argue that the artist now, instead of having failure as a goal, shows the idea of this regressive series of failures, Cartesian logic answers that the idea of infinite regression cannot be shown, but can only be described. This alternative logic sets up its own regressive series, a series of ideas of ideas of the infinite, and so on. This way one can fail without creating a true occasion in the act.[6]

Beckett shows how regressive logic fails to reach or destroy its object, the object of regression, be it language or image. In this he follows Augustine, who argues that things would not be corruptible unless they were good: corruption merely exposes the goodness of its object. This idea is central to Augustine's thought and controls much of Beckett's:

> It was made clear to me that even those things that are subject to decay are good. If they were of the supreme order of goodness, they could not become corrupt; but neither could they become corrupt unless they were in some way good. For if they were supremely good, it would not be possible for them to be corrupted. On the other hand, if they were entirely without good, there would be nothing in them that could become corrupt. For corruption is harmful, but unless it diminished what is good, it could do no harm.

From this Augustine surmises that "whatever is, is good," and so that evil cannot be a substance, or it would be good.[7] In *Watt* Beckett's protagonist supposedly destroys language by mutating it—Ruby Cohn calls his product "anti-language" (*The Comic Gamut* 70–73). Repeatedly he inverts and rearranges the order of letters and words in the sentence, of sentences in the paragraph, and with each attempt his language becomes more opaque, and sounds less like it originally did. For example:

> *Dis yb dis, nem owt. Yad la, tin fo trap. Skin, skin, skin. Od su did ned taw?* (168)

6. This is a version of the problem that language cannot express that which is outside itself, as Wittgenstein says in the *Tractatus*. See Reiss 104–6.
7. *Confessions* vii.12, 148. For Joyce's precise restatement of Augustine's idea, see *Ulysses* 142.

This is pretty good English and reads, as Cohn notes (310),

> What then did us do? Nix, nix, nix. Part of night, all day. Two
> men, side by side.

Watt does not change the language, he only presents it in code, with its
systematic character intact (as Cohn notes, 71). In the end, Watt arrives
at an order so complex that Sam, the narrator, cannot recall an example
of it—but it too, presumably, is systematical and would be understandable, were it reproducible. Watt, ground down by his experiences at
Knott's house, finds that his self too is repeatedly reduced, and examines
the serial diminution that, one might assume, may entirely eliminate
him. But it cannot eliminate him. He discovers that he can always be
reduced but that, by the very same token, he can never be eliminated.[8]

> He saw himself then, so little, so poor. And now, littler,
> poorer. Was not that something?
> So sick, so alone.
> And now.
> Sicker, aloner.
> Was not that something?
> As the comparative is something. Whether more than its
> positive or less. Whether less than its superlative or more.[9]

This is Zenovian regression again, but the very terms it offers, of
infinite reduction, comparative downsizing, guarantee continual being
to the reduced self. So long as it is littler it is there. So Neary's little
hope, his little romanticism, dooms him to hope without end,[10] and
cannot be got rid of:

> There seems really very little hope for Neary, he seems doomed
> to hope unending. He has something of Hugo. The fire will not
> depart from his eye, nor the water from his mouth, as he

---

8. See Ortega's discussion of this in "The Dehumanization of Art" 89.

9. *Watt* 148. This passage echoes Bloom's thoughts in *Ulysses*: "Me. And me now"
(176).

10. For a similarly explicit passage explaining this positive logic, see *Mercier and Camier*
58 (and cp. 11).

Neary's name is an anagram for "yearn," as Rabinovitz notes. Here Neary is described
as "yearning" (201).

scratches himself out of one itch into the next, until he shed his mortal mange, supposing that to be permitted. (*Murphy* 201–2)

Neary "has something," and so his "fire will not depart," though it may be reduced. This logic, in other words, guarantees that whatever is, will remain forever, though it may diminish (cp. Chambers 49). Things decrease, not cease (*Malone Dies* 186). Change is not cessation, discovers the narrator of *Texts for Nothing 2:* "The things too must still be there, a little more worn, a little even less, many still standing" (81). This is what Beckett, in a marginal comment in his copy of Proust's *A la recherche*, calls "*positive* relativism."[11] In *Lessness* Beckett shows again how a thing reduced persists. Like Watt inverting the language, he reshuffles the barest building blocks, something "less," only to reach not an end but endlessness.

This kind of regressive reduction guarantees the Unnamable's progress. The Unnamable stumbles through contradiction on the infinitely regressive system of self-transcendence: "Choke, go down, come up, choke, suppose, deny, affirm, drown," as Malone has it (*Malone Dies* 210). The Unnamable can, for example, be Mahood, then Worm, then one Jones or another, and in speculating about his projections and defining himself against them he can always produce an "affirmation, I mean negation, on which to build" (339). Positing an infinite series of characters to represent himself, he can "think of [himself] as somewhere on a road, . . . gaining ground, losing ground, getting lost, but somehow in the long run making headway" (314). To lose successively more ground is to gain a kind of advance in the face of any odds. No matter how many surrogate selves the Unnamable would produce, he could never reach himself: "I could employ fifty wretches for this sinister operation and still be short of a fifty-first, to close the circuit" (338). But his personified images always admit him as their referent, a "tertius gaudens" responsible for these images' failure to be him (because only he is). As Robert Champigny explains, "If two attitudes are objectified [as Mahood and Worm], a third one is needed to posit them as ego-images, as two of *my* selves. A spectator is needed. And in order to posit this spectator and recognize him as one of my selves, another spectator is needed, and so on ad infinitum" (126). The regressive series of self-images both creates and defers the need for the

11. In *Tome II, A l'ombre des jeunes filles en fleurs* 151. The comment reads: "View of Proust as a representative (Anti-France) of *positive* relativism."

self. Beckett is again explicit on this subject in *How It Is*, though he already implies it in *Molloy*. There, as David Hayman notes, Jacques Moran's son Jacques Moran is, "along with Gaber, one of the novel's unifying principals: the third member of an apparently infinite series of analogical trios" (*Samuel Beckett Now* 144). Hayman considers Moran junior as "the first term of the series concluding with the Unnamable" (145). The trio is the somewhat neglected counterpart to Beckett's couple; *Play* is another example of it: here three figures in their urns seem to carry threesomeness beyond death. In *Not I* Mouth's repeated insistence that its narrative is about "who? . . . no! . . . she! . . . SHE!" (86) reveals all too painfully who the real subject is. Beckett's move in his fiction from third person narration (in the early prose) to the deceptive first person (with the trilogy) pretends to reject the triad, as though the narrating persona were author: not I. For this reason the logic of analogical trios pervades the trilogy all the more. "If at least he would dignify me with the third person, like his other figments," laments the narrator of *Texts for Nothing 4*, "not he, he'll be satisfied with nothing less than me" (92). This is Beckett's general practice with the notion of series—not to show it but to generate it from the couple.[12]

Beckett does the same thing with the human image. The narrator of *The Unnamable* projects deteriorated images of selfhood, first Mahood and then the lipoidal Worm, a crawling mouth. "But what then is the subject? Mahood? No, not yet. Worm? Even less. Bah, any old pronoun will do, provided one sees through it. Matter of habit" (*The Unnamable* 343). A succession of pronouns substitutes for the noun as successive projected selves stand in for the narrator. Each positive subject is "even less" adequate than its predecessor, and must maintain its explicit fictionality in order to be discarded for another. None is expected to do, but is only created in order not to do. These selves are the conventional or habitual concealment of shapelessness, the naming of the unnamable. Presumably one would see the true subject through them all at once, but this is not the case. The late fiction abounds in images of what seem reduced human beings; in *Ping*, for example, one sees a "head haught nose ears white holes mouth white seam like sewn invisible" (71). These images are again seen through. They are, as Daniel Albright says, "objects in the process of dissolving themselves, a phantasmagoria of

---

12. The notion that being is triplicate helps Beckett to imagine the divine, the "pretty three in one" (*Texts for Nothing 12* 134), "the everlasting third party, he's the one to blame" (*The Unnamable* 375). See Chapter 5.

descriptions that fail to constitute themselves into recognizable images, that insist on giving no satisfaction to the reader's appetite for representation" (164). Yet these images, however harshly reduced, cannot shake the idea of the human. Mere proto-beings, a mouth or "ears white holes," conjure and reconstitute the human image. As Enoch Brater says, "One of the great ironies of Beckett's attempt to 'desophisticate' language in *Worstward Ho* is the uncanny way his words have of resurrecting themselves. . . . Images, no matter how cryptically rendered, keep insinuating their immediacy into this supposedly empty text" ("Voyelles" 171). Even Beckett's perception of fragmentation presupposes the idea of unity and conveys the human need for it (cp. Cameron 4). Beckett's assaults on human images do not destroy the idea of the human, but finally emphasize it.

It would not do to argue that Beckett is an optimist whose half-empty glass is really half-full, too. But it does just as little good to argue that because a character in a book is insane the book is mindless, or that because a narrator says that he is at a loss and getting nowhere, so is the work.

Beginning to Mean Something

Beckett manipulates failure to construct a positive logic of persistence and control. But most of Beckett's critics argue that, though his themes are consistent, he does not weave them together into a larger narrative. It is generally agreed that Beckett begins with more realistic works that portray nearly believable characters and a regular landscape, and goes on to reduce his characters and to abstract their settings (Federman 13; Rabinovitz 176–78). His work begins with a brilliant and allusive style (in the early stories and in *Murphy* and *Watt*) but trades its flashiness for simpler, more direct language as it develops (Rabinovitz 176). After *The Lost Ones* his works are simple and scenic like tableaux and tend to present single situations. Such terms do not tell much about Beckett's purpose or design; indeed, most Beckett critics reject the notion that his work can be read systematically at all. Hugh Kenner, for example, warns that Beckett's universe is "permeated by mystery and bounded by a darkness; to assail those qualities because they embarrass the critic's professional knowingness is cheap, reductive, and perverse" (*Samuel Beckett* 10).[13] Some readers even think that the last addendum to *Watt*,

13. This is a common critical response to Beckett's work. Abbott warns that Beckett's

"no symbols where none intended," is the author's warning to that effect.[14] One is asked to accept as relevant to Beckett's work his admonition to readers of *Work in Progress* not to be "analogymongers"— not to identify Joyce's work with the "philosophical abstraction" that underlies and organizes it (*Exagmination* 3–4).

These appeals to Beckett's writings reflect the fact that their author himself has consistently disavowed complicated interpretation of his work. About *Endgame* he wrote Alan Schneider in 1957: "We have no elucidations to offer of mysteries that are all of their [the exegetes'] making. . . . If people want to have headaches among the overtones, let them" (quoted in Bair, 470). So the narrator of *Dream of Fair to Middling Women* says authorially that "the only unity in this story is, please God, an involuntary unity" (118). The Unnamable explains in his first discussion of method that "the thing to avoid, I don't know why, is the spirit of system" (292); "if it begins to mean something," he says later, "I can't help it" (400). And in *Endgame* Hamm wonders, "We're not beginning to . . . to . . . mean something?" (32). Beckett's claim that *Endgame* is about "fundamental sounds" (in the letter to Schneider) recalls not only his praise for *Work in Progress* but also the Unnamable's suggestion that instead of speaking he might equally utter meaningless sounds (408). Hamm's statement, in particular, shows the concern for meaning that these characters, unaccountably wise about their stage being, share with their author. Beckett cannot be called dishonest, but he cannot be made accountable to his characters' words either. These words, the characters' and Beckett's, do not simply deny (or affirm) systematic meaning so much as show a concern for meaning.

Beckett, in fact, has often said that his works form a series. About *Watt* he wrote his agent, George Reavey: "It is an unsatisfactory book . . . but it has its place in the series, as will perhaps appear in time" (1947 letter, Bair 364). To his longtime friend Thomas McGreevy he wrote that "*Molloy* is . . . the second last of the series begun with

---

allusions and overtones are not "clues" to "elaborate structures of meaning"; they suggest allegory, which is "the kind of coherence [Beckett] has striven to avoid" (9, and see 94). Instead, "the beauty lies in the absence of explanation" (11). Bair says that before the war Beckett "had no coherent literary purpose and no philosophical foundation for his commitment" (346); generally in his fictions he "has no system, no easy answer for anything, and he won't allow the reader to find one either" (331). Knowlson and Pilling feel the same: "If one thing is certain where Beckett is concerned, there is no key that will unlock every problem thrown up by his work, no formula that will elucidate every aspect of his *oeuvre*" (xii). I cannot think of any writer for whom this would be possible.

14. Rabinovitz condemns this, 162.

Murphy, if it can be said to be a series" (1948 letter, Bair 372), and about *Malone meurt* he wrote that it was "the last I hope of the series *Murphy, Watt, Mercier & Camier, Molloy*, not to mention the four nouvelles and *Éleuthéria*" (1948 letter to Reavey, Bair 379). He had thought that *Malone Dies* would be the last book in that series but then saw the necessity of yet another book and wrote *The Unnamable*. About his late work he said that it is "residual" in relation to other work it survives and also "in relation to whole body of previous work" (Beckett to Brian Finney, in Mercier 10). Just how true this is shall be seen later. Evidently Beckett thought of his work as serial or consistently developed before he had completed the sequence on which he was working at the time. From his comments it also appears that he thought of his work as serial throughout his career, and not only in his early years as a writer.

Beckett has also conceded a second premise important to his project, that his work is "formal." Formal terms help organize and develop a reading of his work. Some of Beckett's most quoted words claim an overriding interest in the "shape of ideas":

> I am interested in the shape of ideas even if I do not believe in them. There is a wonderful sentence in Augustine. I wish I could remember the Latin. It is even finer in Latin than in English. "Do not despair; one of the thieves was saved. Do not presume; one of the thieves was damned." That sentence has a wonderful shape. It is the shape that matters. (Hobson, 153–55)

Many discussions of Beckett's work (especially in the 1960s and 1970s) say that they address its shape or formal properties.[15] These discussions invariably focus on symmetry, repetition, circularity, and opposition, qualities that do characterize Beckett's work, but the critics do not relate this sense of structure to a larger interpretation of Beckett's work.

---

15. Among these are Abbott's *The Fiction of Samuel Beckett: Form and Effect* (1973), Hesla's *The Shape of Chaos* (1971), States's *The Shape of Paradox* (1978), and Worth, ed., *Beckett the Shape Changer* (1975). The subject has also occasioned many articles, including Andreasen's "Form and Philosophy in Samuel Beckett" (1969), Gontarski's "Samuel Beckett and Intrinsic Form" (1979), Kern's "Structure in Beckett's Theatre" (1971), Louzoun's "Fin de partie de Samuel Beckett: Effacement du monde et dynamisme formel" (1977), and Rothenberg's "A Form of Tension in Beckett's Fiction" (1982). Friedman's summary of the discussions of the structure of *Waiting for Godot* (25–26) illustrates the kind of attention the subject has received.

The Virtual Object

How can one understand the notion of shape as it is expressed in
Beckett's work? The words he attributes to Augustine imply a symmetry of meaning and syntax, an impasse between the good and the bad,
both of which can be equally affirmed. Likewise Beckett's formal
experiments, such as his use of repetition, represent the shape that
informs his content.[16] This equation may also be read to mean that form
is the true artist's subject. Content is really part of art's formal
organization. Nietzsche puts this construction at the core of genuine
poesis: "One is an artist at the cost of regarding that which all non-artists
call 'form' as content, as 'the matter itself.' To be sure, then one belongs
to a topsy-turvy world, for henceforth content becomes something
merely formal—our life included" (quoted in Tanner). Event matters in
as much as it manifests pattern, systematic relation. Beckett, however,
does not simply coerce particularity in the service of abstraction. The
shape of content is, for Beckett, not its narrative or generic pattern but
something built-in, an element of material constitution. Circularity and
duality are important in his work because they reveal the organization or
shape of life. This reading claims for Beckett's enterprise an idealistic
bent (a Neoplatonic one, I will show later), which, on the surface, seems
alien to his representation of the world. Beckett's work is often thought
antigeneric, decomposed, decentered, and Beckett is considered the
writer of meaningless particulars in essential nonrelation. Nevertheless,
Neoplatonic idealism is fundamental to Beckett's project. I take up this
subject directly in Chapters 5 and 6.

More extremely than most writers, Beckett reduces his material to
virtual presence. Content is often abstracted in his fiction, removed by
its artificiality and starkness from recognized or normative material
settings and presented as pure visual resemblance or *Schein*, in Schiller's
sense. The world is present in Murphy's mind as "virtual, or actual, or
virtual rising into actual" (107). Beckett's image is denied an immediate
function; instead it is there, a Heideggerian thing. Susanne Langer
explains the nature of an object reduced to its semblance: "Where we
know that an 'object' consists entirely in its semblance, that apart from
its appearance it has no cohesion and unity—like a rainbow, or a
shadow—we call it a merely virtual object, or illusion. In this literal

16. For Beckett's use of repetition, see especially Connor, *Samuel Beckett: Repetition,
Theory, and Text*, and Henning, passim.

sense a picture is an illusion" (49). One does less well to consider the four-eyed crawlers of *How It Is* and the limbless torso of *The Unnamable* as unfortunate humans than to think of them as images. Molloy's knife-rest is an object rendered with Conradian impressionism. That is Watt's original state too, "a roll of tarpaulin, wrapped up in dark paper and tied about the middle with a cord" (*Watt* 16). Mr. Hackett in *Watt* first appears as "a virtual character like a line drawing" (Pearce 46). Such objects can serve an abstract design, as Langer explains:

> The function of "semblance" is to give forms a new embodiment in purely qualitative, unreal instances, setting them free from their normal embodiment in real things so that they may be recognized in their own right, and freely conceived and composed in the interest of the artist's ultimate aim—significance, or logical expression. (*Feeling and Form* 50)

Beckett's fiction pushes to an extreme the freedom to manipulate intellectual objects as though they were dissociated from their contexts. His characters have few histories and obligations that the reader knows of, free to change identities or suffer abuse as though they existed in an eternal present. Watt may visit the stations of the cross (Robinson 31), but he twists along straight roads and into circular compounds like a toy train on its rail. Later works like *All Strange Away* and *Ghost Trio* present highly stylized, geometrical images, at once manipulable and intangible, suggesting in their shadowy semblance matter that is yet "not for the eyes made of words" (*How It Is* 45).

  Beckett develops this concept of his object early in his career. In *Proust* he argues against simple mimesis, "the grotesque fallacy of realistic art" (57). This kind of art—a kind of thinking—is inferior because it deals only with "line and surface," outer form that suppresses the dynamic quality of the object. Abstraction does better. But in "Dante... Bruno. Vico.. Joyce" he praises Joyce's attempt to create the "sense which is for ever rising to the surface of the form and becoming the form itself" (*Exagmination* 14). Here is the logical expression ("sense") of which Langer speaks, which controls content; here too is the dynamic quality, the process of becoming, which Beckett values and which he finds lacking in "realistic" art. With Proust (as he sees him) Beckett argues for formal abstraction; with Joyce he requires material presence. The object and the image are made synonymous in Beckett's discussion. While Beckett here explicitly differentiates form and content, he sees them as bound, combined in the process to realize sense or logic through the image.

So conceived, the object, according to the logic of Beckett's discussion, subsumes surface in the process of descent, of unveiling, and at the same time shows any revealed depth to be itself a surface, superficial. The object has no interior, because its interiors are revealed to be surfaces, but it has no surface either, because any surface is a veil for the object that hides below. It is a *mise en abîme*, an image that contains itself. Flann O'Brien plays with this concept in *The Third Policeman*, where the infinity that is only hypothetically possible in the image is suggested concretely by a series of chests within chests.[17] This phenomenon is part of Beckett's logic of inexhaustible diminishment. As Miller explains,

> Without the production of some schema, some "icon," there can be no glimpse of the abyss, no vertigo of the underlying nothingness. Any such scheme, however, both opens the chasm, creates it or reveals it, and at the same time fills it up, covers it over by naming it, gives the groundless a ground, the bottomless a bottom. (*The Linguistic Moment* 399–400)

This is related to the fundamental problem of the Unnamable, Beckett's quintessential subject: whatever it perceives of itself is by definition object and not the subject. The subject cannot perceive itself: whatever "me" the "I" perceives—whatever it perceives—becomes other. Descartes neglects to consider this when he doubles his "I": I think, therefore "I" am. "Strictly speaking," says Weiskel, "for all we can know, I am *only* when I am thinking. . . . Thinking appears to yield no possibility of an 'objective me,' and all other mental processes are heuristically in doubt." Descartes's "I," he says, "is first treated as a quasi-objectified essence, and then the resultant 'me' is simply identified with the 'soul' . . . Descartes has slipped across the threshold from the subjective 'I' to the objective 'soul' by going through the portal 'me'" (Weiskel 151). Beckett knows this problem, as he shows in *Texts for Nothing*, a commentary on the logic of *The Unnamable*: "One, meaning

17. 69–74. O'Brien tells, for example, of a device whereby one can see one's past: "If a man stands before a mirror and sees in it his reflection, what he sees is not a true reproduction of himself but a picture of himself when he was a younger man." Constructing "the familiar arrangement of parallel mirrors, each reflecting diminishing images of an interposed object indefinitely," a subject may view his or her past (64–65). Beckett told me that Joyce saw him as O'Brien's pessimistic twin.

me, it's not the same thing" (95); "I tried throwing me off a cliff, collapsing in the street in the midst of mortals, that led nowhere" (87); "His life, what a mine, what a life, he can't have that, you can't fool him, ergo it's not his, it's not him, what a thought" (92); "It's the same old stranger as ever, for whom alone accusative I exist" (91).[18] In *The Unnamable* the self is presented as a surface, an image or object that confesses to be only a cover for another self-image like it. Its polarity of outside and inside, container and contained, surface and depth, repeatedly reverses itself and so dissolves.

To see properly for Beckett is to see *from both sides*, as the four-eyed mud crawlers of *How It Is* substantially demonstrate. "I'm up there and I'm down here, under my gaze," says one narrator (*Texts for Nothing 1* 77). This is again a bit of romantic inheritance—that the actor is the acted upon—though it comes also from the hermetic conception of micro- and macrocosm, the one containing the other and vice versa. So Blake:

> What is Above is Within, for every-thing in
>   Eternity is translucent:
> The Circumference is Within: Without, is formed
>   the Selfish Center
> And the Circumference still expands going forward
>   to Eternity.
> And the Center has Eternal States! these States we
>   now explore.
>   (*Jerusalem*, plate 71, lines 6–9)

Like Beckett, Blake (who represents a kind of thinking here) speaks of the subject as a "formed" microcosmic center, and uses the spatialized trope of surface ("Above") and depth ("Within") to represent it. Time itself, according to one Beckett narrator, is a "plane" on which events removed in time can be associated (*First Love* 11). One's experience is on the surface, in the present. Depth on the other hand is temporal hierarchy, diachronic unfolding. Depth is history: we think of the past as preserved inside us, structuring our development and filling it with substance—"a way of refusing loss and separation," according to Jean Starobinski (Cameron 91). So Krapp reels back in time to find his younger self; similarly the work of art, as Beckett says in *Proust*, is

18. For Descartes's discussion see "Discourse on the Method" I, 101.

"discovered, uncovered, excavated, pre-existing within the artist, a law of his nature" (64). Note again the assumption that matter is inherently formal: art is in the artist like form in stone, and "poetry," in consequence, and in the words of Eugene Jolas's manifesto, which the young Beckett signed, "is vertical."

Periodicity in *Waiting for Godot*

Beckett's image is virtual, but his work articulates a vision of periodicity. *Waiting for Godot* is a work about time, but Beckett buried the particular historical references in the play to emphasize its timelessness, and then suppressed them further in his translation of the play into English. In consequence, *Godot* has been read as a world of simulacra, appearances that have no reality but only mask the lack of the real (cp. Baudrillard 11–12). Alain Robbe-Grillet popularized the notion that *Godot* is nonrelational in "Samuel Beckett, or 'Presence' in the Theatre" (1957). He praises Vladimir and Estragon for being *"there,"* without historical consciousness, without a real sense of loss or of futility. They are, he says, unthinking: "Thought and eloquence . . . figure in the text only in the form of parody" (112). In *Endgame* Beckett could not sustain the depthless image of *Waiting for Godot*, of people without humanity, but instead succumbed to a tragic vision, to tragic depth. Hamm is a cripple, confined to a chair in a room, "enduring a fate" (114), equipped with "a kind of future" (115). He exists in time, and the threat of a "future" annuls his present. This tragic development, according to Robbe-Grillet, threatens to bring Beckett's literature of "non-meaning" into a system of meaning. The notion that the world of *Waiting for Godot* is ahistorical has since become standard doctrine in Beckett criticism. As John Peter says, "Vladimir and Estragon do not have a fictional past: the play is written in such a way as to function in an endless present." "There they are," he says, echoing Robbe-Grillet, "in no particular place and no particular time."[19] Vivian Mercier's one-liner has summed up the consensus: "In *Godot* nothing happens, twice." *Waiting for Godot*, however, is fundamentally about historical process. This historical process suggests the continuous reversibility and repeatability of temporal events, a cyclical vision that undermines the distinction in Beckett's work between presence and history.

In *Waiting for Godot* depth is process (historical and social), surface is

19. Peter 17. See Esslin, *Theatre* 45, Morrison 9, and Peter 8, and also 16–17 and 34.

"being-there," and the two are conjoined. Vladimir and Estragon are rooted to the public road. While Pozzo and Lucky drive "on," Vladimir and Estragon wait. Each state requires the other to be what it is:

> ESTRAGON: (*anxious*). And we?
> VLADIMIR: I beg your pardon?
> ESTRAGON: I said, And we?
> VLADIMIR: I don't understand.
> ESTRAGON: Where do we come in?
> VLADIMIR: Come in?
> ESTRAGON: Take your time.
> VLADIMIR: Come in? On our hands and knees.
> ESTRAGON: As bad as that? (13)

Estragon's idiomatic expressions have lost their social and historical meaning for Vladimir, who takes them literally. Vladimir does think through the question; were he uncomprehendingly literal minded he would have answered Estragon's direct question, "Where," instead of reading it to mean "how." Still he reads the surface meaning of the words. Estragon's language shows dynamic historical depth, while Vladimir's more dissociated interpretation is literal and superficial. But immediately the two reverse positions: to Vladimir's description Estragon replies, "As bad as that?" accepting the literal answer as valid on its own level. A similar reversal happens with Pozzo and Lucky, who are tied together with a rope: in the first act Pozzo appears to drive Lucky, while in the second Lucky seems to lead Pozzo (Guicharnaud 243). But does not Lucky lead Pozzo in the first act too? and does not Pozzo drive Lucky in the second? They do, but that could not be seen without the reversal in their roles.

The idiomatic language that Vladimir—and apparently Estragon too—could only understand literally, outside its conventional history, is "given" in the world of the play, a legacy of a past that has at some point become discontinuous with the present (cp. *The Unnamable* 324–26). The two remark on this past and its gift of "all the dead voices" that rustle on and off in the play (40). This gap, this seemingly absent process whereby the present lost its past, time lost history, is the depth that underlies the play. In *Godot* the gap between time past and time present is the gap between the postwar world and the idealistic society that existed somewhere before the wars. Beckett has removed references to this past from the original French version; what is striking about this process of removal is that it is substantially the subject of the play. Several of the references removed from or altered in the play refer specifically to Beckett's own past.[20] More particularly, Beckett's war years experience (the play was written around 1949) is associated with the social transformations of the first half of the twentieth century. So the process of eroding history from the play—an incomplete erasure, as shall be seen—is also Beckett's conscious attempt to remove his personal history from it.

Beckett's history, together with another set of historical references that Beckett altered in his "translation" of *Godot* into English, signify a particular historical crisis. Estragon's reference to the Rhône (35) is in the French original a reference to "la Durance," a Rhône tributary in the Vaucluse province where Beckett, who had worked for the resistance, hid from the Gestapo during the war. "Macon" is substituted for "Vaucluse" in a later dialogue (39). A peasant colloquialism from that region, "peuchère" ("mon Dieu"), is omitted from Lucky's mono- logue.[21] These topical references explain the "red" landscape of Vladi- mir and Estragon's past (40), which dangles oddly in the English edition: the soil in the Vaucluse is reddish, the peasants there were predomi- nantly leftists politically, and Beckett lived there in the village of "Roussillon" (just "a place" in the English edition, 40) from 1942 to 1944, whose name suggests "red." These memories, Beckett's, are given in the play as Estragon's "private nightmares" (11); they suggest the period of the war as Beckett experienced it. But there is another set of references in the play that point, in their turn, to an earlier period. "What's the good of losing heart now," says Vladimir. "We should have thought of it a million years ago, in the nineties" (7). The gap between the present and the irrevocable past of the 1890s seems disproportional, mythological, qualitative. The French text is more explicit: "Il falait y penser il y a une éternité, vers 1900" (10). The gap is named as eternal, that is, timeless, because it is perceived from the other side, a place without, or outside, time. The French text also mentions "la Roquette" (13), a Paris prison in operation 1830–1900, reinforcing the notion that the year 1900 was the point of transition. These references indicate that

20. See Stempel for the historical claim made for the play, and for several extended parallels that may carry its historical referentiality too far. Cohn discusses the play's English and French versions in "Samuel Beckett, Self-translator" and in *From Desire to Godot*.
21. See Brée and Schoenfield's annotations in their edition of *En attendant Godot*.

the period in which humanity lost its sense of time began around the turn of the century and culminated in World War II. The consequence of this transition is figured in the reference to the Eiffel Tower, built in 1889, a symbol of the new age of positivist and mechanical materialism:

> VLADIMIR: Hand in hand from the top of the Eiffel Tower, among the first. We were respectable in those days. Now it's too late. They wouldn't even let us up. (7)

The Eiffel Tower is—as in Robert Delaunay's famous paintings—an epiphany of social progress. Humanity cannot be elevated spiritually, just as it is no longer possible to go up the Eiffel Tower. "Now it's too late." Now is another time, a later world. There is no bridging the gap to a prelapsarian world.

The golden age spanned the decade following 1889, when the Eiffel Tower was built, but preceding the symbolic and strangely decisive turn of the century. In the French text Estragon tells Pozzo his name is "Catulle," or Catullus, not "Adam," as in the English: Beckett removes the temporal reference to the Roman poet, and substitutes for it a mythical world that existed before the fall into human time. The world somewhere before "the nineties" is Edenic, timeless, compared with the postlapsarian world following the war. Seen through contemporary eyes, that golden age seems dross; none of the earlier ideals remains relevant. Nor does past literature seem relevant. The Irish revival is an easy target: "Pah!" says Estragon, "The wind in the reeds" (13), alluding to Yeats's book of poems of 1899, *The Wind Among the Reeds* (the date is again significant). Yeats is probably again the target when Vladimir recites the ditty, "A dog came in the kitchen" (37), which includes a couplet reminiscent of the last lines of "Under Ben Bulben": "And wrote upon the tombstone / For the eyes of dogs to come."[22] We've already seen about turning "resolutely toward nature" (41). These bits of history, and historical depth, are as insistently present in the play as they are vigorously rejected.

This historical gap is reenacted through the changes that take place between the acts of the play. Pozzo's transformation exemplifies the

---

22. Esslin says that this song is an old German students' song (*Theatre* 76); the song presents a regressive series. Cohn notes that the dog song is a *mise en abîme* (*From Desire to Godot* 142).

process whereby the present assumes surface being. When he delivers his twilight speech in act 2—which Robbe-Grillet valorizes as an emblem of Beckett's "presence"—he is already fallen, transformed. In act 1 he is, with one important relapse (to which I shall return), the type of man who brought about that fall. He is, he says, "not particularly human, but who cares?" (19). He styles himself a successful divinity: Vladimir and Estragon are of an imperfect likeness to him (16), he is a shepherd of humans, demands reverential attention, dispenses rewards and promises, and cultivates his breath (the Word).[23] He is the spirit, driving the body Lucky before him, his carrier. Lucky "used to be . . . my good angel . . . and now . . . he's killing me" (23), a rebel Titan, "Atlas, son of Jupiter":[24] Pozzo styles himself God in a Manichean world, with Lucky as his fallen counterpart. Here Pozzo finds Vladimir's statement that "time has stopped" (24) a threat to his time-bound identity—"Whatever you like, but not that." In act 2, when Vladimir asks him when it was he became blind, he is again adamant, but for a different reason:

> (*violently*). Don't question me! The blind have no notion of time. The things of time are hidden from them too. (55)

He says he "woke up one fine day as blind as Fortune" (55). Along with this loss of the sense of time comes loss of memory:

> I don't remember having met anyone yesterday. But tomorrow I won't remember having met anyone today. So don't count on me to enlighten you.

Blindness, the loss of light (reason) or vision (ideals), brings about the loss of time, which in turn brings about the loss of memory. That is the historical process that informs the play. In act 2, surprisingly, Pozzo becomes much like Vladimir and Estragon, timeless as a prelapsarian. The two acts can be read in reverse, the second preceding the first as the innocent atemporal world preceded fallen temporality. If in the first act Pozzo is fallen, in the second he is innocent again, not because he

---

23. In recent revisions Beckett seems to want to eliminate the vaporizer from the play as inessential to it, but then Pozzo would lose the device of his divine breath.

24. In Alan Schneider's production (Grove) these words seem to apply not to Lucky but to Pozzo, but the text allows for this reading as well.

reformed or was elevated spiritually, but because of another fall, as it were—because of the entropic process that, as Lucky explains in his monologue, erodes "the labors of man." This suggests that before his superior condition—as he sees it—of act 1, which is in fact a fallen condition, Pozzo was abased, without time, as he would be in act 2. His fall into time, he confesses in that exceptional instance in act 1, occurred "nearly sixty years ago," that is, around the turn of the century. That is what his relapse in act 1 suggests. Attacked by Vladimir and Estragon for his inhumanity to Lucky, he complains about Lucky's behavior to him. "I'm going mad," he says (22). But soon after he takes it all back: "Do I look like a man that can be made to suffer?" (23). Similarly, in the first act Vladimir recalls Pozzo and Lucky: "How they've changed!" he says. "Yes you do know them" (32), he tells Estragon, who has forgotten them. Pozzo and Lucky had been different, more like their second act selves, one suspects, and they had already passed before the two tramps.

The result is a world of eternal recurrence: the protagonists wait for the future, but keep returning to the past. Pozzo can have his relapse in the first act because he can remember something of his former self that is suppressed in act 1, a self that appears again in the second act; Vladimir, who cannot recall Pozzo in the first act, remembers him in the second. The characters both know and do not know the magnitude of their fall.[25] A third act would repeat the first; a fourth, the second; a fifth, the first again; and so on. The world of the play is not only cyclical but also periodic. In each act the characters must appear to reenact an old scenario as though for the first time; at the same time, the acts must suggest the fall into surface, the process of falling from process, from time. The play insists, by the very erasure that conceals this information, that humanity has fallen tragically from time into a world of simulation. At the same time, it shows that this process repeats itself, reversing itself, so that the seeing and powerful Pozzo of act 1 is at once a specimen of postwar time and of humanity before the fall out of time to the ahistorical world of Vladimir and Estragon. Each state is a fall from the other. Tragic depth in *Waiting for Godot* is this process—both history (a process) and its representation (itself a process). This sense of time is important to Beckett's project as a whole.

---

25. Chambers recognizes the relevance of the tension between attainment and deferment to the structure of *Godot*: "C'est ce *double* mouvement de rapprochement continuel de l'instant éternel qui donne à *En attendant Godot* sa structure essentielle" (53).

Literalizing Metaphors

Waiting for Godot, and Beckett's work generally, present an image that,
as Vladimir explains to the messenger, is there to be seen; and in that
image or object are combined depth and surface, history and virtual
semblance. How is Beckett's object or image both virtual and conno-
tative? It is tempting to think of it as an icon or concrete symbol that
leaps beyond its context, but this interpretation is limiting. Consider for
example the scene of *Waiting for Godot*. Vladimir expects that Estragon
would "recognize the place," but Estragon rejects his friend's "landscapes" because there is nothing to recognize (39). Vladimir says only
that this place does not bear any resemblance to another place (the
Macon country), which he cannot name (39–40). Later, when the blind
Pozzo wants to know where they are, Vladimir confesses he couldn't
say; the two fail to name the place; and Vladimir says it cannot be
described:

> (*looking round*). It's indescribable. It's like nothing. There's noth-
> ing. There's a tree. (55)

Naming, description, and resemblance fail to explain the scene. But
Vladimir's self-contradictory retort does contain an answer: there's a
tree. The tree is like a cross, one meaning of the word "tree."[26] As a
cross, it marks the "spot," possibly designating it as the "place" where
the two were to wait (10); it represents the crucifixion of Jesus and of the
thieves (8–9); it is a crossroads for the wayfarers, who may choose to
leave; and it is the gravestone that presides over life ("Where are all these
corpses from?" 41). A cross is a symbol; were there a cross on stage it
would have only the meanings restricted to it as a symbol. But the tree
is not a symbol: it is a real tree (a willow, possibly, 10), one that is *like*
a cross, a tree from which the duo might hang themselves, and which
manifests the cycle of natural death and regeneration. So the play
develops a simile through the tree—the tree is like a cross—a simile that
preserves the identity of the tree.

A simile, Paul Ricoeur says, following Aristotle, is a developed
metaphor.[27] Where a simile presents analogy, a metaphor would specify

26. As Guicharnaud notes, 247 n. 10. In *Murphy* Beckett describes the form of a "T"
as "a decapitated potence" (166). The cross is "potent"—sexually potent, too.
27. *The Rule of Metaphor* 24–25. Frye also argues for the metaphor as a simile, in

identity: the tree is a cross. *Waiting for Godot* suggests a simile with the tree, but that simile subsumes or elaborates an identity. And this identity is borne out in the play. Reviewing what the play makes of the tree *as tree*, one finds that the tree serves as if it were a cross. Vladimir and Estragon propose to hang themselves from it; and it supposedly shows the "miracle" of regeneration, as does a cross. While Vladimir is right that the tree is virtual ("There's nothing. There's a tree"), it also embodies the metaphor that the simile "a tree is like a cross" develops. The place of the play is to the tree as salvation is to the cross—hence waiting by the tree; leaves are to the tree as regeneration is to the cross—hence the miracle of their sprouting; sexual erection is to hanging on the tree (the duo hope to be stimulated by hanging, 12) as spiritual erection is to the cross.

Beckett's tree embodies the metaphor. This direct embodiment substitutes in the play for the failures of language to name or describe directly. For Beckett the literalized metaphor is not a unit of primitive language, a language of *"things"* such as Swift's Laputan academicians use in *Gulliver's Travels,* or the original poetic noun-language as Shelley and Emerson and Nietzsche conceive it.[28] Language in the world of *Waiting for Godot* is abstract; when Vladimir and Estragon understand their own speech literally, they deal innocently with sophisticated language. The literalized metaphor is not primitive vision, but elaborates a world that seems simple because it is abstract and wordless: the concrete or literalized metaphor *is* that which it portrays or explains. In this it combines mind and world, form and content. And this is the source of its lyrical power, that it is removed by its directness, its literal-mindedness, from the complexity it embodies.

Knott's pot in *Watt* is another example much like that of the tree in *Waiting for Godot:* "It resembled a pot, it was almost a pot, but it was not a pot of which one could say, Pot, pot, and be comforted. It was in vain that it answered, with unexceptionable adequacy, all the purposes, and

---

Anatomy 123, and see Robert J. Fogelin, *Figuratively Speaking* (Yale University Press, 1988).

28. *Gulliver's Travels* 230. Nietzsche's concept is similar to Beckett's, but he leans toward "nameless things"—things without concepts. "It is our peculiar modern weakness," writes Nietzsche, "to see all primitive esthetic phenomena in too complicated and abstract a way. Metaphor, for the authentic poet, is not a figure of rhetoric but a representative image standing concretely before him in lieu of a concept" (*The Birth of Tragedy* 55). Beckett presents nameless things, but attaches to them conceptual complications.

performed all the offices, of a pot, it was not a pot" (81). It is and is not a pot; it is one of the "things of which the known name, the proven name, was not the name, any more, for him" (81). Other things and events in Watt's life resemble little else and defy naming—the piano-tuning Galls, father and son (80), for example—but to understand the pot Watt searches not only for the name but for the proper metaphor that would provide "semantic succour" (83): "Thus of the pseudo-pot he would say, after reflection, It is a shield, or, growing bolder, It is a raven, and so on" (83). He seems to think like a Greek—Aristotle also compares a bowl to a shield (*Rhetoric* 1412 b 34). Watt tries on names "almost as a woman hats" (83): he is a Don Quixote in search of embodied analogies, thinking of his pot as a shield, trying it on like a hat as the Don tries on a brass basin (*Don Quixote* 160–64). Knott's pot defies Watt's metaphors, as the barber's defies the good knight's. And yet the pot is presented as a concrete metaphor for a head and, metonymically, for a person.[29] The Latin *testa*, or "little pot," becomes the French *tête*.[30] Watt tries the name for "pot," and failing there he tries to borrow a name for the thing, but the problem with pot is that it *is* something else, a metaphorical head at least.

Malone's room, Joe's room in *Eh Joe*, and in principle all of Beckett's rooms and houses are literalized metaphors for the head. This holds also for the egglike universe of *All Strange Away* and the loose-knit enclosure of *Ill Seen Ill Said*. Even the head becomes for the Unnamable a metaphor for the head—"that head in that head" (*Worstward Ho* 22). Watt may have learned to call himself a man, but "he might just as well have thought of himself as a box, or an urn" (83). Watt's pot reflects in miniature the universe (the head head, as it were) and vice versa, micro- and macrocosm. His failure to name the pot is a failure to name the self and the world at large; that is Vladimir and Estragon's failure too. In *Watt* Beckett is still conventional in his use of images of serial contain-ment: the pot is in the house which is in the walled garden. These are the serial and self-containing surfaces of the self-as-object, the mind-as-

29. The pot contains, like Mr. Knott's body, the sum of all that Mr. Knott eats, in mockery of the idea that "you are what you eat." This joke figures in *Waiting for Godot*. In the English, Vladimir simply says, "One is what one is" (14). In the French he says, "On reste ce qu'on est" (24). Here the unsounded ending of "est" defeats the rhyme, reste-est; but the rhyming sound does make sense in German: ist-iβt. You are what you eat.

30. Ricoeur 290. See also the *OED*: "pot" is often used to describe a person, as in "the pot calling the kettle black" and "pot head." The *OED* also lists "pot" as a seventeenth-century word for "helmet."

world. So Mr. Falkland's secret, the secret of his character, his name in a sense, is in a trunk in a private apartment in his library in his house in Godwin's *Caleb Williams* (131); Poe's cat is in the wall of a chamber in the cellar of a mansion; and Lucy Snow wraps a roll of letters and puts this into a jar which she seals hermetically and buries with mortar in Brontë's *Villette* (380). I will show in Chapter 2 how Beckett's head/room metaphor participates in a larger issue, as a figure of cosmic revolution, wandering and return.

The pot in *Watt* and the tree in *Godot* are simple objects presented directly—they derive their complications from Beckett's conceptual framework. This is another feature of Beckett's metaphors: the world of *Watt* and *How It Is* is conceptually complex, but its metaphorical images or objects are simple and abstract. The world's underlying complexity informs the metaphor. This is not the regular relation between the two: Beckett reverses a long-standing relationship between the literalized metaphor and its world. The metaphor is traditionally itself complex, and its lesson informs and elaborates the given world. When Alcithoe tells the story of Salmacis and Hermaphroditus in Ovid's *Metamorphoses* (101–4), she does not set out to explain the physical or psychological condition called hermaphroditism but "how the fountain Salmacis acquired its ill repute and why its enervating waters weaken and soften the limbs they touch" (101). She tells how Salmacis's wish for the young Hermaphroditus was fulfilled in their literal union; but Salmacis disappears from the scene after this union—she becomes a part of Hermaphroditus. The literalized metaphor or image of Hermaphroditus's "double nature" (104) shows or embodies the weakness of heterogeneity that this corrupting experience brings to the pure boy, a descendant of Atlas who "did not know what love was" (102). Alcithoe relates through her complex metaphor a version of the corruption of man through sexual knowledge. Only now can the metaphor's context, the story's pretext, be understood: why the waters of the Salmacis fountain weaken the body. This fountain, whose weakening properties are "well known" (101), is itself metaphorical, the fountain of life, maturation, human knowledge. Alcithoe's literalized metaphor—nothing like a simple pot or tree—complicates, informs, and explains the world.

Modern writers tend to use metaphors in this way. In Goethe's *Elective Affinities* landscape architecture is a literalized metaphor for chemical psychology: it shows in detail how the mind's blank landscape might be arranged. This is also somewhat true in Huysmans's *Against Nature*. In these two works the literalized metaphor takes up so much space that it practically overwhelms its world. Kafka's *The Metamorphosis* demonstrates with supreme clarity this relation of the metaphor to its world. In *Snooty Baronet*, Kell-Imrie describes a puppet, a "hatter's automaton," that is "more real than live people" (133), so that he too comes under its spell. This is a controlling metaphor in the book; Lewis could not simply say, "People are puppets," and hope to shape our sense of the world as he can with the metaphor—but to create it he must take much of a chapter. In Cortázar's *Hopscotch*, Talita's role in the relationship between the friends Oliveira and Traveler is literalized when she crawls in her bathrobe on a bridge between their apartment windows (250–72). The bridge is made of two overlapping planks, which she must tie together in the precariously overhanging middle; she links Oliveira and Traveler, while preserving a gap or distance between them. This compound bridge metaphor expresses the relations between the three: the trope informs the action. For Beckett it is the reverse.

In Beckett's fiction the literalized metaphor expresses the world, but that world must explain it. In itself the metaphor is dumb. This circular dependence accounts for much of his work's difficulty: what purpose does that pot serve in *Watt*? It does not explain itself. One needs to know Beckett's language in order to decipher its individual words. Because metaphor lies, or pins the wrong name on its object,[31] it provides indirect speech for things that, as Watt discovers, cannot be spoken of directly. But when it is literal, it represents ideas directly. It is, like every part of Beckett's work, at once abstract and particular.

31. Aristotle, *Rhetoric* 1457 b 7; Ricoeur 18–20; de Man, *Allegories of Reading* 151–52.

2

Home and Away

For Beckett, wandering can be done at home. For this reason the wandering and return in his fiction represents the workings of the mind, and conversely, of the universe. As his fiction develops it argues progressively that world and mind are the same. Beckett's landscapes represent and embody thought, abstraction—the contents of mind. To understand how the landscape, images of things, come to be thought, the relation of mind and world in Beckett's work needs to be examined. This relation expresses an aesthetic of figure and ground and involves almost invariably the act of telling. Telling becomes an act of engagement with the world, an engagement made possible precisely because of the dissociation of mind and anti-mind that rules Beckett's world. Like the logic that overcomes the antagonism of anti-mind, this engagement renders radical dissociation inconsequential. There is, then, an association between differentiation (of figure and ground) and the wandering of the word (telling) as expressions of the world and mind; this complex suggests that there is a metaphysical argument to Beckett's work that is expressed here only in aesthetic terms.

Figuring the Mind

For Beckett epistemology precedes metaphysics: how one perceives determines what is. There is a correspondence between Murphy and the

stars—but Murphy is "the prior system."[1] For Beckett, as Wallace
Stevens put it, "Description is revelation," and hence "the word is the
making of the world."[2] In consequence the physical world can be stated
psychologically. Conversely, aesthetic truth has its material correlate.
This idea underlies a famous exchange between Neary and Murphy:
"All life is figure and ground," says Neary. "But a wandering to find
home," replies Murphy (*Murphy* 4). Plotinus, too, defines "being" as
"motion and rest, identity and difference": wandering and home,
ground and figure, respectively (*Enneads* II.6.1). Beckett governs his
work consistently with these terms.[3] First "all life" is stated in aesthetic
and perceptual terms, as a question of differentiation or difference. "All"
is a key word here: the whole cannot exist without differentiation—only
a part can appear whole, defined against other parts. Being somehow
depends on division: this supposition is of passionate concern in
Beckett's work. The correlate of this binary division is that one is either
home or away. All that is needed to come and go on this earth,
according to one narrator, is "a little resolution" (*Texts for Nothing 6*
102). Ground cannot eliminate figure and become "all life"; if ground
becomes figure it must displace figure, and the latter necessarily
becomes ground. Figure and ground cannot take place at the same place.
Shelter, similarly, does not efface the road: "The way was long that led
back to the den, over the fields, a winding way, it must still be there"
(*Texts for Nothing 2* 83). The two cannot occupy the same place literally,
but they can do so metaphorically, and that metaphor presents an image
of both figure and ground. Wandering can be done at home, through
metaphor.

For Beckett the quintessential figure is the head, with the world as
ground.[4] The head, of course, is part of the body, a part of anti-mind,
and not of mind. But the head is more than just a figure for the mind—it
also contains the mind and somehow defines it. The problem, at least
provisionally, is that the place of the mind is uncertain: if, as Descartes

1. *Murphy* 183. A wise man, says Robert Burton in *The Anatomy of Melancholy*, will
rule the stars (206).

2. "Description without Place" VI, 1.121; VII, 1.135.

3. "Repeatedly the narrative or thematic pattern in Beckett's work is the journey out
and return, the going and coming," says Gontarski ("Molloy and the Reiterated Novel"
60), but in the same essay he claims that Beckett's aesthetic "rejects the teleology, the
overall, all-embracing metaphor characteristic of modernism" (59).

4. Barnard, in an introductory study, associates the discussion in *Murphy* of figure and
ground with Beckett's numerous room-as-womb images, including Malone's room and
the Unnamable's jar (44).

worried, the mind is not "extended substance," not the body and not outside it, where is it? Is the mind at home or away? As Wittgenstein says in the *Philosophical Investigations*, "Surely the owner of the visual room would have to be the same kind of thing as it is; but he is not to be found in it, and there is no outside" (No. 399, I, 121). Beckett's metaphorical head both answers and evades the question. Because the metaphorical head is the room, with six planes of solid bone, as Malone says (*Malone Dies* 221), the place of the figure is naturally the home. To journey is to leave home, or the head, and to move, actually or in the imagination, to the world outside. But then this holds also for the movement from world to home. To make "headway," as the Unnamable says, one must gain ground and lose it, get lost, be on a road (314).

Beckett's subject moves out of one room, one container, only to find another shelter—or wanders to shelter only to leave again. In this, Beckett's text appropriates, for its own different purpose, the alternation of roads and shelters, crises and resolutions, that enables traditional narratives like *Jane Eyre*. Among the best examples of the alternation of head-substitutes are Beckett's *First Love*, *The Expelled*, and *The End*, short stories first written in French in 1945. In *First Love*, for example, the protagonist leaves his room at home after his father's death. He wanders to a bench, "covered" from the rear by a mound and surrounded by dead trees and a canal (16). He leaves the bench for a cow shack or "byre" (that is, a bower), returns to the bench, leaves for his friend Anna's rooms, retreats to a couch that he turns to the wall, and finally leaves when Anna gives birth. Other Beckett narratives show this relation of wandering and shelter, but in the later works this relation is increasingly metaphorical. Later, roads and rooms represent more overtly the relation of world and mind. So the narrator of *From an Abandoned Work* (written in 1955) says he travels "old roads" because he does not like "new ground"; he walks "on the dim granted ground," his "feet going nowhere only somehow home" (43). This passage sounds much like the one from *Murphy* about wandering and home, though "granted ground" sounds philosophical, more than earth. The narrator insists that he wanders ("stravaging," "going nowhere") and associates wandering with ground, but finds himself reaching home. The Unnamable, stuck at home, has the opposite complaint: he explains that because he cannot differentiate himself sufficiently from any thing, his words have "no ground for their settling" (386). He cannot go out.

These two narrators present two different, if complementary, relations between mind and world, figure and ground. In *From an Abandoned*

Work the narrator can move in his imagination, in the mental world he
has recreated. In *The Unnamable*, on the other hand, the mind cannot
envisage at any length an independent world; whatever it thinks *is* the
world, at that moment. A change of mind is a change of world. Both
narrators discuss thought as wandering, in terms of figure and ground,
but each seems to have a different kind of thought in mind. Clearly if the
head is to combine wandering and home metaphorically, then the head,
as metaphor, must accommodate these two differing relations of mind
and world.

In Beckett's fiction the metaphorical head, or home, preconditions
and subsumes the metaphorical journey in two ways, through two
models of mind—versions of the relation of mind and world. The first
version (which I tagged as the Unnamable's above) sees the head as
microcosm and equates it with the world. I have mentioned this relation
in the previous chapter—as microcosm the head *contains* the world
outside it so that the world is seen to be within the head.[5] This version
accords thought a magical efficacy: thought materializes that which it
imagines. The second version (articulated in *From an Abandoned Work*,
in the passage quoted) considers that the mind is made of particles that
translate or *reflect* the world. Thinking, on this model, is like traveling
through the world of anti-mind translated into the mind. The first
version or model is favored by Bruno and the Hermetic tradition; Vico
voices a general Hermetic sentiment when he explains that, apart from
"eternal truths," which are independent,

> we feel a liberty by thinking them to make all the things that are
> dependent on the body, and therefore we make them in time, that
> is when we choose to turn our attention to them, and we make
> them all by thinking them and contain them all within ourselves.
> For example, we make images by imagination, recollections by
> memory, passions by appetite . . . and all these things we
> contain within us. (*Autobiography* 127)

Here is the Unnamable all over. Vico emphasizes that these are *things*
that we contain within us, and, in a characteristic move, praises Plato for

5. Harvey says that "the tendency to interiorize . . . creates the microcosm"; he adds
that "the microcosm of the imagination can be not only a place to live but also the little
world of a literary work" (*Samuel Beckett Now* 183). Rose writes that "with the trilogy
novels . . . the narration moves inside, and the place narrated becomes internalized"
("The Lyrical Structure" 226).

giving abstract substances power over corporeal ones (127). The mind, in other words, repeats the Platonic cosmological process whereby the eternal Idea—Plotinus's "Intelligence"—creates matter out of itself (cp. *Enneads* v.9.5–6). The mind's creation is a real thing, and it remains unambiguously within the head. The second model of mind that informs the head metaphor is more ancient, and sees the mind as a mirror to nature. Beckett usually refers to one version of this model, where the mind is not clear and smooth but is made of fine-grained particles.[6] This version is especially suitable for Beckett's purposes because the particles of mind are words, or incorporeal substances, following the Cartesian model. Malone describes his sensations as "reflected gleams" (*Malone Dies* 186), the narrator of *Enough* refers to "gleams in my skull" (54), and in *From an Abandoned Work* the narrator explains that when he was in his "right mind," questions such as appear to him now would have been "atomized . . . before as much as formed, atomized" (44).[7] Knowledge is like a false lighthouse beam, appealing and promising home, "flickering on and off, turn about, winking on the storm, in league to fool me" (*Texts for Nothing 3* 86).[8]

6. See Rorty, especially 42–43. Rorty dates the fine-grained or particle model of the mind to Anaxagoras (42 n. 12). Acheson discusses the relation of mind and world in "Murphy's Metaphysics." See his discussion of Leibniz's idea that the mind is a living mirror to the universe (10). On Leibniz in the context of *Murphy*, see also Henning, *Beckett's Critical Complicity*, especially 50 and 59–61.

7. "Right mind" may also refer to the pictorial side of the brain, the right side; the second typescript for Beckett's short prose *Stirrings Still* begins with the same trope: "As one in his right mind . . ." With "gleams" Beckett brilliantly combines the images of mirror and particle.

8. In the last example, "flickering" suggests a more sensuous, flamelike character for the mind (cp. "flickers of reasoning," *Company* 45). This implies that the mind is, like Munch's subjects, continuously wavering, unstable—"gleams," in contrast, suggests abrupt alternation of clarity and opacity—while drawing on the traditional association between the candle flame and the soul.

Beckett refers to this model of mind often in his work. Mrs. Lambert in *Malone Dies*, for example: "Her mind was a press of formless questions, mingling and crumbling limply away" (217). One sees an image of her mind when she sorts lentils in a saucepan, separating them "from all admixture" as though trying to purify her thoughts. She is agitated, fails to concentrate, sweeps the lentils and lets many drop to the floor (213–14). Krapp sweeps his tapes—his memory—similarly to the ground. In Beckett's essay "La peinture des van Velde ou le Monde et le Pantalon" the mind is a "boîte crânienne" (*Disjecta* 126), which translates nicely as the "brain-pan" (Mercier, *Beckett/Beckett* 102). In Pozzo's celebrated speech, "the light gleams an instant" (*Waiting for Godot* 57) seems to refer to consciousness. In a draft, "Preliminary to *Textes pour rien*," Beckett writes: "car c'est sans bruit . . . dans la tête, quelques grains qui s'en vont" (4th section, 10); and in *Dream of Fair to Middling Women* the brain molecules in Belacqua's mind correspond to what he sees (120).

In the most obvious sense the head subsumes wandering because thought wanders; thought, "moving" from one mental image to another, travels the world. This formulation works only if mental images *are* the world, as the microcosmic model holds. The mirror model resists this notion.[9] In fact these two ideas of mind are similar. Where the mirror model claims that the mind reflects the world, that thought is *like* things, the microcosmic model insists that the mind embodies the world and that thought *is* things. The microcosmic version stands to the mirror version as Aristotelian metaphor stands to simile. Beckett does not restrict himself to either version in a single narrative. So the Unnamable says that

> the words are everywhere, inside me, outside me . . . I'm in words, made of words, others' words, what others, the place too, the air, the walls, the floor, the ceiling, all words, the whole world is here with me, I'm the air, the walls, the walled-in one, everything yields, opens, ebbs, flows, like flakes, I'm all these flakes, meeting, mingling, falling asunder, wherever I go I find me, leave me, go towards me, come from me, nothing ever but me, a particle of me, retrieved, lost, gone astray, I'm all these words, all these strangers, this dust of words, with no ground for their settling, no sky for their dispersing, coming together to say, fleeing one another to say, that I am they, all of them, those that merge, those that part, those that never meet. . . . (386)

In this important passage Beckett brings together both versions of mind. The Unnamable is "like flakes," "a particle," following the mirror model, and also "the whole world," as the microcosmic model prescribes. He describes himself as wandering, "lost, gone astray," but says he is home too, "the walled-in one." He is all words, or thought, and yet he is personified and can meet himself, the exiled Miltonic Satan, in his wandering: "wherever I go I find me." His words, too, are personified

9. This is fundamentally a romantic impulse. Yeats followed Coleridge in disliking the passive mirror-mind—Stendhal's idea of the novelist as mirror, and Locke's notion of the mind as *tabula rasa*—and sought for a freer imagination:

> it was this mimetic metaphor [of the mirror] that had to be transformed, to be replaced by something active, unifying, autonomous. . . . "From the soul itself must issue forth/A light," Coleridge declared in the Dejection ode. "Soul," said Yeats . . . "must become its own betrayer, its own deliverer, the one activity, the mirror turn lamp." (Keane 54)

("these strangers") and can participate, as Mahood and Worm do, in his mental landscape. His words come and go, out from him and back, toward each other and away, in order *to say him*, to tell him. "Motion is being," as Plotinus says (*Enneads* II.6.1): wandering, differentiation, is the condition for telling, and the wandering of words gives being even to the Unnamable.

Both versions of mind also share an emphasis on images or pictures.[10] Here mental images are not different from "real" or physical images— pictures that we draw or images of the world that we see.[11] Physical images are also produced by the mind. In one place the Unnamable explains that we set out from the eye, and to it return (*The Unnamable* 375). The mind, of course, does not depend on the eye—on physical sensation—to convey to it images of the world. "Balls, all balls," puns the Unnamable, "I don't believe in the eye either" (375). The mind is divorced in both models from anti-mind, and anti-mind includes the body and its organs. Sensations are Cartesian, immaterial events. Only words belong both to mind (they are "constituent of mind," in Beckett's formulation) and to the world as physical objects—traces of ink, sound waves. In one place Malone insistently distinguishes between his spoken and written language, emphasizing the latter.[12] So Beckett often associates language with the body, as when Molloy thumps his mother's head in code (one thump means yes, two no, and so on to five; *Molloy* 18) or when the narrator of *How It Is* etches his words into Pim's skin.

10. See Rabinovitz, *The Development of Samuel Beckett's Fiction*, especially 27–31, on the suitability of figurative language to describe mental activity. He says rightly that figurative language describes Belacqua's inner world (29).

11. Mitchell discusses this concept, with special reference to Wittgenstein, in *Iconology* 13–15.

12. It must be over a week since I said, I shall be quite dead at last, etc. Wrong again. That is not what I said, I could swear to it, that is what I wrote. This last phrase seems familiar, suddenly I seem to have written it somewhere before, or spoken it, word for word. Yes, I shall soon be, etc., that is what I wrote when I realized I did not know what I had said, at the beginning of my say, and subsequently . . . (*Malone Dies* 209)

This distinction, and its emphasis on the reified signification of the written word, is close to poststructuralist positions that restate Beckett's idea. If language is the House of Being, as Heidegger says (*On the Way to Language* 135), writing is wandering, the errant son to logos (see Derrida, *Dissemination* 143–46). Malone equates his telling with the original act of divine creation: he repeats several times that it has been over a week since his departure, his last "say"; he mentions a possible "fall" (208), and even says, audaciously, "at the beginning." Derrida speaks similarly of writing that, like a wandering son, has lost touch with its origin.

Some words "you wouldn't throw to a dog" (*The Unnamable* 380). Only words can travel from anti-mind and carry with them images of the world to the mind. "With the plain in my head I went to the heath," says the Expelled (*The Expelled* 13), and the character C in *Molloy* acts "like someone trying to fix landmarks in his mind" (9). One can see the mental, the verbal landmark, and know it even better than one knows the "physical" landmark, only not with the physical eye:

> But now he [C] knows these hills, that is to say he knows them better, and if ever again he sees them from afar it will be I think with other eyes, and not only that but the within, all that inner space one never sees, the brain and heart and other caverns where thought and feeling dance their sabbath, all that too quite differently disposed. (*Molloy* 10)

Not subject to natural law, language creates magically an interior space, a place like Plato's cave world, inhabited by images. But because these are now thought-images, they are no longer simply images of things. They become in effect a language, pictures that have meaning only by convention, as language does.[13]

According to both models of mind, then, to tell a story is to travel, to move in a mental but real topography. In *Texts for Nothing 9*, for example, the narrator is convinced that he could find his way out by saying the right words, a matter of "sequency of thought." If he could *say*, he could get out, "borne by my words."[14] In *Company* a character's

---

13. Ernst Gombrich popularized the notion that the innocent eye is blind in *Art and Illusion*; Nelson Goodman applied the extreme conventionalist position not only to artificial images but also to our mental images of the world, disavowing in consequence any natural order to the world; and both owe something to Wittgenstein's nominalist argument in the *Blue and Brown Books*:

> The pictures that seem to reside in our language, whether they are projected in the mind's eye or on paper, are artificial, conventional signs no less than the propositions with which they are associated. The status of these pictures is like that of a geometrical diagram in relation to an algebraic equation.

See Mitchell, *Iconology,* especially 13–43.

14. *Texts for Nothing 9* 121. This is a magical, Faustian notion: words in the right sequence can transport the self beyond its material boundaries. "Borne" also suggests that the narrator would be born upon leaving. This notion recalls the generative power of the word and compares the head with the womb, both images of generative self-containment. It is also an instance of Beckett's idea that one is given being through wandering, or movement.

crawl is counted "grain by grain in the mind" (49). A character in *Kilcool* equates wandering with text, and Malone can leave one subject and enter upon another.[15] Sapo halts because a voice stops telling—telling him "to go on" (*Malone Dies* 206). Beckett's narrators often equate wandering with speech—a variant of the Chaucerian association—as when Malone says: "I shall hear myself talking, afar off, from my far mind . . . my mind wandering, far from here, among its ruins."[16] He explains that the ground for wandering is the mind's "ruins": continuous wandering erases the head/world distinction. As the narrator of *The Calmative* says, "I have changed refuge so often, in the course of my rout, that now I can't tell between dens and ruins" (27–28). Earlier Malone equates telling with the move out ("out of my hole") and then the return, "the relapse . . . to home" (*Malone Dies* 195), but he also says that telling is the opposite of departure: "I now add these few lines, before departing from myself again" (208). Thought is both fixed and moving, home and wandering, "the brain still . . . in a way . . ." (*Not I* 77). The metaphorical head subsumes both journey and home, and these two, between them, express "all life."

Bram van Velde and the Balance of Mind

There is, then, an equation in Beckett's work between head and world, a balance between mind and anti-mind. The displacement of figure and ground and the metaphorical translation of anti-mind into mind are related to the act of telling. Molloy subtly associates these three. He explains that he never really says what he says he says; he only hears these words (88). But he does not really hear anything either—that would be physical sensation—nor do things merely "seem" to him:

> for it seemed to me nothing at all, and I had no impression of any kind, but simply somewhere something had changed, so that I too had to change, or the world too had to change, in order for

15. "He: We jump about in the book and we wander about in space" (Gontarski, *The Intent of Undoing* 135); *Malone Dies* 220. "Kilcool" is the name of a Dublin suburb, as Gontarski explains; it is also a Hebrew word meaning "deterioration" or "damage," though Beckett told me he did not know this.
16. *Malone Dies* 216. This passage is echoed in *Texts for Nothing 3*: "There's going to be a departure, I'll be there, I won't miss it, it won't be me, I'll be here, I'll say I'm far from here, it won't be me, I won't say anything, there's going to be a story, someone's going to try and tell a story" (85).

nothing to be changed. And it was these little adjustments, as
between Galileo's vessels, that I can only express by saying, I
feared that, or, I hoped that, or, Is that your mother's name? said
the sergeant, for example . . .

The imbalance between mind and world reaches Molloy's consciousness, but not through any sense "impression," and is somehow expressed by his telling. Molloy then links telling to wandering and home.
He continues:

> So I said, Yet a while, at the rate things are going, and I won't be
> able to move, but will have to stay, where I happen to be, unless
> some kind person comes and carries me. For my marches got
> shorter and shorter and my halts in consequence more and more
> frequent and I may add prolonged. For the notion of the long halt
> does not necessarily follow from that of the short march, nor that of
> the frequent halt either, when you come to think of it. (*Molloy* 88)

In consequence of the "rate" or equation between mind and world, that
is, the imbalance redressed by telling, Molloy must increasingly halt,
decreasingly march. Marching and halting alternate like ground and
figure; marching is telling, and halting silence. By telling, Molloy
weighs the balance in favor of wandering and against halting. Presumably, since he tells more, he will need to halt more, to adjust between his
vessels.[17]

The tendency here is to say more and do less. Of course if telling is
marching, then there cannot be less action if more is said. There can,
however, be less real, physical action: the action associated with
telling—wandering—is in the head, metaphorical action. Beckett's early

---

17. In *Murphy* Beckett illustrates the mind-world equation with an amusing "example":

> He [Murphy] was split, one part of him never left this mental chamber that
> pictured itself as a sphere full of light fading into dark, because there was no way
> out. But motion in this world depended on rest in the world outside. A man is in
> bed, wanting to sleep. A rat is behind the wall at his head, wanting to move. The
> man hears the rat fidget and cannot sleep, the rat hears the man fidget and dares
> not move. They are both unhappy, one fidgeting and the other waiting, or both
> happy, the rat moving and the man sleeping. (*Murphy* 110)

Note Beckett's use of the head/room/way/rest motif; there is even a rudimentary version
of the parallel light/dark motif.

works show action, expulsion, wandering, while in the middle works the protagonists increasingly revert to telling about action. But in Beckett's later fiction, beginning with *How It Is* (1961), there is action again. Things are said to be "good"—stable, accepted, given, just—in a way unthinkable in the trilogy. Somehow telling, which in the middle works almost abolished all action, is found in the later works commensurate again with wandering. This is so because as Beckett's career develops he moves from the more conventional epistemology expressed in his earlier works to the more radical idea that thought is thing. In this situation Descartes is no longer so useful: the perceiving subject is *inside* the world it perceives (cp. *Disjecta* 125 and *The Unnamable* 409). The early fiction relies on the mirror model, with anti-mind reflected into mind (re-membered, re-collected); the middle works move to the microcosmic model, culminating in *The Unnamable*, where world is mind. In the later works Beckett sees that the two models are essentially the same: the microcosmic reality—the world fully incorporated—includes both subject and object and is as independent as the reflected world of the earlier works.

The tension between the two models of mind, and its effect on Beckett's landscape, comes out clearly in *Murphy*. Murphy, who believes in the microcosmic model—he thinks that the mind is hermetically sealed from the world—actually lives in a mirror-model world; at the novel's end he finds just what a microcosmic mind might entail. Most of the characters in that novel are puppets, but Murphy is not: "All the puppets in this book whinge sooner or later, except Murphy, who is not a puppet" (122). The others are, in effect, reflections of Murphy's "bodytight" mind, for everything leads to Murphy (66). There is, however, a notable exception to this rule, which damages the mirror model of mind implicit in the novel. Mr. Endon, the mental patient Murphy so admires, is also not a puppet. When Murphy peers into Endon's eyes he does see his own distorted reflection in the cornea, but also that he was unseen by Endon, who could only see himself (248–50). Then comes an extraordinary experience for Murphy. He finds that the mirror model fails in the face of true solipsism. In Endon he finds the undifferentiated all, "ground . . . free of figure" (245). Lying deranged and naked in the grass he tries "to get a picture" of his friends in his head, all in vain.

> He tried again with his father, his mother, Celia, Wylie, Neary, Cooper, Miss Dew, Miss Carridge, Nelly, the sheep, the chan-

dlers, even Bom and Co., even Bim, even Ticklepenny and Miss
Counihan, even Mr. Quigley. He tried with the men, women,
children and animals that belong to even worse stories than this.
In vain in all cases. He could not get a picture in his mind of any
creature he had met, animal or human. Scraps of bodies, of
landscapes, hands, eyes, lines and colours evoking nothing, rose
and climbed out of sight before him, as though reeled upward off
a spool level with his throat. (251–52)

Instead of articulated images, his mind contains a jumble of bits. He
manages to reach his room in a daze, and blows up in an explosion of
gas, "superfine chaos" (253). He becomes the concrete expression of his
thought, the uncomfortable world of a mind containing "scraps of
bodies, of landscapes, hands, eyes, lines and colours evoking nothing."

   The equation of head and world can also be expressed in terms of
figure and ground, as Murphy suggests. Such expression reveals the
aesthetic and figurative quality of Beckett's metaphorical equation. "As
soon as two things are nearly identical I am lost," says Moran (Molloy
156). This search for difference is here explicitly the condition for being,
for what must be considered a fundamental quality of being. So
Company's crawler searches for an obstacle (49), and the narrator
concludes that "No such thing then as no light" (54): "perfect black is
simply not to be had" (Dream of Fair to Middling Women 214). The
all—not less than everything, as Eliot put it—is undifferentiated,
unbounded, undefined, and undefinable. Change is the minimal necessity (Company 51): "all life" would not exist, for us, if it were not visible
as figure and ground, in terms of contrast. For this reason Beckett often
emphasizes the differentiation involved in his characters' movements, as
when Macmann's place "thanks to the hat continued to contrast with the
surrounding space" while Macmann "rolled upon the ground" (Malone
Dies 246). All one needs to come and go on this earth, according to one
narrator, is "a little resolution" (Texts for Nothing 6 102).

   Beckett's evolving aesthetic has a correlate in a set of works that also
show the fragmentation of the world, its translation into mind, and its
subsequent resurrection. These are the paintings of his friend Abraham
van Velde (1895–1981), the abstract painter. Van Velde's paintings are in
several ways like Beckett's work, and have probably influenced Beckett.
They deserve close attention here, not least of all because they are
themselves extraordinary.

Bram van Velde is often mentioned in connection with Beckett, but his work itself is little discussed, possibly because he only painted about a hundred paintings in all (Putman 1960, 47).[18] Beckett wrote several short essays about Bram van Velde (and about Bram's brother Geer, also a painter), recently collected by Ruby Cohn in the indispensable *Disjecta* (117–45). Most critics follow to some extent Beckett's lead and say that van Velde is a painter of absence.[19] Jacques Putman justly distinguishes the consistency of his oeuvre, in words that describe Beckett's enterprise too:

> L'unité de la démarche apparaît: pas de faux pas, pas de toiles sans nécessité, pas de toiles ratées, quelle que soit l'esthétique dont elles se réclament, pas de demi-mesure. Un fil ininterrompu fait d'une incroyable fidélité à soi-même, à ce qui demeure inconnu en soi-même, guide d'un bout à l'autre de l'oeuvre. (1960, 47)

Beckett's essays on van Velde show Beckett articulating his own aesthetic sentiments, not really disguised as praise for the painter's achievement. They show, furthermore, that he admires van Velde's work because he sees the painter much as he sees himself, as a true artist in the only possible sense, an artist who scorns the notion that there can be an object—any signified—for art. [20]

18. Among discussions of his work, Beckett's are most distinguished. See also Duthuit in *Derrière le Miroir* (February 1952); a 1959 monograph by Beckett, Georges Duthuit, and Jacques Putman, published in English by Grove Press (1960); Putmann's [sic] useful "Bram van Velde," *L'Oeil* no. 65 (May 1960): 44–49; Putman's *Catalogue raisonné de l'oeuvre du peintre* (Turin: Edizioni d'Arte Fratelli Pozzo, 1961); Schneider in *L'Express* (25 November 1968); Gaëtan Picon's "Sur Bram van Velde," the introductory essay to *Bram van Velde* (Archives de l'art contemporain 12, 1970); Juliet and Putman, *Bram van Velde* (Paris: Maeght, 1975); and Albright, *Representation and the Imagination* (1977).

19. Picon 14. Picon also describes van Velde's work as having presence; there is movement in his paintings, he says, but not a movement that searches for its form or direction:

> D'un tel mouvement seulement peut-on dire qu'il est là, ou encore que quelque chose l'a laissé fuir, qu'on l'a laissé échapper. Chaque fois, c'est le même acte, disant cela seul qu'on peut dire, non point un acte différent, disant tantôt plus et tantôt moins: à la fois semblable à tous les autres, quelconque—et unique, excepté de tous les autres, comme chaque respiration, chaque battement du coeur est en même temps sans identité et sans pareil. (9)

20. Bair says that Beckett found in van Velde "a visual counterpart for the futility of

Art today has three options, Beckett explains in "Peintres de l'empêchement": it can return to the old naïveté of representational painting, it can accept its own defeat, or else it can acknowledge, as van Velde's painting does, the absence of rapport and the absence of the object.[21] The latter is the only true way, and Beckett saw himself as following it. Daniel Albright suggests that in his 1945 essay, "La peinture des van Velde ou le Monde et le Pantalon," Beckett praises the painter much as he had praised Proust: "The compliments Beckett used for Proust in 1931 are adapted to van Velde: he is the hero who has turned his eyes from the exterior chaos of time, from spatial representation, in order to seize the [internal] 'ideal real'" (Albright, "Plates," Plate 6). Like Proust, van Velde is the model artist for Beckett—and Beckett has always striven to be himself the ideal artist. Bair reports that some in Georges Duthuit's *transition* circle in Paris, with which both van Velde and Beckett associated, feared that Beckett's theoretical talk would inhibit the painter, but says that "if one examines the paintings of van Velde since 1950, it is obvious that Beckett had little influence upon him" (*Samuel Beckett* 394). This may be true, though his painting continues to develop during and after the fifties (Beckett's late "middle" period) much as Beckett's work develops. It is certainly possible that the painter influenced the writer; and their respective works developed along similar lines well before they knew each other's work. Van Velde's work may have served Beckett, up to a point, as a generative system, a structuring device which helped him conceptualize and work through his own systematic enterprise.[22]

Van Velde's work begins with expressionistic landscapes that are soon made entirely abstract, then moves to abstract representations of the head, and finally to abstract landscapes again, which are now seen

---

expression he encountered in his own writing" (*Samuel Beckett* 394), Albright calls van Velde "a plastic Samuel Beckett" (160), Rosen calls the painter Beckett's "artistic surrogate" (215), and Robinson calls him Beckett's "counterpart" (36).

Beckett told me that he felt while writing exactly as van Velde appeared to him to feel when he painted, as a man plunging into deep water without knowing how to swim.

21. In *Disjecta* 137. Beckett was commissioned to write this essay for *Derrière le Miroir*, the publication of the Galerie Maeght in Paris, where it appeared in June 1948.

22. As indeed his essays on the van Veldes suggest. Leach and Kirkpatrick explain and discuss visual generative systems that contemporary writers use to organize their texts. Morrissette warns against the notion that these writers relinquish their control over their texts when they use external generative systems (26)—though that is what Beckett is said to have done in making *Lessness* (he supposedly shook sentence-fragments and spliced them).

FIGURE 1.   "Paysage" (1922). 85 x 100. S. Spierer, Geneva (© 1992 ARS, New York/SPADEM, Paris)

within the head, a mental geography. He began painting in an expressionist artists' colony in Worpswede, Germany (1922–24), and his early paintings, like "The Cyclist" and "Paysage," show the frightening, wobbly, and familiar visible world. In "Paysage" (1922), for example (Figure 1), there is a blurring of boundaries, but the boundaries are there; there are shaded blotches and paint masses, but one readily recognizes a road, center back, and some growing things, left. There is a crude perspective. One can already distinguish the geometrical patterns that dominate the later works, a triangle at upper center and another at bottom left, but these are here legitimate parts of the landscape. These early paintings show the world of anti-mind, the world of early Beckett fiction. Both artists, working at least in part within the expressionist framework, show a world wavering under the pressure of mind, and both combine compassion with a brutal tearing up of things. So in the jejune *Assumption* (*transition* 16–17, 1929), the protagonist dies of his expressionistic hunger, swept from life and his woman by the mind-bent world:

> Then it happened. While the woman was contemplating the face that she had overlaid with death, she was swept aside by a great storm of sound, shaking the very house with its prolonged, triumphant vehemence, climbing in a dizzy, bubbling scale, until, dispersed, it fused into the breath of the forest and the throbbing cry of the sea. (Jolas 44)

This is not the best literature, but it is pure expressionism. In *Walking Out* (*More Pricks Than Kicks*, 1934), similarly, Belacqua pauses "not so much in order to rest as to have the scene soak through him"; he *takes in* the scene "in a sightless passionate kind of way" (101). The world's surface in these works seems permeable, susceptible to suggestion, and inclined to penetrate the self, but there is no question of actual penetration. In *First Love* (written 1945) the mirror-model mind again recollects the past: "The day itself [of his birth] comes back to me, when I put my mind to it" (11). Tenderness seems fundamentally unstable: "how tender the earth can be for those who have only her" (35); "I set out in the morning and was back by night, having lunched lightly in the graveyard" (11). In these stories the landscape is a primary concern, but things are permeable, seen into. A field, for example, is "richer on the surface in nettles than in grass and in mud than in nettles," but its subsoil is "perhaps possessed of exceptional qualities" (21).

Between 1925 and 1930, in Paris, Bram van Velde painted abstract and fluid portraits and still lifes. These are titled, dated, and recognizable: "femme, iris, tulipe, rue de Paris, portrait," as Picon says. "Les choses sont encore là" (8). Soon after, however, he painted more abstract landscapes like "Two faces" of 1932 (Figure 2), where vaguely geometrical forms are crowded together with more Matissean figures like the swan head and neck (at top right) and the ornamental leafed stems (just left of center). Here the recognizable figures are embedded in their surroundings, like fossils or foreign objects impressed into mud. These more geometrical works, where the canvas is cut up into interlocking dark and light segments, show van Velde's development and foreshadow his imminent breakthrough. They have their Beckettian correlatives in *Watt* (written 1942–44) and *Mercier and Camier* (written in French in 1945), both works where near-human characters are embedded in abstracted, geometrical landscapes. In *Watt* the topography

FIGURE 2. "Two faces" (1932). 81 x 100. Jacques Putman, Paris. This work is entitled simply "Figures" in the 1970 *Musée National d'Art Moderne* (Paris) edition (© 1992 ARS, New York/SPADEM, Paris)

consists almost entirely of straight roads, circular rooms, and square gardens. Watt himself is given borderline reality—he is at least presented as real, more or less—but no such trouble is taken with his world: the locked door that opens, Mr. Knott's rotating furniture, or the Lynch family. Watt's world, according to the addenda to *Watt*, is a "soul-landscape" (249). In *Mercier and Camier* the landscape is mostly made up, like van Velde's canvases, of field parcels divided by hedges. This work's "pseudo-couple" are even more virtual than Watt, like complementary material correlates of an idea.

After the war van Velde worked in his mature style,[23] but he had

23. All sources agree that van Velde did not paint during the war, but Beckett insisted to me that van Velde did paint during the war and said that Beckett and his wife used to watch him paint in his atelier in Paris in 1940 or 1941.

made the decisive move in that direction before the war, even as early as the middle thirties. He had started with human figures in expressionistic settings, moved to abstract the settings and enmesh his figures in them, and then, in the middle thirties, began to paint his landscapes *as figures*. More specifically, he painted human heads, but not heads in a landscape: he painted heads as landscape. This is much what Beckett does with his virtual figures. A key, transitional work for van Velde here is the 1934 "Masques" (called only "Peinture" in Putman's 1960 *L'Oeil* article; Figure 3). The painting still distinguishes between figure and ground, with a discernible squarish head occupying most of the canvas, bottom center. The ground is a set of flat line-drawn masks at top, and also a flat surface around the perimeter, top left, and some vaguely ornamental squiggles at top right. In themselves these differentiated lines and surfaces can be considered figures, but they produce an extreme flatness that gives the "head," with its dark eyes and triangular shadowing, some depth, in contrast. This head is clearly made of landscape, the kind of segmented topography that characterizes "Two faces." In 1938 van Velde was imprisoned for a month in Bayonne, France,[24] and this experience evidently accelerated his interest in the head as his controlling image. Jacques Putman says that his imprisonment impressed the painter forcibly. In prison he drew some of his most explicit heads, using envelopes or other throwaway paper (see "Dessin," Figure 4). The head represents here his incarceration, a den like Beckett's prison-heads; van Velde's experience attaches him to a kind of tradition important to Beckett, a group of imprisoned visionaries that includes Boethius and Bunyan. Through the late 1960s, van Velde painted many heads, some very explicit as heads, others more schematic. These heads take center stage (as the figure) and sustain a tension with their ground. Often the ground is scarred like the head (as in "Dessin," 1938, Figure 4). In some of these the head is just a perimeter line drawing imposed on the landscape. The heads of the fifties and sixties are made of thicker lines: some float forward in dark grounds while others merge with their grounds (Figure 5).

Whether their interiors merge with and are the "exterior" world, or merely reflect the world, they resemble in principle Beckett's middle-period works. In *Molloy* (written 1947) the world still wobbles under the

---

24. He had just returned to France and had failed to renew his "papiers de résident" (Putman, "Introduction"). Compare Molloy's similar experience when he cannot produce his "papers" and is interrogated by the police.

FIGURE 3. "Masques" (1934). 100 x 80. Galerie Maeght, Paris. Van Velde's
theme is not the mask but masking itself: how many masks beneath the mask?
(© 1992 ARS, New York/SPADEM, Paris)

FIGURE 4. "Dessin" (1938). 17 x 17. Jacques Putman, Paris (© 1992 ARS, New York/SPADEM, Paris). Note the geometrical vortex lying at right angle to the masklike layers, which are predominantly perpendicular (especially at left). For Beckett's use of the vortex see Chapters 4, 5, and 7 below.

expressionistic pressures of the mind. Moran changes, in a sense, from an artist or critic who thinks that things have their proper names and places, to an expressionist Molloy whose world oozes around and revolts him. Malone in *Malone Dies* (written in French in 1948) heightens the tension of mind and world, returning to the head, living in the head, but "going out" to ground in his telling. He can be compared to the artist who, like Kandinsky, still believes in the object, even if it is "only" a mental object. In *The Unnamable* (written in French, 1949) the world is entirely interiorized, mind is world. "How all becomes clear and simple," says the Unnamable, "when one opens an

FIGURE 5. Untitled gouache (1958). 123 x 92.5. Private collection, Geneva (©
1992 ARS, New York/SPADEM, Paris). The "sloppy" overlay of paint areas
(especially bottom left) helps fuse the head with its ground.

eye on the within, having of course previously exposed it to the without, in order to benefit by the contrast" (342–43).

Beckett is said to have told Israel Shenker in 1956 that he had failed to surmount his trilogy difficulties with *Texts for Nothing* (written in French in 1950). But Pilling is right that the *Texts for Nothing* "occupy a genuine median point between *The Unnamable* and the works that have come after them."[25] In *Texts for Nothing* Beckett's protagonist narrators still hold an underground position in relation to the other characters told about (Coe 80), but the topography of figure and ground is reestablished. This development, which anticipates the later fiction, is consistent with Beckett's movement in the trilogy. In *Texts for Nothing* Beckett undermines the tension created by a mind conscious of its own isolation.[26] The narrator in *Texts for Nothing 1* recalls the "failure" in *The Unnamable* to go on: "Suddenly, no, at last, long last, I couldn't any more, I couldn't go on" (75). Then he explains why he could not remain in the head, and how the world of anti-mind was resurrected:

> I could have stayed in my den, snug and dry, I couldn't. My den, I'll describe it, no, I can't. It's simple, I can do nothing any more, that's what you think. I say to the body, Up with you now, and I can feel it struggling, like an old hack foundered in the street, struggling no more . . .

That is the teller ("hack") on his road ("in the street"), on the way; he can perceive himself now. "I say to the head, Leave it alone, stay quiet, it stops breathing, then pants on worse than ever." He talks, in other words, both to body and to mind (here represented by its container), and both try to obey, then fail. He commands both because he is neither, or both, as he explains ("it's truly one to me"); he need not wander (body) nor stay (mind) because he is both body and mind and can take either position against the other. This is radically unlike the Unnamable's impasse:

> I am far from all that wrangle, I shouldn't bother with it, I need nothing, neither to go on nor to stay where I am, it's truly all one

---

25. Knowlson and Pilling, *Frescoes of the Skull* 43. Pilling argues that *Texts for Nothing* makes *How It Is* possible (41–60).

26. For this reason perhaps Pilling says that in *Texts for Nothing* and in *How It Is* Beckett moves to abolish the divisive distinction between subject and object (*Frescoes of the Skull* 69–71); where the subject moves as a real object inside himself, it is both subject and object. This logic already figures in earlier works.

to me, I should turn away from it all, away from the body, away
from the head, let them work it out between them, let them
cease, I can't, it's I would have to cease. (*Texts for Nothing 1* 75)

Rose argues that the thirteen texts show, in sequence, the outer scene
(*TfN 1*), the mind (*TfN 2–4*), solipsism (*TfN 5*), the move out again
(*TfN 6–8*), and then the voice's struggle to free itself and its reasoned
reconciliation with continuity ("The Lyrical Structure" 230). If this is so,
these texts follow and review the chronological development of Beckett's fiction up to this point. The *Texts for Nothing* do not abandon
ambivalence, the play between mind and anti-mind, but Beckett's
narrator is now willing to acknowledge that he is both.

Bram van Velde's work follows this development. Along with the
heads of the late 1930s and after, he also paints abstracted, geometrical
worlds, resembling the early abstract paintings, though more intensely
woven. His ruling medium after the war is gouache, more fluid and
more raw than the earlier oil. His world seems interior, epidermal:
"C'est un espace du dedans, mais ce n'est pas l'espace mental. . . . Ici
s'étend le lourd espace qui s'ouvre une fois traversée la surface de l'eau,
une fois percé l'épiderme du corps" (Picon 9). In several works the
image of the head is superimposed, overlaid on the landscape (Figure 6).
Elsewhere no head stares through things: there is only landscape (Figure
7). These latter works are strikingly like the early abstracted landscapes
(Figure 2, for example), though they are more abstract, geometrical, and
fluid. Van Velde paints these undifferentiated landscape images and his
head images (both mirroring and embodying world) during the same
postwar years; in Beckett's case, the chronology is more sharply
demarcated. But when van Velde's work from before the war is
considered, his development seems less ambiguous. Van Velde's move
to the landscape again is prefigured in Beckett's writings, although it
appears that van Velde was there first.

Metaphors of Travel, Travel of Metaphor

Beckett's radical dissociation of mind and world, and the displacement
of figure and ground, mandate that all traveling in Beckett's fiction is
metaphorical: mind cannot participate in anti-mind as figure cannot
participate in ground, except through metaphor. It should already be
clear that Beckett literalizes this metaphor, erasing the mind-world
division, and he does so with the metaphorical journey. Metaphorically

FIGURE 6.   Untitled gouache (1962). 122 x 147. Musée d'Art et d'Histoire,
Geneva. This work portrays the head through its vertical lines and its "eyes," eye
shapes more or less aligned horizontally at the top. The wandering of human
features recalls Picasso's similar practice.

the head contains the world, and so *is* the world. Consequently for
Beckett travel or movement along the world's surface can represent
cosmic revolution. And because the only movement in the head is the
movement of thought, this cosmic revolution is endowed with thought:
the self is imposed on the landscape, which is otherwise so exclusive of
mind. This leads, on the one hand, to classical and magical ideas about
the world—the globe is alive, it thinks—and also to a Dantean view that
the spiritual and the geographical journeys are the same. In several
instances Beckett describes the body in terms of the world, as in *From an*

Figure 7. "Composition" (1966). 130 x 195. Musée National d'Art Moderne, Centre Georges Pompidou, Paris. There is still some hint of the old head/world division here, which can be seen along the perimeter, top and sides, but unless one knows to look for it, it would not be obvious.

Abandoned Work, where a pregnant belly is a cavernous mountain (34), and in *Malone Dies*, where Malone is the world, with his arse in Australia (235). More often, this superimposition of figure and ground takes the opposite form—the world is endowed with human features. One may find oneself lost "on the face of wind-swept wastes" (*Malone Dies* 227), a road is "blind" (182), the terrain has "folds" like skin or a cloak (*Molloy* 11), and the world is "corpsed" (*Endgame*). This is in part Viconian projection, which sees a hill as having a brow, shoulder, back, and foot. But Beckett is not here concerned with naming *per se*, but with the geographical combination of self and world.

Beckett uses the wandering of thought to represent cosmic revolution—a connection that the head-as-world metaphor suggests directly. While many modern writers shun those epic and mythopoeic organizing devices favored by classical and Renaissance writers, Beckett's work reflects unremitting concern for cosmic and topographical schemata. In this he is substantially indebted to Joyce. Joyce's world is "solarsys-

temised, seriolcosmically, in a more and more almightily expanding
universe under one, there is rhymeless reason to believe, original sun"
(*Finnegans Wake* [II.2] 263.24–27). Bloom the returning wanderer sets
out from his house on the sunny side of the street, and imagines
traveling "round in front of the sun" (*Ulysses* 57). He lives on Eccles
Street, reminding the reader of the phrase from *Ecclesiastes* that Beckett
echoes in the beginning of *Murphy*.[27] Beckett uses the sun's movement
to elaborate the geographical aspect of his metaphorical journey. He
links both telling and wandering with the daily cycle. The wandering
cycle is diurnal: "the feet going nowhere only somehow home, in the
morning out from home and in the evening back home again" (*From an
Abandoned Work* 43). And the narrator of *From an Abandoned Work* says:

> But let me start as always with the morning and the getting out.
> When a day comes back, whatever the reason, then its morning
> and its evening too are there, though in themselves quite
> unremarkable, the going out and the coming home, there is a
> remarkable thing I find. So up then in the grey of dawn, very
> weak and shaky after an atrocious night little dreaming what lay
> in store, out and off. (46)

Telling ("let me start"), like wandering, follows a solar cycle: both start
with the morning and the move "out." Morning and evening mean little
separately, but together they are significant, because night returns the
traveler to a "home." Like the sun, the narrator gets "up" at dawn,
though "out and off" has a double significance—the sun's movement
includes both revelation and extinction, coming out and going out,
getting off and turning off. Similarly in *Company* dark lightens while the
voice sounds, "deepens when it ebbs" (19); see how subtly Beckett
includes geographical movement ("ebbs") in the quality of his voice.

This wandering of Beckett's teller, then, is essentially diurnal.[28] So
numerous Beckett characters are associated particularly with the sun. In
Watt the narrator is "in the sun. . . . I was the sun" (42), and Mr.

27. For the Eccles-*Ecclesiastes* association, see Seidel, *Epic Geography* 37. He discusses
Joyce's interest in the solar epic and its classical sources, and the diurnal structure of
Ulysses in general (especially 24–27). Seidel gives the lines from Joyce I quote here.
28. Hoffman notes that "in the case of Dante's Belacqua, the issue [of motion from
place to place] is met in indolence; he will wait, while the sun moves. Beckett's persons
move, and assume (at least in collaboration with it) the diurnal motion of the earth"
(*Samuel Beckett* 101).

Knott is in several places described as the sun, rising and setting (e.g., 86–87). Molloy associates wandering and rest with the daily cycle (67), as does the narrator of *The Calmative*: "But up with me again and back on the way. . . . it's west I must go" (45–46). The sun opens the story of *Murphy*: "The sun shone, having no alternative, on the nothing new."[29] Murphy, rocking up, down, and up again in his chair, resembles the sun. And the Unnamable imagines that he moves his head in and out of his jar in tandem with the diurnal cycle: "And often at dawn, having left it out all night, I bring it in" (*The Unnamable* 331). The sun's east-west axis figures prominently in Beckett's topography—it is the line of travel, for example, in *How It Is* (123). Getting worse is also going west, as the title of *Worstward Ho* implies—"In me thou seest the twilight of such day / As after sunset fadeth in the west." That the sun's axis curves presents no difficulty, because the straight line is in fact a curve, as Beckett notes that Bruno explained ("Dante... Bruno.Vico..Joyce," *Our Exagmination* 6). So Molloy rues the sun's rising in the east, but then admits that he confuses east and west (19). An infinitely large circle would have a straight line for circumference, and this, with Brunovian logic, holds for the smallest circle as well (*Our Exagmination* 6). To journey is to move in a circle, in principle, or at least in a curve—and the gentle slope, conversely, is a plateau (*Malone Dies* 246). Like the sun, Beckett's protagonists travel "the arc of a gigantic circle" (246), "not in a straight line . . . but in a sharp curve" (*The Unnamable* 316): "How often round the earth already" (*Company* 15).

That the metaphorical journey should have a diurnal quality seems perfectly logical, given the geographical interpretation of the self, the head-as-world. Less obvious is Beckett's unobtrusive insistence that flowers belong in this context. Flowers, like the sun, reflect the diurnal quality of Beckett's landscapes: they line the path of thought in the metaphorical head. Flowers serve as images of the mind, if only because, like the mind, they are enclosed in their vases, the "flowers of rhetoric" (*The Unnamable* 379). In *First Love* the protagonist asks for a living flower in a pot, which then dies, leaving a half-buried bulb (32). It is perhaps in this context that one should read Beckett's lyrical rendition of a *pot de chambre* as "vase de nuit" in *Premier Amour* (44). The home/head motif of the chamber pot incorporates the flower vase and night/day

29. Cp. Thackeray, "On the second day . . . the sun rose as usual" (157), and Auden, "the sun shone / As it had to on the white legs disappearing into the green / Water" ("Musée des Beaux Arts").

motifs too.[30] Watt is an old rose (no longer afraid of the gardener; *Watt* 253), and the Unnamable says that his head is a sprouted bud (354), a sheaf of flowers in a jar: "Stuck like a sheaf of flowers in a deep jar, its neck flush with my mouth, on the side of a quiet street near the shambles, I am at rest at last" (327). As cut flowers the narrator is finally at rest; living flowers, in contrast, make the "horizon" and "ground" of traveling, a "moving carpet" (*Enough* 55). Their trajectory encompasses the mind's horizon.[31] Flowers are trod underfoot (*Watt* 135–36, *Enough* 55, 56). Flowers line the path of travel (*Malone Dies* 206). In *Murphy* Beckett opts for flowers called "traveller's joy" (258). Flowers cover the walls of the room/head, as Malone tells it,

> wall-paper still clinging in places to the walls and covered with a writhing mass of roses, violets and other flowers in such profusion that it seemed to me I had never seen so many in the whole course of my life. (*Malone Dies* 223–24)

Malone specifically refers to the "whole course" of his life, the metaphorical way that is the walls of his world. Like the sun's course, the flower path figures the wandering of mind, subsumed in the head. Flowers do not embody wandering but serve as useful emblems, appealing figurations of the geographical journey. Their diurnal character makes them cosmic or geographical figures. Beckett's flowers are often heliotropes, mirroring and following the sun. They open to the sun (*Molloy* 67), and they fade like darkness falling (*The Calmative* 45). Joyce's Bloom is a good example of heliotropism, a wandering flower.[32] For Beckett, flowers and the sun embody, in other words, the quality of the journey itself.

30. See Kristeva 158 n. 1. In *Premier Amour* the narrator says that he had always loved the words "vase de nuit," which remind him of Racine or Baudelaire. This passage is missing in the English.

31. For this sense of "horizon," see Karl Jaspers, "Existenzphilosophie," from *Reason and Existenz*, in Kaufmann, especially 184–94.

32. Joyce draws on the literal meaning of "Bloom" often in *Ulysses*. Beckett takes a pot-shot at the Joycean protagonist in *Dream* through the Empress Wu of China: "'Bloom!' she cried to the peonies, 'bloom, blast you!'" (99). In *Finnegans Wake* II.1 Joyce associates the heliotrope directly with troping, the diurnal cycle, and with pilgrimage (248–49).

See *A Portrait of the Artist as a Young Man* for another image of the flower-strewn path: Stephen, like Malone after him, stares "at the great overblown scarlet flowers of the tattered wallpaper . . . imagining a roseway from where he lay upwards to heaven all strewn with scarlet flowers" (221–22).

In Beckett's scheme of things, geographical movement, metaphorical wandering, is the process of differentiation, producing figure and ground, home and the way, mind and world, subject and object. This process of displacement (or emanation, in Chapters 5 and 6) is the defining action of metaphor—metaphor is "the displacement of nouns," as Jacques Derrida puts it ("White Mythology" 33). Beckett's trope for this metaphorical division of "all life," for the equation of mind and anti-mind, for the alternation of road and shelter, is division, translation, alternation—it is the trope itself. The metaphorical journey is the process of metaphor. Such practice makes Beckett a literalist of the imagination (Yeats's judgment of Blake): his images embody concretely the intellectual process that underlies his world. As he writes in *Proust*, "The Proustian world is expressed metaphorically by the artisan because it is apprehended metaphorically by the artist" (67). His topography, one might say, is intelligent. Like the heliotrope that lines the way of wandering in the head, the sun is, to borrow Derrida's phrasing, "the paradigm of what is sensible *and* of what is metaphorical: it regularly turns (itself) and hides (itself)." Metaphor, continues Derrida, "therefore means heliotrope, both movement turned to the sun, and the turning movement of the sun."[33] So Beckett's Unnamable confesses that he is a sprouted flower-head: as such he is a "mechanism," he declares, that first makes visible and then extinguishes (*The Unnamable* 354). The heliotrope is machinelike, predictable and systematic. Like the Unnamable, the sun makes visible but hides itself and cannot itself be seen directly. This is the aesthetic of a world that is ruled by tropes. The process of seeing, of making seen (showing), the differentiation of things, brings things into being, makes what is. "Art," Beckett says in "Intercessions by Denis Devlin," "is the sun, moon and stars of the mind, the whole mind" (94).

The sun in its diurnal cycle embodies the movement from home to wandering to home again, the halting and marching of telling, the revelations and denials of Beckett's narrators. Both sun and self parallel in their wandering the self's movement to unveil itself, whereby it alternates between its states (Blake's term) of subjectivity and objectivity. And finally, like the journey, Beckett's metaphorical head or home is also a metaphor for the metaphorical process that underlies Beckett's

33. "White Mythology" 52. Paul de Man also emphasize the natural, self-originating quality of flowers, which, he argues, makes them metaphors for poetic language ("Intentional Structure of the Romantic Image" 68–70).

work. The home is a metaphor for metaphor: "expropriation, being-away-from-home, but still in a home, away from home but in some-one's home, a place of self-recovery, self-recognition, self-mustering, self-resemblance: it is outside itself—it is itself" ("White Mythology" 55). These lines could have been written explicitly to explain Beckett's work. Wandering and home together reconstruct the metaphorical and topological relation of mind to anti-mind in the steps of Beckett's epistemology, and express the metaphorical, periodic, self-revelatory logic of his world. What process underlies Beckett's world? It is displacement, translation, periodicity, concealment, revelation.

3

Landscapes of Pilgrimage

I have discussed wandering as Beckett's agent of differentiation, an agent of a binary worldview. Wandering is purposeful in the scheme of Beckett's work, but does it lead anywhere? As the narrator of *From an Abandoned Work* says, "I have never in my life been on my way anywhere, but simply on my way" (39). Because to wander is to move in a circle, there may appear little sense in it as directed behavior: one returns eventually to the head, as Malone says (*Malone Dies* 236), or travels "so many times already round the earth," to speak geographically (*Company* 23, and see 15, 21, 60). Where are we when we are "nowhere in particular on the way from A to Z" (*Company* 23)? Beckett's travelers are directed even when not going somewhere special: the protagonists of *How It Is*, for example, travel east—not exactly a place but not exactly not a place either. In *The Lost Ones*, when the ladders do not serve as "vehicles to the niches and tunnels," they still lead somewhere, if only "clear of the ground" (25). A ladder leads up, whether or not it leads up to something.

Journeying in Beckett's fiction of the first thirty years usually represents the subject's search for the place of the object. In his earlier fiction Beckett pursues this goal in the exterior, surface world; he then moves to depth, into his subject. Finally, the "place" of objectivity is found in the tension between the two movements: the gap between subject and object is transformed into a threshold or doorway. The subject's search for unity can be thought of as the figure's search for ground, an attempt to annul the differentiation that wandering creates,

to efface the perceiver and perceived. The search is an attempt to abolish
searching, a move to abolish movement, just as Malone's telling is a search
for final silence. There is nothing "paradoxical" here, any more than it is a
contradiction to journey in order to reach home. But the solution to the
subject–object problem lies not in abolishing one of the terms; rather, it lies
in a dialectical third condition enabled by the tension between them.

I

The Union of Subject and Object

Beckett's critical writings—*Proust* and the *Three Dialogues*, especially—
are often considered to prophesy his poetics of failure.[1] These works do
express admiration for a kind of failure, but they also set the terms of
Beckett's pilgrimage. In *Proust* Beckett gives the definition of reality
as "the adequate union of subject and object" (57). He says that this
old story is "Baudelaire's definition," but it is his choice of it that
is important. This passage in *Proust*, less noticed than several of his
pronouncements on art, is one of the most important in Beckett's early
writing (and if, as Nicholas Zurbrugg says, Beckett "systematically
misrepresents Proust's vision by reducing it to Beckettian terms," all the
better for the purpose of studying Beckett).[2] Speaking of Marcel, who
has just left the library, Beckett writes:

> So now in the exaltation of his brief eternity, having emerged
> from the darkness of time and habit and passion and intelligence,
> he understands the necessity of art. For in the brightness of art
> alone can be deciphered the baffled ecstasy that he had known
> before the inscrutable superficies of a cloud, a triangle, a spire, a
> flower, a pebble, when the mystery, the essence, the Idea,
> imprisoned in matter, had solicited the bounty of a subject

1. Read ("Artistic Theory in the Work of Samuel Beckett"), Trezise (6–10), Pilling
("Writings on Literature and Art," *Samuel Beckett* 13–24), Knowlson and Pilling ("A
Poetics of Indigence," *Frescoes* 241–56), and especially Dobrez (chapter 1) provide useful
discussions. Zurbrugg protests that Beckett's fictional world is "anti-Proustian" (*Beckett
and Proust* 45).
2. Zurbrugg, *Beckett and Proust* 103.

passing by within the shell of his impurity, and tendered, like Dante his song to the "ingegni storti e loschi," at least an incorruptible beauty:
> "Ponete mente *almen* com'io son bella."

And he understands the meaning of Baudelaire's definition of reality as "the adequate union of subject and object," and more clearly than ever the grotesque fallacy of a realistic art—"that miserable statement of line and surface," and the penny-a-line vulgarity of a literature of notations. (*Proust* 57)

Beckett suggests that the artist's task is to seek this reality, the union or reconciliation with the object. This union cannot be attained by propositioning the object logically but through intuition, a "mystical experience" (57) described in religious terms. Marcel experiences the pure Idea descending into matter in clear vertical progression (cp. Jolas's manifesto): first "a cloud" (the holy-mystical godhead, pure Idea), then "a triangle" (godhead's perfect Platonic and occult representation), descending to "a spire" (the spirit's architectural representation), then "a flower" (rooted and natural perfection, worthy of Beatrice), and finally to clay and clod, mere matter, now charged with grandeur.

For Hegel, the union of subject and object is the goal of Spirit achieving full self-consciousness, journeying to incarnation or self-revelation through the dialectical process of history. Here is a version of this model from the "Revealed Religion" section of the *Phenomenology of Mind*:

> There is something in its object concealed from consciousness if the object is for consciousness an "other," or something alien, and if consciousness does not know the object as its self. This concealment, this secrecy, ceases when the Absolute Being *qua* spirit is object of consciousness. For here in its relation to consciousness the object is in the form of self; i.e. consciousness immediately knows itself there, or is manifest, revealed, to itself in the object. . . . It is . . . at home with itself. (759)

Hegel's thesis is an extreme statement of an idea that Beckett found compelling on a different level.[3] One thinks of Joyce disclaiming the

---

3. See Hegel's *Phenomenology* VII.C-VIII, especially 789–91. Beckett's reference to Schopenhauer regarding this matter (*Proust* 8) shows that he paid some attention to

psychological accuracy of his internal monologue, or of Yeats endorsing his Vision as "stylistic arrangements of experience" that "have helped me to hold in a single thought reality and justice" (*A Vision* 25). This claim, as Richard Ellmann has noted, is far from modest, appropriating more than literal truth ("W. B. Yeats's Second Puberty" 14).

Beckett's project should be considered in this light. The union of subject and object is of course also the romantic paradigm where perceiver and perceived are one,[4] and here Beckett's general connection with romanticism emerges clearly. He is not following specific influence, a Wordsworthian guidebook: his thought is itself ruled by romantic logic. In the *Biographia Literaria* Coleridge makes the reconciliation of subject and object the premise of his metaphysics, the "primary ground" of his theory of knowledge. As Meyer H. Abrams explains,

> In the *Biographia Literaria*, when Coleridge came to lay down his own metaphysical system, he based it on a premise designed to overcome both the elementarism in method and the dualism in theory of knowledge of his eighteenth-century predecessors, by

---

Hegel's view, though I suspect his apology for *Film*'s debt to Berkeley would apply here as well: "No truth value attaches to above, regarded as of merely structural and dramatic convenience" (*The Collected Shorter Plays* 163). For some discussion of Beckett and Hegel in this context see Rosen ii.3. Rosen (169) quotes Kierkegaard's dissenting position from his *Concluding Unscientific Postscript*: "The systematic idea is the identity of subject and object, the unity of thought and being. Existence, on the other hand, is their separation." Beckett's subject cannot find unity in this life (in "existence"), but because it is only half alive (see Chapter 5), it persists beyond life and can unite with the object there.

On Hegel and Kierkegaard in the Beckett context see also Dobrez 122–28, and Kern, *Existential Thought* 56–57. Beckett mentions Hegel in *Murphy* (222).

4. On Romanticism and Neoplatonism see Abrams, *Natural Supernaturalism*. That the actor is the acted-upon in romantic ideology—as in Byron's "Childe Harolde's Pilgrimage" iii.lxxv, Emerson's "Brahma," Stevens's "Tea at the Palaz of Hoon," Swinburne's "Hertha," Whitman's "There Was a Child Went Forth," Wordsworth's "Nutting," etc.—need not be argued here. There is also a Neoplatonic version of this idea: "intelligence is simultaneously the object thought, and the thinking subject" (*Enneads* v.4.2), and "intelligence is both thinker and thought" (*Enneads* vi.9.2). The Intelligence is below Unity in Plotinus's scheme—the Intelligence is double, while Unity is above number (*Enneads* vi.9.3). And then there's Flaubert:

> Everything that is rational is real. In fact there is nothing real but ideas. The laws of the mind are the laws of the universe. . . . Therefore the absolute is at once subject and object, the unity in which all differences come together . . . the organism only remains in being through the destruction of the organism; throughout there is a dividing principle, a linking principle. (*Bouvard and Pécuchet* 213)

converting their absolute division between subject and object into a logical "antithesis," in order to make it eligible for resolution by the Romantic dialectic of thesis–antithesis–synthesis. (219)

This resolution anticipates and probably contributes to Beckett's solution to the problem of the alterity of anti-mind.[5] Coleridge's ambition can be restated in Beckettian terms: because the subject confronts an alien objectivity as mind confronts anti-mind, some common ground is wanted to reduce anti-mind to mental terms. Beckett's solution is to translate anti-mind into language, which is compatible with mind. Coleridge's solution is remarkably similar. Abrams continues:

> The "primary ground" of his theory of knowledge, he says, is "the coincidence of an object with a subject" or "of the thought with the thing," in a synthesis, or "coalescence," in which the elements lose their separate identities. "In the reconciling, and recurrence of this contradiction exists the process and mystery of production and life." And the process of vital artistic creation reflects the process of this vital creative perception. (219)

Coleridge develops, as Beckett does, something like a microcosmic model of mind, where thought is thing. This concept makes possible, as Coleridge puts it, the reconciliation of "the idea, with the image" (Abrams 220).

Coleridge and Beckett both think of this translation of anti-mind as the artistic process itself. The artist's effort to achieve "the adequate union of subject and object," as Beckett suggests in his *Proust* essay, is what Coleridge calls "the process and mystery of production," which exists in "the reconciling" or "coalescence" of subject and object. But the translation of anti-mind and the unity of subject and object are not identical. Unity presents a new entity, "in which the elements lose their separate identities," as Coleridge says. Translation merely asserts the priority of mind, which must be protected from anti-mind. Similarly the subject does not look for an object as one might look for a face in the metro; rather, it seeks a condition where there is no more disparity or relation between subject and object, hence no subject and no object. On

5. For a reference to Coleridge in Beckett's work, see *Murphy* 214–15. This passage refers in part to literary influence.

the other hand, it is not misleading to think of union and translation together. One might be tempted to say, following Beckett's two models of mind, that translation is a weaker form of unity, reflecting union; but in fact for Beckett the artistic process, verbal translation, is a *means* to the coveted unity.[6] The Beckettian subject is an artist who seeks union with the object through artistic process. So in the passage from *Proust* Beckett discusses the role and necessity of art. Art conveys the baffled ecstasy of the artist–perceiver, "when the mystery, the essence, the Idea, imprisoned in matter, had solicited the bounty of a subject passing by within the shell of his impurity" (57). The artist is not struck by the surface of the object but by its inner essence or mystery. "Realistic art" is a "grotesque fallacy," inadequate to a truth that lies beyond appearances. An idealist notion, and a world away from Robbe-Grillet's fancy that Beckett's ideology is one of pure surface. Beckett's experience is with surface, but his ideology is not. Here too is one reason why the visual arts are valorized in Beckett's scheme of things: the artist perceives the object directly and is struck by it, while the writer only translates this experience into inevitably compromising language.[7]

So the object's essence, which solicits the artist, is couched in matter just as the mind is buried in Kafkaesque body, "within the shell of his impurity." There is some obscure rapport between the perceiver and perceived, but they are separated by an inessential materiality. This concreteness, however, is not the only thing that obstructs. Perception also contributes to obstruct the union of subject and object, in two ways. First, it sophisticates and mystifies the object, endowing it with categorical ideation, idealization. All qualities are fundamentally ideal: stones are not hard in themselves, but we make them so. No union with the object is possible with these interfering perceptions around. In "Dante...Bruno.Vico..Joyce" Beckett says that in *Work in Progress* "Mr Joyce has desophisticated language" (*Our Exagmination* 15); with Joyce (as he presents him in that essay), Beckett needs to desophisticate the perceived, to strip it of its false cognitive clothing. The senses also color the perceived. Beckett associates with Proust the wish to overcome the sensible habits that "interfere [their] prism between the eye and its object" (*Proust* 15). This notion appeals to the epistemological

6. Cp. Read 20.
7. As Beckett writes in *Proust*, "The artist has acquired his text: the artisan translates it. 'The duty and the task of a writer (not an artist, a writer) are those of a translator.' The reality of a cloud reflected in the Vivonne is not expressed by 'Zut alors' but by the interpretation of that inspired criticism" (*Proust* 64).

skepticism of David Hume, who observed that all perception is contaminated by the body. Thus Clov uses a Humean telescope to peer outside his head/room, emphasizing the instrumentality of perception. An image may at first sight seem clear, "but as the eye dwells it grows obscure. Indeed the longer the eye dwells the obscurer it grows" (*Company* 22). The eye is a problem. The object's concealing materiality, then, is to some extent a product of perception, both a cognitive projection and a sensible addition. With Proust and Hume, Beckett wants to overcome the objectivity or material interference of the subject. With Joyce he wants to overcome the subjectivity or projected quality of the object. These opposite obstacles resist the artist's quest for reality, or union. In "Peintres de l'empêchement" Beckett terms these opposite obstructions "l'empêchement-objet et l'empêchement-oeil" (*Disjecta* 136). (Note the visualizing function associated with the subject as eye.) The pure object hides behind veils; fully defrocked it may itself be nothing at all. The pure subject lies so deeply within the instrumentality of the self that, were it found out, it might be incapable of perception. The artist must overcome these *empêchements*—and the task of finding the worthy object is equalled only by that of becoming a worthy subject.

Beckett admires Proust's solution to this problem. The object cannot be real or present because "imagination . . . is exercised in vacuo and cannot tolerate the limits of the real" (*Proust* 56). But intellectual contact with the object is not possible either, because ideation endows the object, which then "loses its purity." Proust's solution is his famous "reduplication," as Beckett calls it. Remembrance, re-membering, is "real without being merely actual, ideal without being merely abstract, the ideal real, the essential, the extratemporal" (56). The remembered object is experienced again, it has presence without being material, and essence not marred by cognition. The problem for Beckett is that this kind of union does not last. For a moment, transported by this vision, the subject is outside time, outside experienced continuum, exalting in a "brief eternity" (57). But then material and cognitive presence returns. Returning from absence to time and space, the subject finds in art a means to decipher its "baffled ecstasy." Because a Proustian, epiphanic rapport with the object cannot last, the artist must turn to art, to what Coleridge calls "the process and mystery of production." So must Beckett, whose subjects find even approximate union with the object difficult. Malone and the Unnamable try, with exemplary failure, to get lost in their stories. Victor (in *Éleuthéria*) and Murphy succeed all too briefly, too intermittently.[8] Vladimir and Estragon, whose anecdotes and dreams disintegrate as soon as the two begin to reminisce or dream, succeed least. Beckett's subjects cannot obliterate time in epiphany. This search, and the "process of production" it entails, become perforce among Beckett's central concerns.

Beckett often alludes to the pursuit of the object in these terms. Watt, for instance, has premonitions of "imminent harmony, when all outside him will be he" (*Watt* 40). In *The Unnamable* the narrator speaks of pursuing an object, first an "immediate object," then others (367). In *Company* a subject endowed with an ideal voice is imagined as "more likely to achieve its object" (34). And in *Film*, which deals plainly with the famous Berkeleyan concept that being is being perceived ("*esse est percipi*"), the character E (or eye) pursues O (or object) in order to perceive him. *Film* is based in part on Unamuno's "The Other," where Cosme, like Beckett's protagonist, is "pursued by the one he calls The Other. . . . He doesn't want to be seen. And he's had all the mirrors in the house covered over" (253). Beckett's earlier designation for O was "One," not "Object":[9] in seeking the object, the subject pursues oneness or union, a state beyond either subject or object. Cosme in "The Other" explains that when The Other looked into his eyes, he seemed to dissolve and "to un-live . . . as in a film run backwards" (257). Beckett makes clear in his comments on *Film* that O's "place" is "a different world": "He [O] gets into his vestibule, and we enter a different world immediately" (Gontarski, *The Intent of Undoing* 190, 189). Beckett needs to find the right way to get to that place.

Bunyan and Céline: The *Visio* and Psychological Landscape

The subject's search for union is a movement at once physical and spiritual. These motions are related, in part because in Beckett's work the physical world usually embodies psychological conditions. That is

8. Jones claims that "there are certainly four and probably five occasions where he [Murphy] apparently succeeds in detaching himself from physical reality and enters into communion with 'The accidentless One-and-Only, conveniently called Nothing'" (40). He says that these four occasions take place (1) in the mew, (2) in Hyde Park, (3) with Endon, and (4) in the garret. The fifth is implied by the repetition of "When he came to, or rather from." But it is unclear whether these experiences are more than elaborate trances.

9. The original notation, "For Eye and Him who does not wish to be seen," was revised to "For Eye and One who would not be seen" (Gontarski, *The Intent of Undoing* 105). The script had once been titled "*The Eye*" (Alan Schneider 65).

not to say that, strictly speaking, Beckett's world is entirely allegorical.[10] The carrots in *Waiting for Godot* are, after all, only carrots. But
Beckett does rely on the allegorical tradition, and especially on Bunyan
and on Céline. While writers such as Kafka and Malcolm Lowry may be
counted with Beckett as modern explorers of spiritual landscape,
Bunyan and Céline provide Beckett with specific terms that help
articulate a topography endowed with cognitive qualities and spiritual
significance.

Beckett's connection with Bunyan is fairly well established. *Molloy* in
particular is thought to have been influenced by *Pilgrim's Progress*, partly
because that novel employs the device of the wicket gate (*Molloy* 52,
127). John Fletcher thinks that *Molloy*'s two parts are inspired by the two
books of *Pilgrim's Progress* (Fletcher 133), and Robinson suggests specific
correlations between events in the two works.[11] *How It Is* has also been
mentioned in relation to Bunyan (Barnard 78). But there is also a logic
to Bunyan's presence in Beckett's text.

First, of course, Bunyan uses the metaphorical journey to portray
spiritual pilgrimage. In such a world physical event is a function of the
pilgrim's psychological condition; surface action reflects an inner landscape (Fish 255). This is Beckett's practice as well. For Bunyan the
subjugation of *physis* to *psyche* leads to radical and abrupt manipulations
of the physical world, as it does for Beckett. So for example after
Apollyon injures Christian in head, hand, and foot ("understanding,
faith and conversation," explains Bunyan's marginal gloss), Christian
chases him away (with a "deadly thrust," oddly) by remembering aloud
to rely on God's power (*Pilgrim's Progress* 93–94). Similarly the depth of
the Slough of Despond varies according to the doubts of Bunyan's
sinners. For Beckett, too, things can materialize as they are required,
virtual objects unencumbered by a history of causes. In *Molloy* a feather
duster appears suddenly in the hand of Lousse's valet (43; cp. Abbott,
Form and Effect 106), and in *First Love* a character does the same: "She
wasn't there, then suddenly she was, I don't know how, I didn't see her

10. If a strict allegory is not found in the modern (Murrin xi), a looser notion of
allegory may be more useful for modern literature.

11. Robinson writes that "Gaber takes the place of Bunyan's Evangelist and Molloy's
arrest and subsequent treatment at the hands of an enraged populace is reminiscent of the
pilgrims' seizure in *Vanity Fair*. Both Molloy and Moran directly recall Bunyan's famous
gateway. Molloy escapes from Lousse and Moran begins his journey, by passing through
a wicket-gate into the world beyond. However, Moran's re-entry into his garden at the
end of the novel points the circular, hopeless nature of their pilgrimage in search of the
Self against Christian's discovery of paradise" (154).

come, nor hear her, all ears and eyes though I was" (26). In an earlier version of *Comment c'est* the narrator says: "Ils [objects] se présentaient d'abord sous forme d'image, plus ou moins nette, à l'instant même où j'en avais besoin."[12] Such spontaneous materialization prompts one of the Unnamable's humorous quips: "Did I say I catch flies? I snap them up, clack! Does this mean I still have my teeth?" (332). The Unnamable's word makes and unmakes matter (here dentition). As Beckett writes in *Proust*, "The world being a projection of the individual's consciousness (an objectivation of the individual's will, Schopenhauer would say), the pact must be continually renewed, the letter of safe conduct brought up to date" (8). For Beckett, such correlation of thing and thought as would have delighted Oscar Wilde is possible, as it is for Bunyan, because mind is not matter, the word is not the way, and sensibility is dissociated from the world.

Both Bunyan and Beckett undermine the linear and visual quality of the journey and involve the reader in this questioning process: both make a pilgrim of the reader and educate her or him not to believe too literally in concrete images. As Stanley Fish argues, convincingly, there is no real physical advance in *The Pilgrim's Progress* but repetition of trial and solution until Christian can learn to forgo the linear-physical terms of his existence in favor of the way of the spirit (Fish 232–33, 237–38). This kind of subversion is everywhere in Beckett. Not only does he frustrate narrative closure and the reader's expectations (Abbott 19), but also his wandering for home is circular and leads back to the self. As Fish puts it, writing of Bunyan, "Fleeing from place to place is no way to escape a foe who lives within" (230). Both writers also undermine the visual quality of the journey by contrasting the narrator's dream vision, which is had at home, with the physical vision, which the narrator experiences as the wandering protagonist. The narrator—say, Malone—presents himself as confined in a room, envisioning self-substitutes such as Macmann on their way, and writing down his vision. In *How It Is* the narrator presents himself as the author, documenting what is revealed to him ("I say it as I hear it"), namely how he is or was himself the protagonist, on a journey. The writer is in the head, and his image somewhere outside. Bunyan's narrative is also presented "in the similitude of a dream," and the narrator presents himself as the dreamer, confined in a "den" (Bunyan 39). The dreamer, however, is left outside

12. "On Way to *Comment c'est*," Reading University Library, Catalogue No. Acc 1655, 4th text, 4.

the Celestial City at the end of the pilgrims' journey, leaving behind his dream *visio*, to which the author is scribe (Fish 263). The narrator's dream undermines the reader's attempts to see clearly more than some of the things some of the time, because the reader is kept out with the pilgrim in the fantasized world of wandering.

Bunyan, then, may acquire a modest reputation as one of Beckett's literary ancestors, together with Louis-Ferdinand Céline. Deirdre Bair cites a 1933 letter to his friend Thomas McGreevy in which Beckett expresses interest in Céline's *Voyage au bout de la nuit* (*Samuel Beckett* 165). Beckett did not read the novel until 1938, six years after it first appeared and too late for it to have influenced *Murphy* (written 1935). At that time, Bair says, he told Peggy Guggenheim that it was the greatest novel in French or English (275). The critical literature, however, makes little of the connection.[13] But Céline is important; like Bunyan, he provides Beckett both with props and devices and with good reasons to use them.

The details common to Beckett and Céline, massed together, reveal a conceptual affinity between the two that runs deeper than the common platitudes suggest (both writers pursue humanity's death in life and the agony of telling it, etc.). In most cases where Céline's work suggests a parallel to Beckett's, this resemblance is carried further to include Beckettian nuance. The metaphorical journey, for example, also reflects mind's power over matter. In his prefatory remarks Céline says: "*Our journey is entirely imaginary. That is its strength. It goes from life to death. People, animals, cities, things, all are imagined.*" His journey, like Beckett's, takes place largely in the present, and is defined against some golden days of the prewar period when rest was possible (as in *Krapp's Last Tape* and *Waiting for Godot*). But because it is internal and imagined it also involves the tension between told images and the words that tell them: "Nothing was happening except inside me, still asking myself the same questions" (Céline 251). Bardamu, the protagonist, often sounds like one of Beckett's characters: "We won't be easy in our minds until

13. Vivian Mercier brings up Céline in order to favor the French novelist Raymond Queneau instead (142); Robinson quotes a phrase from Céline in passing (182); and Hoffman says only that Beckett does not wish "to prove a hateful thesis, like that of Céline" (73). Rosen, on the contrary, argues that Beckett eschews consolation even more than Céline does (44–46), and considers him in Beckett's tradition (74, 92). Friedman also lists Céline among Beckett's precursors (4), and Barnard says that Céline's novels "show a very similar emotional attitude [to Beckett's novels]. They express powerfully the feeling of the futility and sordidness of life and that combination of disgust at bourgeois ideals and pity for the down-and-out misfits of society which Beckett shows in his *Trilogy*" (4).

everything has been said once and for all, then we'll fall silent and we'll no longer be afraid of keeping still. That will be the day" (282). Céline understands the double power of words much as Beckett does: they reduce hostile things to innocuous mental terms, but such freedom remains outside the world. "When someone comes to see you," says Bardamu, harping on the loathed disturber theme so dear to Beckett, "quick, reduce him to nakedness. . . . There won't be anything left but ideas, and there's nothing frightening about ideas. With ideas nothing is lost, everything can be straightened out" (290).

At the same time, "Everything's permissible internally" (39). Events corroborate mental conditions. The doppelgänger Robinson provides a good example:

> The conversation started up again, about this and that. "My trouble is that drink doesn't agree with me." A bee in his bonnet. "When I drink, I get cramps, it's unbearable. Worse!" And by throwing up several times he demonstrated that even our little *cassis* that afternoon hadn't agreed with him.
> "See what I mean?" (258)

Conversation has turned into proof, matter, something to be seen. To reinforce the projected and virtual quality of his objects, Céline gives persons and places allegorical names like "Barbigny," as in *barbant*, or "boring," anticipating Pynchon's "Stencil" and "Slothrop," all possibly descended from Flaubert's "Bovary." His landscape too suffers from willful reconstruction, raveled and unraveled by association, condensation, and displacement, as the narrative requires.[14] Seen through the lens of Beckett, Céline is a modern Bunyan. His projected landscape

---

14. Manheim's useful annotations to his translation of *Voyage au bout de la nuit* point out Céline's recurrent manipulations. Here is a representative passage from Céline, followed by Manheim's note.

> In Paris the rich live together. Their neighborhoods adjoin and coalesce, so as to form a wedge of urban cake, the tip of which touches the Louvre and the rounded outer edge is bounded by trees between the Pont d'Auteuil and the Porte des Ternes. That's the good part of the city. All the rest is shit and misery. (61)

Manheim comments: "Céline's geography is as free and easy as his history, though he knew Paris like the back of his hand. Both extremities of the wide end of the wedge are slightly displaced, the one linguistically, the other geographically. Pont d'Auteuil should be Porte d'Auteuil, which is far away, and Porte des Ternes should be Porte Maillot, which isn't far at all. Then you get the eastern edge of the Bois de Boulogne, hence the trees" (439). Hewitt also discusses Céline's projected topography (75, 203).

anticipates Beckett's, his place names recall Beckett favorites like "Hole" (*Molloy*), and his personal names probably contributed to Beckett's "Lynch" (*Watt*) and "Krapp."

Such a projected world is insane,[15] but insanity has its uses in visionary fiction. More important, in its representation Céline contributes to Beckett's topography. Robinson's question—"see what I mean?"—is also Céline's. It refers to the literalization of metaphor—the writer's technique—and to its consequent world. In such a world, nouns like "war" and "insanity" are put on a par as "true manifestations of our innermost being" (359). Language, unanchored, cannot express truly; but the alternative to lying is death. "The truth is an endless death agony. The truth is death. You have to choose: death or lies. I've never been able to kill myself" (173). This is a trouble several Beckett characters, such as Molloy, discover. It leads Céline to search for inner refuge. As Monsieur Baryton, administrative head of an asylum, says,

> What I want, Ferdinand, is to try and lose my soul, as you might try to lose a mangy dog, your stinking dog, the companion who disgusts you, and to get far away from him before you die . . . To be alone at last . . . At peace . . . Myself . . . (378)

As in Beckett's early fiction, especially *Murphy* and *Watt*, insanity is a retreat from time and space and at the same time a condition where word is made flesh, thought is thing.[16]

---

15. As Coleridge has it, "When a man mistakes his thoughts for persons and things, he is mad. A madman is properly so defined" (*Table Talk*, 25 July 1832).

16. For Céline's obsession with the madhouse motif see the soldiers' insane asylum (50ff.), and the "loony bin" (365–68), a tempting place of liberation. The following passage in particular recalls the microcosmic and hermetically sealed mind depicted in *Murphy* and the madhouse in the garden of *Watt*. It is called a "Rest Home" and is "in the middle of a big garden, where the nuts went walking on nice days":

> When the patients spoke of their mental treasures, it was always with anguished contortions or airs of protective condescension that made you think of powerful and ultrameticulous executives. Not for an empire would those lunatics have gone outside their minds. A madman's thoughts are just the usual ideas of a human being, except that they're hermetically sealed inside his head. The world never gets into his head, and that's the way he wants it. A sealed head is like a lake without an outlet, standing, stagnant. (357)

Céline returns to landscape as the proper metaphor for the lunatic mind.

Céline, however, enlarges the spatial domain of the asylum to yield the Zone, a useful term with which to engage Beckett's topography. Céline's "Zone" (206) refers to a specific area in Paris, a strip of land, first vacant, then developed with impoverished neighborhoods, between the Louis Philippe fortifications of Paris (built 1841–44) and the city suburbs. By using "la Zone" as an allegorical middle space outside the set terrain of bourgeois values, Céline participates in a tradition to which Beckett also belongs. This tradition may have its beginning in the first chaotic space between water and earth of *Genesis*, on which Milton draws to make the domain Satan must cross to reach earth. Bunyan's way from the City of Destruction to the Celestial City passes such a Zone, as his follower Thackeray understands.[17] Dickinson uses the word to designate perfect place or order (as in poems 871 and 1056), but Rimbaud and Apollinaire (in "The Drunken Boat" and in "Zone," both works which Beckett translated into English), and then Eliot ("The Waste Land"), model a new Zone, a world of stony rubbish and broken images.[18] For Céline the Zone is a place where society's disease finds its objective correlative in liminal figures—tramps, vagrants, "half-assed barbarians, undone by red wine and fatigue" (206). Bardamu finds an apartment at the edge of the Zone, and his patients, whose illness is both the cause and effect of their condition, are "mostly people from the Zone, that village of sorts, which never succeeds in picking itself entirely out of the mud and garbage" (287–88).

This objectified dis-ease started, Céline suggests, around 1900. Things are no longer as they were in the old days (399). As Baryton says, "I saw the human mind, Ferdinand, losing its balance little by little and dissolving in the vast maelstrom of apocalyptic ambitions! It began about 1900 . . . mark that date!" (366). Beckett marks the date well in

17. In chapter 51 of *Vanity Fair* Thackeray writes of Becky Sharp's counterfeit glory, the success of her pilgrimage to the false City and its false god: "Ah, my beloved readers and brethren, do not envy poor Becky prematurely—glory like this is said to be fugitive. It is currently reported that even in the very inmost circles, they are no happier than the poor wanderers outside the zone; and Becky, who penetrated into the very centre of fashion and saw the great George IV face to face, has owned since that there too was Vanity" (493).

18. Pynchon appropriates the tradition in *Gravity's Rainbow* as the occupied zone in postwar Europe. Cortázar uses the Zone as a projected mental topography in *62: A Model Kit*, as does Rushdie in *Grimus*, following a Dantean model. For a discussion of the Zone see McHale, especially 45–58. Chambers uses the word to signify the no-man's-land of Beckett's characters (45–46).

Waiting for Godot, as I have shown.[19] Here a city is, like Bunyan's frustrated way, a systematic expression of humanity's fallen state, "an abominable system of constraints, of corridors, locks and wickets, a vast, inexpiable architectural crime" (177). Beckett adopts these Bunyanesque terms. Just as Bram van Velde allows Beckett to visualize his work, so Bunyan and Céline enlarge Beckett's projected mental landscape. Céline's Zone is a liminal landscape where the subject is always hemmed in by its own inexpiable sin made concrete, seeking escape from uncertain ground. Bunyan's subject is similarly positioned, constantly betwixt and between.[20] Céline, then, creates a quest landscape guided by a logic much like Beckett's, a larger spatialized representation of the condition where thing, place, character, and action are literalized aspects of mind.[21]

Beckett takes up from Céline and from Bunyan this projected system of constraints. This system is the product both of *empêchement-oeil*, the habit of mind, mental projection made concrete, and *empêchement-objet*, the object's material sheath, which never completely dissolves. To bridge the gap between subject and object, the subject searches for a way out of this division to reality, its underlying ideal. Bunyan and Céline develop a language that exhibits its own inadequacy, rejecting its imagery and involving the reader in the search for new terms, a way out of false surface being. For Beckett's subject, this way out is a point of passage, a threshold to the place of the object.

19. Around 1900, says Baryton, "we've started buggering each other for variety" (366), a phrase that recalls *Waiting for Godot*. Elsewhere Bardamu reports that some furniture was "too good for us—genuine '1900' pieces" (400), again suggesting Vladimir and Estragon, who once had gone up the Eiffel Tower, whereas now they would not be allowed up. On the other hand, the past is also best forgotten. As Bardamu says, in a passage that sounds much like talk in *Waiting for Godot*: "Was yesterday such a bargain? Or last year? . . . What did you think of it? . . . Regret what? . . . I ask you! . . . Youth? . . . You and I never had any youth!" (327). Hewitt discusses the importance of the date 1900 for Céline (9, 84–85, 88–94, 196). Céline is especially interested in the Universal Exposition of 1900.

20. As Bercovitch says, citing Victor Turner, "The ritual that Bunyan adopts leads Christian into what anthropologists call a 'liminal state,' a sort of cultural no-man's-land, where all social norms may be challenged" (25).

21. Other similarities between Beckett's work and Céline's include Céline's use of the protagonist couple Bardamu and Robinson. That Bardamu traveled in the mud ("liquid manure") with tuna cans (37) is also striking, considering the protagonists' parallel situation in *How It Is*. When in Detroit, Bardamu is unemployed but supported by his solicitous whore, Molly (e.g., 199), a situation that recalls Murphy. For Bardamu, as for Murphy, there is a vacuum between the penis and mathematics (361).

II

Liminal Passage in the Beckett Country

Beckett's fictions form a series because they develop systematically the subject's pursuit of union and the return from that state. Each work explores new aspects of this search, addressing problems left unresolved by the works that came before and raising new issues to be resolved, and so the continuum of works itself presents an argument. It both investigates the nature of the subject-object relation and demonstrates how such an investigation unfolds. In this, Beckett's project suggests the triadic structure of Hegelian dialectic: the subject, Hegel's abstract "in-itself," defines itself particularly and negatively, against the object, to become what Hegel calls the "for-itself," only to realize that the object (or anti-mind) is part of the mind, simply a larger conception of what constitutes it. It then becomes the "in-and-for-itself," a unity of subject and object. This process can be repeated again and again because Hegel's object is particular, the "other" of the subject's given circumstances. The subject, or Spirit, stops unfolding only when it has been incarnated, as Hegel would have it, in everything. For Beckett the object, broadly conceived, cannot be so limited: it is all that is not mind. There cannot be anything after the union of subject and object, unless the whole be refracted again—which is exactly what Beckett's later work suggests. When Beckett talks in *Proust* of a specific object appealing to the perceiver, he presents a general principle in understandable, limited terms. There is no "isolated" object, no table or tree out there—there is only an appeal from otherness. As Beckett claims in his anatomy of Marcel's experience, that appeal comes not from the pebble or the flower or the cathedral but from something beyond, from a supersensible or "mystical" realm. Beckett visualizes that realm, the place of the object as it appears to us, in Schopenhauerian terms, as turbulent and incomprehensible, and this is how it appears in his earlier works, a world of the Will, musical and abstract.

It is possible to explain the questing in Beckett's fiction with conceptual frameworks other than that of his early aesthetic work.[22] Whatever the subject's goal, the All or nothingness or chaos or God, it is a condition and not a thing: for this reason it may be considered a

---

22. Several critics have argued—as Sen does—for the influence of Eastern religion on Beckett.

"place," and even equated with its place. But the paradigm of subject and object that Beckett develops early on is the one that organizes his fiction. Beckett works with these terms throughout his career; the essays on van Velde come sixteen years after the essay on Joyce (1929), fourteen after *Proust*, spanning a period that includes several of Beckett's most substantial prose works. But it should also be clear that Beckett's "shape" that matters, his virtual landscape and literalized metaphors, his emphasis on the image, his figure and ground—all argue for a specifically aesthetic underpinning to his metaphysics; they construct the quest in his works in terms of perceiver and perceived, subject and object. It is not a coincidence that many Beckett characters look for the place of the object in others' eyes. The eye underscores the fact that both of Beckett's models of mind frame a visual world where not to be means not to be seen: in the All, figure and ground are indistinguishable.

Beckett's subjects try to find the object outside and inside the self, following Proust's two ways in his *recherche*. The two van Velde brothers, Geer and Bram, reinforce Beckett's sense that he is on the right track, and in "Peintres de l'empêchement" he proclaims their divergent approaches as the only ones available to modern art (*Disjecta* 137). To look for the object in the exterior, as Watt does, is to follow Geer's way. This is the Joycean project of Beckett's early works, defrocking the object. To look for the object within the self, as the Unnamable does, is to follow Bram's way.[23] That is the Humean project of the later works, leading to *How It Is*, overcoming the habits of the self. In his early fiction, *Dream of Fair to Middling Women* (written in 1932) and *Murphy* (1935), Beckett tries to look for the object, as it were, both ways at once, and this attempt contributes to these works' disjunctive quality. The stories of *More Pricks Than Kicks* belong to this period (1934). With *Watt* (1942–44), *Mercier and Camier* (1945), and *Molloy* (1947), Beckett launches a more consistent ichnography of the way, beginning with the search in the exterior. *Molloy* is the boundary work, where the exterior world dissolves more insistently, leading to the opposite search in the interior. *Malone Dies* (1948) and *The Unnamable* (1949) constitute this phase, the latter quickly leading to another transition point, to a liminal state taken up by *How It Is* (1959–61) and several short works including *The Lost Ones* (1965). Later works like *Ill Seen Ill Said*, *Worstward Ho*, and the *Fizzles* form the fourth and last phase.

---

23. Beckett wrote in a drafted letter to Duthuit regarding Bram van Velde that "Ce qui m'intéresse c'est l'au-delà du dehors-dedans où il fait son effort" (3 September 1949; at the Reading University Library).

A Dream of Divine Presence

Written with glib if choppy irony, in spurts and stabs, *Dream of Fair to
Middling Women* parades a large cast of unformed characters, many no
more than names, over 215 or so typewritten pages. No character is
fully introduced or placed, no relation spelled out; characters appear and
disappear like marionettes. The work cries out Beckett's impatience
with normative expectations and dislike for good behavior. But the
novel is far from anarchic. It reflects Beckett's dissatisfaction with "the
grotesque fallacy of a realistic art—'that miserable statement of line and
surface'" (*Proust* 57); its coherence lies in its argument. The substance of
the book is divided into three rough parts.[24] In the first part (1–100) the
unsavory Belacqua returns from Germany to Dublin and his beloved,
the Smeraldina-Rima, only to be reminded why he wanted to keep away
from her in the first place. Then comes a crucial short discussion of
novelistic art and metaphysics (100–111). This section is like the
all-important sixth chapter that bisects *Murphy*, the one chapter that
Beckett was least willing to change to get that novel published (1936
letter to George Reavey, *Disjecta* 103). The action continues when
Belacqua, wandering in the city, turns to pursue "the Alba," another
woman;[25] this part culminates in a party at the house of Frica, where
Belacqua meets the Alba. The two abandon the party and go to her
house, but then Belacqua leaves to wander again. This wandering is
given a separate section in the novel under the heading "*AND*" and
begins: "It began to rain again" (213). So the action of the novel is
divided into two parts of roughly equal length separated by an abstract
theoretical discussion that heralds the novel's second part as the first's
"colleague" (105).

Belacqua's interest in the Smeraldina-Rima and in the Alba turns
on the conventional assumption, dismissed in the course of the novel,

---

24. *Dream of Fair to Middling Women* is as yet unpublished. Its typescript is at the
Samuel Beckett Archive at Reading University. The text is divided into five parts:
"ONE," p. 1; "TWO," pp. 2–98; "UND," pp. 99–126; "THREE," pp. 127–212; and
"AND," pp. 213–14, continued on the reverse of p. 214 in red ink. There is an additional
typed version of the ending, similar to the other, with page numbers 197–99.

Page numbers from *Dream* in my text refer to this typescript.

25. Beckett may have coined the Alba's name after Francisco de Goya's mistress, the
Duchess of Alba (though Marion Chapman's then popular *The Loves of Goya* was
published only in 1937). Harvey notes that the "Alba" is a twelfth-century lyric that
protests the coming of light as the end to lovemaking.

that there is a connection between sex and heaven, located in Woman:

> "Now" said Belacqua "at last I can say what's on my mind."
> A convulsion of attention pealed down the Mandarin.
> "In the old town" said Belacqua "correct me if I am wrong, a certain Fräulein Anita Furtwängler sits by her window."
> "Wisdom gleams through me" cried the Mandarin, "I shudder and kindle."
> "The perfection of her limbs" pursued Belacqua "has been weighing me up to the peace of Jerusalem. I have the address of Abraham's bosom."
> "Zahlen!" cried the Mandarin. "Telephone for the Grauler!"
> "The true Shekinah" said Belacqua "is Woman."[26]

The Mandarin receives Belacqua's message with religious and sexual fervor—shudder and convulsion. The ideal is found in the particular; divine presence has a street address. Belacqua, unfortunately, is seeking this presence in fair to middling women. Smeraldina-Rima is clearly the middling, "snuffling and muttering" (97). At one point the reader is told that Belacqua cannot be presented as a stable character of the Balzac and Austen type (110–11): "He is no more satisfied by the three values, Apollo, Narcissus and the anonymous third person, than he would be by fifty values, or any number of values."[27] These two of his identities are worked out in his relation to the Smeraldina-Rima and to the Alba. To the Smeraldina-Rima, the body, he is Apollo pursuing Daphne. He is intellect, she Weib. (Belacqua is not a humanist.) Finding insufficient Presence in the Smeraldina-Rima, Belacqua turns to the Alba, who, the "Fair" of the title, seems to "transcend beauty" (according to the narrator of *What a Misfortune* 116). But whereas the Smeraldina-Rima has too low an opinion of the true, the Alba succumbs at the opposite end by believing, a little like Binx's aunt in Percy's *The Moviegoer*, in an unchanging truth of the soul. Belacqua, in contrast, is nothing fixed:

> But she, [*sic*] does not really care about moving (must we drum that drum for ever?), she puts not her trust in changes of scenery,

26. *Dream* 94. In quoting from *Dream* I try to preserve Beckett's form. Each speaker and the narrator begin a new line when they speak, but without indentation. There is only one space after periods, and paragraph indentation is usually eight spaces.

27. 111. Compare the serial nature of the Unnamable, which would not be exhausted by fifty names.

she is too inward by a long chalk, she inclines towards an absolute moral geography, her soul is her only poste restante. Whereas he does care, he prays fervently to be set free in a general way, he is such a very juvenile man. But he will get over all that. (157)

Belacqua has moved from the bodily to the spiritual woman, but the Alba, for all her superiority to the party crowd at Frica's, is too fixed an embodiment of the ideal to harbor divine presence. The narrator explains that, "just as we have feared the Alba and Co have turned out to be as miserable a lot of croakers as Belacqua at his best and hoarsest and the entire continental circus" (159). The reader is told that the story would not permit Belacqua to stay overnight at the Alba's home (213), and he must wander out again. It seems that Belacqua moves from the exterior body inward, from the Smeraldina-Rima to the Alba, who is "not heavy enough to hang herself" (153). She plays Echo to his Narcissus, pursuing him to her home, he finally escaping. But Belacqua cannot be fixed in any one identity; he has to abandon his role as pursued Narcissus, just as he had to relinquish his former Apollo self. Echo may be purer than Daphne, but neither is Shekinah. As Kierkegaard knew, moral geography is no closer to divinity than is aesthetic appetite. Belacqua has to "get over all that" (157), either his juvenile desire for freedom or the *empêchements* to the condition where the ideal is fully present.

Why does Belacqua expect to find divinity in women? He expresses the same idea differently in a poem to the Smeraldina-Rima. Here he is the spirit incarnating in matter, the subject uniting with its object:

> At last I find in my confusèd soul,
> Dark with the dark flame of the cypresses,
> The certitude that I cannot be whole,
> Consummate, finally achieved, unless
> I be consumed and fused in the white heat
> Of her sad finite essence, so that none
> Shall sever us who are at last complete
> Eternally, irrevocably one,
> One with the birdless, cloudless, colourless skies,
> One with the bright purity of the fire

of which we are and for which we must die
A rapturous strange death and be entire,
Like syzygetic stars, supernly bright,
Conjoined in One and the Infinite!

(63)

Belacqua is the spirit, and his friend the "sad finite essence" necessary for
his own eternal completion.[28] He describes the union in visual terms as
"One with the birdless, cloudless, colourless skies," that is, an undifferentiated One, all ground without figure. So Mr. Kelly's kite becomes
one with the sky in *Murphy*. Belacqua's poem is ugly—he is not meant
to be antipathetic so much as beyond sympathy altogether. He is like
one of those divine Jackson Pollock paintings, a natural, amoral force:
"For we assume the irresponsibility of Belacqua, his faculty for acting
with insufficient motivation, to have been so far evinced in previous
misadventures as to be no longer a matter for surprise. In respect of this
apparent gratuity of conduct he may perhaps with some colour of justice
be likened to the laws of nature. A mental home was the place for him"
(*Love and Lethe* 89). Insane behavior is coherent and formal; Beckett's
insane manifest nature directly, not interfering with it through organized sensibility. They have lost their *empêchements*.

Belacqua's inhumanity, it turns out, is something like Schopenhauerian Will. Schopenhauer, in whom Beckett was always interested—he is
mentioned by name in *Dream*[29]—considered that there is an abstract
amoral power governing the world, the Will, and that music can express
it directly. Proust had a similar notion, as passages Beckett scored in his
copy of *A la recherche* show.[30] In *Dream* Beckett combines this notion

28. Kroll sees in *Dream* the idea that women "can somehow lead to a reunification of
man with his essential nature or source": love unites the masculine and feminine
principles, producing a Platonic unity (22).

29. *Dream* 55, 75. Beckett quotes from Schopenhauer's *Von Seiden der Welt* in a
notebook recently acquired by the Reading University Library; his entry was made
between 1977 and 1981.

For his career-long interest in Schopenhauer, see Henning, Rosen, and Pilling's *Samuel
Beckett* 115–27. Kern rightly sees Schopenhauer behind Proust's occupation with music in
A la recherche (*Existential Thought* 77) and sees Beckett's interest in music in Proust in this
light (167).

30. Here, for example, is part of a passage Beckett marked in his copy. It is from *Du
côte de chez Swann*, vol. 1, part 2, 34. All underlinings are Beckett's, in ink. Brackets are
mine.

with the Pythagorean idea that the earth is part of a Ptolemaic cosmological harmony, participating in and surrounded by the music of the spheres (see Hollander 28–31, 38–41, 262–64). This perfect harmony is in Beckett's synthesis the Will purely expressed; the human world of perception and thought is a world of fallen notes, musical fragments, bits broken from harmony, ruined melody. These fragments, which Beckett calls "lius," are like single notes or electrons (100) that clash and do not constitute a system, a harmony:

> The lius do just what they please, they just please themselves. They flower out and around into every kind of illicit ultra and infra and supra. Which is bad, because as long as they do that they can never meet. We are afraid to call for the simplest chord. Belacqua drifts about, it is true, doing his best to thicken the tune, but harmonic composition properly speaking, music in depth on the considerable scale is, and this is a terrible think [sic] to have to say, ausgeschlossen. (*Dream* 104)

The novel lacks a coherent plot because its different notes cannot be ordered into a melody. Belacqua thickens the tune because he associates, more or less, with other characters, other notes, giving rise to occasional musical mutations. The wandering personae of the novel are "refractory constituents," refracted, that is, from the implied original unity, the whole of "One and the Infinite," into a universe where solar bodies, like their namesake animals, "scatter and stampede":

> Much of what has been written concerning the reluctance of our refractory constituents to bind together and give us a synthesis is true equally of Belacqua. Their movement is based on a principle of repulsion, their property not to combine but, like heavenly bodies, to scatter and stampede, astral straws on a

---

Et le plaisir que lui [Swann] donnait la musique . . . ressemblait . . . au plaisir qu'il aurait eu à expérimenter des parfums, à entrer en *contact avec un monde pour lequel nous ne sommes pas faits*, qui nous semble sans forme parce que nos yeux ne le perçoivent pas, sans signification parce qu'il échappe à notre intelligence.

Swann's search leads to a revelation much like Belacqua's:

quelle *étrange ivresse il avait à dépouiller son âme la plus intérieure de tous les secours du raisonnement et à la faire passer seule dans le couloir, dans le filtre obscur du son.*

time-strom, grit in the mistral. And not only to shrink from all that is not they, from all that is without and in its turn shrinks from them, but also to strain away from themselves. They are no good from the builder's point of view, firstly because they will not suffer their systems to be absorbed in the cluster of a greater system, and then, and chiefly, because they themselves tend to disappear as systems. Their centres are wasting, the strain away from the centre is not to be gainsaid, a little more and they explode. Then, to complicate things further, they have odd periods of receuillement, a kind of centripetal backwash that checks the rot. . . . To the item thus artificially immobilised in a backwash of composure precise value can be assigned.[31]

This backwash of pure essences is the kind of "character" created by Balzac and "the divine Jane" (106), a character that can be discussed with consistency, albeit an illusory one. In this Beckett takes his cue partly from Unamuno, who told his readers in the "Epilogue" to "The Novel of Don Sandalio, Chessplayer," "do not look for the coherent world of so-called realist novels" (226).

The unity from which these characters or "lius" strain away is a "centre" that cannot hold.[32] These characters are "a collection of Kakiamouni wops, scorching away from their centres. . . . What would Leibnitz say?" (159). Leibniz would have agreed to condemn their decentered microcosms.[33] At their centers they are whole, pure, unrefracted. They are, in other words, themselves cosms, "syzygetic stars" as Belacqua puts it (63). This agrees with the geographical view of the self found in Beckett's work; the narrator excuses his discussion of "the liu business" on the ground that "we were once upon a time inclined to fancy ourself as the Cézanne, shall we say, of the printed page, very strong on architectonics" (159). Like the cosmos, the individual is a "system" that tears itself apart, centrifugal force checked by centripetal backwash, but also something other, pure, unnamable. Belacqua is "at his simplest . . . A trine man":

Centripetal, centrifugal and . . . not. Phoebus chasing Daphne, Narcissus flying from Echo and . . . neither. Is that neat or is it

31. 105–6. This passage and its immediate continuation are in *Disjecta* 46–47.

32. Beckett roughly acknowledges his connection with Yeats elsewhere: "[a butterfly,] it was inscribed above on the eternal toilet-roll, was to pern in a gyre about a mixed pipi champêtre" (116).

33. For discussions of Leibniz in connection with Beckett, see Dobrez's first two chapters.

not? The chase to Vienna, the flight to Paris, the slouch to Fulda, the relapse into Dublin and . . . immunity like hell from journeys and cities. (107)

This *is* neat. There is a condition, the center, where Belacqua is immune from the move out and in, from journeys and cities, from wandering and home. It is otherworldly, "like hell" (a concept that Beckett takes literally—see Chapter 7). Instead of "wandering about vaguely, thickening the ruined melody here and there" (105), Belacqua can be in pure harmony without cause or reason. His being "trine" only reinforces this possibility: like the Christian divinity he is at once fragmentary and whole. Phoebus and Narcissus are the polar extremes of his continuum of being, distinguished clearly only from the "other" condition defined negatively as "not": "In this Kimmerea not of sleep Narcissus was obliterated and Phoebus (here names only, anything else would do as well, for the extremes of the pendulum) and all their ultra-violets" (109). "Kimmerea" (which may be read as the adjective "Cimmerian") also suggests an otherworldly hell. Belacqua does not have only three values, "centripetal, centrifugal and . . . not," but like the divinity, an infinity of values along the continuum between them. Here Zeno meets Euclidian geometry. But no matter how regressive the individual's chain of being, there is one still center flanked by two infinities where the spectrum's ultraviolets and all other lights succumb to darkness. This center is expressed in *The Unnamable*, where it leads out of the impasse of the two regressions to the place of union; it is right to expect that the threshold to the object would be at that liminal center point because that point alone denies the regressive line that always promises subjective regressions beyond it.

Beckett describes Belacqua's "other" identity, or anti-identity, in a passage that looks back to Schopenhauer and forward to *Murphy*:

> The third being was the dark gulf, when the glare of the will and the hammer-strokes of the brain doomed outside to take flight from its quarry were expunged, the Limbo and the wombtomb alive with the unanxious spirits of quiet cerebration, where there was no conflict of flight and flow and Eros was as null as Anteros and Night had no daughters. He was bogged in indolence, without identity, impervious alike to its pull and goading. The cities and forest and beings were also without identity, they were shadows, they exerted neither pull nor goad.

His third being was without axis or contour, its centre everywhere and periphery nowhere, an unsurveyed marsh of sloth.
(107–8)

This third being is a place or condition, a Limbo or wombtomb where
outside is expunged. To enter it Belacqua must "go under," "be sucked
down and abolished" (108). It is portrayed as antigeography, though in
geographical terms: "unsurveyed marsh," a "dark gulf" without "contour." To arrive at this place is to abandon the topography of wandering
for unchartable boundlessness where "the gin-palace of willing" (109) is
given up to the natural "wombtomb" principle of death and becoming.
The "gulf" is also a crucial term in *Murphy*, where it serves more clearly
to define and set apart that other being. And the "goading" of the will
resurfaces in Beckett's works in *Act without Words II*, where a goad prods
two characters enwombed in sacks. That dramaticule frames its sack
shelters against a desert flooded with light, just as Belacqua's retreat
shelters him from being "hauled . . . out like a crab to fry in the sun"
(108). Belacqua is not merely the indolent Dantean character who
exemplifies the disinclination to get going; his indolence is not a trait but
traitlessness.

The narrator warns us not to suppose "that this third Belacqua is the
real Belacqua any more than that the Syra-Cusa [a minor character] of
the abstract drawing was the real Syra-Cusa" (108). His reason for this,
however, is evasive: "There is no real Belacqua, it is to be hoped not
indeed, there is no such person." Belacqua is a fiction, so he is no more
"real" in his anti-identical third being than in the linear and regressive
continuum of his identity. But Belacqua's emancipation from identity
"suits his accursed complexion much better than the dreary oscillation
that presents itself as the only alternative." This identity is a "place"
where he would have liked to "settle down" (109):

But when, as rarely happened, he was drawn down go [*sic*] the
blessedly sunless depths, down and down to the slush of angels,
clear of the pettifogging ebb and flow, then he knew, but
retrospectively, after the furious divers had hauled him out like a
crab to fry in the sun, because at the time he was not concerned
with such niceties of perception, that if he were free he would
take up his dwelling in that place. (108–9)

Belacqua knows his good fortune only retrospectively, ask does Proust's
Marcel, and his experience down under is like Marcel's epiphanic

remove from time and space, only more prolonged. Earlier in *Dream*
such an experience is described in detail:

> The labour of resting in a strange place is properly
> extenuating. The first week and more went to throwing up a ring
> of earthworks; this to break not so much the flow of people and
> things to him as the ebb of him to people and things. It was his
> instinct to make himself captive, and that instinct, as never before
> or since, served him well and prepared a great period of beatitude
> stretching from mid-October to Xmas, when deliberately he
> escaladed the cup so scooped out of the world and scuttled back
> to the glare of her flesh, deserting his ways of peace and his
> country of quiet. But for two months and more he lay stretched
> in the cup. . . . lapped in a beatitude of indolence that was
> smoother than oil and softer than a pumpkin, dead to the dark
> pangs of the sons of Adam, asking nothing of the insubordinate
> mind. He moved with the shades of the dead and the dead-born
> and the unborn and the never-to-be-born, in a Limbo purged of
> desire. They moved gravely, men and women and children,
> neither sad not [*sic*] joyful. (38)

Belacqua's private retreat is a geographical Limbo where shade-
characters wander. Here desire, Schopenhauer's nemesis, is purged.
This is Belacqua's "pure" or truest condition because it is instinctual, and
it offers divine presence, the "beatitude of indolence." Diagram 3.1
shows what Belacqua's trine being might look like.

Belacqua's "cup," like Watt's pot, represents the mind and its
container. Being in the mind, one is neither of the body nor of the
world. Belacqua's Shekinah, finally, is the condition where the mind is
a refuge for itself, the self translated into itself.

> If that is what is meant by going back into one's heart,
> could anything be better, in this world or the next? The mind,
> dim and hushed like a sick-room, like a chapelle ardente,
> thronged with shades; the mind at last its own asylum, disinter-
> ested, indifferent, its miserable erethisms and discriminations and
> futile sallies suppressed; the mind suddenly reprieved, ceasing to
> be an annex of the restless body, the glare of understanding
> switched off. The lids of the hard aching mind close, there is
> suddenly gloom in the mind; not sleep, not yet, nor dream, with

Narcissus   Phoebus
(in)   (out)

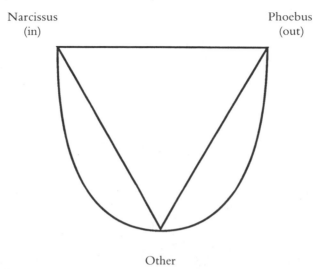

Other

Diagram 3.1.

its sweats and terrors, but a waking ultra-cerebral obscurity,
thronged with grey angels: there is nothing of him left but the
umbra of grave and womb where it is fitting that the spirits of his
dead and his unborn should come abroad. (39)

Belacqua's condition could not be bettered "in this world or the next."
It belongs neither to one nor to the other but is somehow between the
two, a liminal space like Céline's projected landscape. (Why the dead
and the unborn should populate this liminal space shall be seen in
Chapter 5.) The mind in this state is not "an annex of the body" but an
indefinable space of its own, in the Cartesian sense. Finally, the mind's
optical or visual essence is borne out by its "lids."

Belacqua's third being, then, is a condition between death and life, an
inner place literalized as a room or cup or tunnel: "in the umbra, the
tunnel, when the mind went wombtomb, then it was real thought and
real living, living thought. . . . live cerebration that drew no wages
and emptied no slops" (39). This condition is beyond subjective
empêchements—both "erethisms and discriminations," stimuli coming in
and judgments projected outward—beyond the sensible appearances of
time and space.

Murphy's Rapture: The First Landscape of Freedom

Dream of Fair to Middling Women articulates a program for much of Beckett's later fiction. Belacqua, the wavery subject, seeks Shekinah first in the embodied exterior (the Smeraldina-Rima), next in the interior (the Alba), but finds both stationed along a continuum of unacceptable states, and desires a third being—to live, if he could, in a liminal place of pure subject-lessness.

The problem for Belacqua, as for other protagonists to follow, is that one cannot will oneself into that "other" place. Belacqua remembers his pleasant tunnel after the event, but cannot return there (110). "How could the will," asks the narrator, "be abolished in its own tension?" It cannot will will-lessness. Instead, Belacqua "remains, for all his grand fidgeting and shuffling, bird or fish, or, worse still, a horrible border-creature, a submarine bird, flapping its wings under a press of water." He can't be helped, says the narrator, and must simply wait "until the thing happens." This is not completely true, as the narrator hints: "What we are doing now, of course, is setting up the world for a proper swell slap-up explosion. The bang is better than the whimper. It is easier to do. It is timed for about ten or fifteen thousand words hence. We shall blow him out of the muck that way" (158). Such an explosion is Murphy's unpleasant apotheosis, but ten thousand words later (at the end of the novel) there is no explosion. Belacqua comes out of the Alba's in a discombobulated state of mind that resembles Roquentin's when he leaves his tree. The passage parodies "The Dead": "and the rain fell in a uniform untroubled manner. It fell upon the bay, the champaignland and the mountains, and notably upon the central bog it fell with a rather desolate uniformity" (213).[34] But it is uncertain whether Belacqua experiences a revelation, as Gabriel Conroy does. This problem remains unsolved until the end of *The Unnamable*. After *Murphy* and *Watt*, where approximate unions of subject and object are achieved with deliberately unsatisfying sleights of hand, Beckett must explore the continuum of identities, seeking a way out. This movement is so difficult to accomplish because to abolish the subject, differentiation of figure and ground, is to kill the pilgrim. How else can one attain "ultra-cerebral obscurity"?

Beckett wrote *Murphy* three years after *Dream of Fair to Middling*

---

34. Joyce's story, in turn, echoes the two opening paragraphs of Bret Harte's novel *Gabriel Conroy*.

Women, and only one after *More Pricks Than Kicks*. *Dream* and *Murphy* appear substantially different one from the other. *Murphy* is more restrained, leaving fewer strands to dangle and with less ostentation. In *Dream* the characters butt and fall off, refusing to make melody; in *Murphy* each character has a counterpart—Murphy, Mr. Kelly; Celia, Miss Counihan; Endon, the Old Boy—giving the work symmetry and balance. *Dream* contains many subplots of varying length and importance—some of them dropped by the sardonic and self-conscious narrator. In *Murphy* the subplots—the search for Murphy, Celia's relation with Mr. Kelly, and the story of the Old Boy—mirror and corroborate the main plot. Nevertheless both works make a similar argument in strikingly similar terms.

Murphy wants to "enter the landscape," where he would be "improved out of all knowledge"; there his will would be "dust in the dust of its object" (*Murphy* 79, 105). This is described, as was Belacqua's desire for unity, in religious terms, as an improvement beyond the grave. Murphy imagines that his mind is made of three "zones," corresponding roughly to the social world, the intellectual, and neither (*Murphy* 111–13). He wishes to inhabit the "third" zone, analogous to Belacqua's "third being," where all is "a flux of forms, a perpetual coming together and falling asunder of forms" (112), where Murphy is "a mote in the dark of absolute freedom. He did not move, he was a point in the ceaseless unconditional generation and passing away of line." This place is a "pure" or "unconditional" maelstrom, a Platonic cave of being where "line," the continuum of fixed states of being, degenerates and reemerges; the dark zone contains "neither elements nor states, nothing but forms becoming and crumbling into the fragments of a new becoming, without love or hate or any intelligible principle of change" (112). It is like Belacqua's "umbra," where the dead and the unborn are generated (*Dream* 39), and like Belacqua's third being it is a condition without human will or reason. Subjectivity is given over to an objective "will-lessness" (113). Whereas the light zone of Murphy's mind contains figures, "the world of the body broken up" into pieces, and the half-light zone contains "states of peace," the dark zone contains neither—neither subject nor object, only the "absolute freedom" obtained when there is no freedom at all, no subjective being. Murphy's mistake is Belacqua's, that he wants to apperceive himself "into a glorious grave" (21), and he too must fail because the will cannot will its own destruction (cp. 185). Belacqua tries to achieve this state through his "cup"; Murphy's third zone is clearly a part of his mind, and he searches for it in his rocking chair. (The swilling motion of waters ebbing to the rim and flowing back to the center in Belacqua's cup is like the swing of Murphy's chair.) The chair's swing or pendulum represents the continuum of experience, of states, but unlike most things it does not slow down to stop: it rocks faster and faster as its arc shortens, nearing the pendulum's center, and then stops. At that centerpoint Murphy is supposed to enter the third zone of "non-Newtonian" (113) being. When the chair is finally still it is rocking infinitely fast, along this equation: the problem, predictably, is how to get from movement—the chair's swing, the linear world of states—to stasis, the pure center, the stateless condition of generation.

Belacqua's quest for his third being is expressed in a correlate search for Divine Presence in Woman, and that is the case with Murphy as well, up to a point, though Belacqua's prior example makes Murphy's case stand out more clearly. Murphy's two women are the fleshly Miss Counihan and the heavenly Celia. His involvement with Miss Counihan occurred in Dublin, before the story begins, as is revealed by her prized letters (231–32). Like the Smeraldina-Rima, she cares only for her own fortune, which she expects another to safeguard (255–57). Murphy escapes from Counihan to London—she believes that he is going to find work there to support her, which shows how little she knows him. In London he meets Celia, who appears at first to be another Miss Counihan, because of her old profession. She is introduced as a set of bodily measurements. But whereas Counihan would not acknowledge that she is a *de facto* prostitute, Celia takes prostitution for granted as a social necessity. Unlike the mechanically calculating Counihan, Celia appears beatific. In her presence Neary and Wylie are "petrified" and feel "more and more swine before a pearl" (232, 231); they attend her as though "at Divine Service" (233). Celia's beauty is only an aspect of her perfection. So Murphy's movement from Miss Counihan to Celia can be considered a move from the exterior inward, from the first or light zone of his mind to the second or semidark zone. This transition foreshadows his movement to the dark zone at the Magdalen Mental Mercyseat, a place beyond reason.

But since *Dream* Beckett has simplified his argument. The Smeraldina-Rima and the Alba were Daphne and Echo, retreating from Belacqua and pursuing him, and Belacqua was Apollo and Narcissus, pursuing and retreating. Murphy does not relish the Apollonian role; he is pure retreat. He leaves Miss Counihan for the West Brompton mew and Celia, and Celia for the asylum and Endon (or "within," in

Greek). Murphy, the "seedy solipsist," is "Narcissus," drawn to the charming Endon (186, and see 228). And both Celia and Miss Counihan are like Echo. One expects Celia to be Echo, given Beckett's paradigmatic movement from the outside in, from Daphne to Echo, and she does pursue Murphy, demanding that he find employment. Miss Counihan, who according to the *Dream* model should be like Daphne, is clearly also Echo. She pursues Murphy from Dublin to London, and often echoes Murphy, as in this scene, when she confronts Celia:

> "One of the innumerable small retail redeemers," sneered Miss Counihan, "lodging her pennyworth of pique in the post-golgothan kitty."
>
> But for Murphy's horror of the mental belch, Celia would have recognised this phrase, if she had heard it. (232)

On another amusing occasion she continues word for word a soliloquy learned from Murphy—an "excellent reception," according to Wylie, in which Neary detects "no trace of fading" (see 218–19). Both women, then, are Echo-like, though Miss Counihan is worldlier.

This simplification allows Beckett to concentrate on Murphy's retreat. Murphy rightly recognizes the asylum as the place where he could enter his third zone. Up to this point the novel has involved, with some exceptions, only a general topographical consciousness: spatial constriction, the topos of wandering and home. Here Beckett increasingly relies on topographical devices to articulate his argument. The institute is "ideally situated in its own grounds on the boundary of two counties" (156): it is a liminal zone, a pure (or "ideal") place of unity (or "ground") where subjectivity (the figure) has no hold. This is Murphy's "Belacqua fantasy": a place for "those that lay just beyond the frontiers of suffering"—that is, the insane who are beyond this world—"the first landscape of freedom" (78). The asylum's padded cells are microcosmic: "Within the narrow limits of domestic architecture he had never been able to imagine a more creditable representation of what he kept on calling, indefatigably, the little world" (181). Better yet, the cell is a place where time, the fourth dimension, does not exist (181). The cell, as Neary explains to the sergeant, is "next best thing to never being born" (44), a place like Belacqua's umbra.

The asylum mirrors Murphy's mind, for Murphy. He thinks of his mind as a sphere (110); "his mind functioned not as an instrument but as a place" (178). Trying for his third zone, he must become himself like these denizens of the little world. This is the reverse of the hospital's declared purpose:

> The function of treatment was to bridge the gulf, translate the sufferer from his own pernicious little private dungheap to the glorious world of discrete particles, where it would be his inestimable prerogative once again to wonder, love, hate, desire, rejoice and howl in a reasonable balanced manner, and comfort himself with the society of others in the same predicament. (177)

"Wonder" and will are linked to wandering; "glorious" shows that the institutional vision transposes heaven to the outside from its rightful place at home, in the middle (cp. "Heaven in the midst," 176). Murphy, in contrast, wants to translate himself into the mind from anti-mind, the social dungheap. To do so he must bridge the "unintelligible gulf" (240) that he feels exists between himself and the inmates (236), but he cannot, any more than the institution can succeed in getting the inmates out: "It was as though the microcosmopolitans had locked him out" (240). He needs a key to enter the dark zone: he must turn the gulf into a door to unlock.

Murphy considers his mind a "cave" in which to behold "beatific idols" (178). It is, as it were, Plato's cave turned inside out to contain the divine, especially the idol-like Endon, "an impeccable and brilliant figurine" squatting "tailor-fashion" (241), whose "speck" Murphy decides that he is (250). This may be an ironic version of the "toys" that Murphy considers people in the outside world to be.[35] At any rate, it is not surprising to find divinity in the asylum. Murphy hurries "back westward down" to Endon—every word follows Beckett's topographical argument—"with his master key at the ready" (242). Later, Murphy's dead body is associated with "key" (257, 260): only in death can Murphy find his object. In their chess game, where Endon develops and then returns his pieces in a meaningless formal pattern, disregarding the socially transactive purpose of the game, Murphy cannot correspond with Schopenhauerian Will, which disregards him despite its (or Endon's) apparent interest (this is explained in 241). "There is no return game between a man and his stars" (85): Endon, like Murphy's stars,

---

35. Compare Watt's reaction to senseless incidents: "And Watt could not accept them for what they perhaps were, the simple games that time plays with space, now with these toys, and now with those . . ." (75)

appears accessible, but is not. (The game with the stars is chess; Ticklepenny is "the merest pawn" in it.) Murphy is absorbed into Endon's system, but this process occurs involuntarily: after the chess game his eyes are "captured" like a chess piece by the brilliant Endon and all dissolves into ground "mercifully free of figure" (245). That is the effect of the Mercyseat and its grounds. Murphy collapses in a positive but not atemporal peace—an incomplete Proustian epiphany— and Endon, free to wander from his cell, plays a precise "amental pattern" (247) on another cell's light switch. Still "a prisoner of air," Murphy looks into Endon's eyes "across a narrow gulf of air" (248). These eyes, a generative "ballrace" (249; cp. the Unnamable's "all balls"), are everted like Murphy's cave-mind to contain the outside, including Murphy's image: Murphy's mind is scrambled in this organized mindlessness or anti-mind, and he stumbles to his garret cell to explode in chaos (the heating gas). Murphy is like Cosme in Unamuno's story, after The Other has looked into his eyes: "I began to live backwards. . . . And my whole life passed before me and once again I was twenty years old, and then ten, and five, and I became a child . . . I was unborn . . . I died . . . I died when I reached the age of birth" (Unamuno 257–58).

In Endon's eye Murphy discovers pure ground without figure, objectivity without subject. Beckett's subplots lead to the same conclusion; indeed, as parallels they emphasize the novel's argumentative nature. Miss Counihan and her helpers cannot recognize Murphy, who has practically lost his identity in the explosion. This is a problem of vision above all—"How various are the ways of looking away!"—as their eyes stray and mingle "among the remains" (264). Murphy's ashes end up "freely" scattered on the floor or ground (275). The Old Boy, who lived in the room above Murphy and Celia, is a lesser Murphy or Endon who finds suicide the only way out, though it is hard to decide the case conclusively. He had been a porter—a liminal figure guarding the frontier, or besieging it. Like an inmate he retired to a room and never left it, and Celia is anxious to exchange her room for his, as Murphy envied Endon's. He was served his meals in his room, anticipating Malone and other Beckett protagonists who are served in theirs. But he seems to have been a searcher, as his constant pacing shows, and his suicide is like that of some Mercyseat patients who cut their throats with razors (236).

Kelly's story is the most evolved of these parallels. Like Murphy he is chair-bound, in his wheelchair (see 277 for this comparison; Murphy ultimately exchanges his chair for the Mercy-seat). Kelly journeys from his room to Kensington Gardens—a ground, though the word is not used—which is surrounded by a "boundary" with wickets in it, an allusion that adds a touch of Bunyan to his pilgrimage. To reach the park Celia intends to cross the water by "Rennie's Bridge": this recalls not only Murphy's desire to bridge the gulf into his third zone, but also chess, the game of queens (*reine*) and kings—"Kensington" is mentioned in the same sentence (150). Mr. Kelly flies his kite above the Round Pond, which stands to him as Endon does to Narcissus-Murphy. The wind and the pond correspond to Endon's mind. The pond is a "palace of the wind" (151), both amental energy and divine presence, and the kites are "specks against the east darkening already" (152), like the speck Murphy in Endon's unseen, with darkness recalling the third zone inhabited by Endon, coveted by Murphy. In the park the leaves and the kites move in a frenzy, seeking freedom and ground, "a sudden frenzy of freedom at contact with the earth" (150), like Murphy's chair defying general practice by moving faster and faster and then stopping. Mr. Kelly's kite disappears in the sky, figure lost in ground, to its owner's "rapture," a religious connection with the absolute. This connection also has a sexual aspect, as did Murphy's relation with Mr. Endon when he held the inmate as though in a butterfly kiss; of Mr. Kelly, Beckett writes that "so great was his skill that in five minutes he was lying back, breathing hard and short, his eyes closed of necessity but in ecstasy as it happened, half his line out, sailing by feel" (279). He holds his kite by its "line," all of linear history, it is made clear (see 279–80), the line and surface of the visual world, disappearing into objectivity. He wants to measure the "point" where seen and unseen meet, the frontier between himself and the other. But Mr. Kelly dozes and his kite escapes, no longer a prisoner of air, to vanish in the dusk (282).

Like Mr. Kelly, Murphy does not really bridge the gulf between himself and the object: disoriented by his experience with Mr. Endon he is still "dimly intending to have a short rock and then, if he felt any better, to dress and go, before the day staff were about, leaving Ticklepenny to face the music, MUSIC, MUSIC, back to Brewery Road, to Celia, serenade, nocturne, albada. Dimly, very dimly" (252). He still desires and wills, though "dimly," nearing his dark zone, and desire remains the subject's problem in Beckett's next work. But in *Murphy* Beckett abridges the task of locating the place of the object. He does not evade the question, as the ending of *Dream* does, but Murphy need only turn away from the social world at large to find the sanctuary of the All (see 240), and within it a very approachable version of the unassimilable and irreducible Other. Then he need only look at ordered Nothingness to be sucked into the inner vacuum of chaos. Somehow the whole process of getting to the place of the object is belittled: in *Murphy* Beckett still explores the idea that there is such a thing. In *Watt* Beckett can assume that there is a place of unity and engage the more difficult problem of reaching it.

Watt: Obstruction and Desire in the Linear World

In *Murphy* Beckett already narrows the nature of his search for unity. *Dream* represents the paradigm of wandering and home, subject and object, with actual wanderings and homes, but it does not really *figure* the search, as *Murphy* does. But when Beckett wants to show the movement to the object he finds that his two ways, the centrifugal and the centripetal, are at odds. Murphy seeks an object outside himself, embodied in Endon, but as the Greek word "Endon" suggests, that final encounter leads to a change "within." Murphy's topographical movement into the asylum and into Endon's cell, which appears so crucial, is merely symbolic, analogous to the real change inside Murphy. There is no union of subject and object for Murphy; the object remains outside and can only merge with Murphy through the microcosmic incorporation of the world. Somehow the terms of the search must change for the union with the object to be shown, if it could be shown. *Watt* is Beckett's attempt to do just that.

In *Watt* (1942–44) Beckett concentrates on the possibilities of centrifugal motion, the surfaces of things. There is never any talk of a transcendent change in Watt himself, the perceiving subject, and although the whole of the book's world can be thought of as a mental landscape, it presents a traditional, corruptible Watt contemplating the absolute, what Beckett calls in *Proust* "a mobile subject before an ideal object, immutable and incorruptible" (6). Watt believes in reason and tries to explain the order in which he participates; but order in itself is not meaningful and does not explain itself. Watt, in other words, explores the world of form and surface (*Watt* 73), of line, for what is pure and nonlinear, and it soon becomes obvious that he will fail.

Watt is the first of Beckett's works to emphasize place over action. In *Dream* there is much theoretical talk of the place of unity—Belacqua's "cup"—but it is never embodied; in *Murphy* Beckett literalizes the mental home, but wandering still gets the greater share of the action. In *Watt* Beckett emphasizes Knott's house and grounds, described much as Murphy's third zone and Belacqua's umbra are. Knott's house inspires awe (36). It is a place of fixity (199) where incidents "of great formal brilliance and indeterminable purport" (74) occur. Arsene describes it to Watt as the place of unity, "this state or place on which my hopes so long were fixed" (49). Knott himself is not human (202), a master who cannot be known directly (67), served by generations of transient servants.[36] Each of these servants takes the "place" of the other, Watt replacing Arsene who had replaced Vincent, Erskine replacing Walter to be replaced by Arthur (56, 148). Knott's bedroom and the music room exemplify the nature of the place. The bedroom is a solar system with the bed apparently fixed in the center (207); Knott rotates the room's furniture like planets in a motion that is "both absolute and relative" (204), both around the bed and around themselves. The music room is bare and white (71), and receives the only visitors to cross Knott's threshold (70), the two piano tuners. The piano tuning, so called, has form (presence) but no meaning (causal sense):

> Thus the scene in the music-room, with the two Galls, ceased very soon to signify for Watt a piano tuned, an obscure family and professional relation, an exchange of judgments more or less intelligible, and so on, if indeed it had ever signified such things, and became a mere example of light commenting bodies, and stillness motion, and silence sound, and comment comment. (73)

Knott's bedroom furniture and the piano-tuning incident show the nature of Knott's, a place of Schopenhauerian Will that is both cosmic and musical. They are two versions of formal nothing, of the "presence of what did not exist" (45). Watt, trying to make sense of these events, is the impure subject who "insists on giving a figure to that which is ideal and invisible, on incarnating the Idea in what he conceives to be an appropriate paradigm" (*Proust* 71). Like the artist of the *Three Dialogues*, he is "obliged, because of his peculiar character, to enquire into what they meant" (75). Instead he finds at Knott's the "comedy of substitu-

---

36. Knott's name, which denotes a knot in the world of line, derives from "ball" in Icelandic (Skeat 280)—which one might have expected—and also from "Knout," a scourge or whip. Joyce's friends knew his *Work in Progress* as WIP, which makes Joyce the Knott/master, and Sam his servant. Beckett uses the word "knout" in the sense of "whip" in *Molloy* 93.

tions" (*Proust* 16), "the simple games that time plays with space" (*Watt* 74).

Arthur's story of Louit, a researcher into the mathematical intuition of the "Visicelts," and of his specimen Mr Nackybal, supports Knott's distinction. Actually the whole affair is fake, made up by Louit to cover up his smuggling operation, and Mr Nackybal is really a Mr Tisler who lives in a room on the canal (198). Nackybal is supposed to be like Endon, "a moron from a different crawl of life" (181), with only a "pale" music in his mathematical mind (174; cp. the white music-room). He is said to know the cube root of any number, though in fact he simply has a method of cube-rooting (198), and he supposedly exists "in an ecstasy of darkness, and of silence" (175). In other words, he fakes being Endon, or Knott, living in what Murphy calls the third zone. This episode goes to show that the qualities of Knott's place are in fact as unique as Watt thinks they are: "For outside Mr Knott's house, and of course grounds, such incidents were unknown, or so Watt supposed" (75). Knott's is "the right place," as Arsene calls it (40).

To reach the place of the object one must cross a threshold, a borderline that gives access to a different state or condition, dividing the state of unity from the world of experience. "Threshold" is easily one of Beckett's most important concepts, and *Watt* is Beckett's first work to give it control over the narrative. In *Dream* Beckett does not conceive of a threshold because he denies the possibility of willful movement to the object; in *Murphy* and *Watt* he does acknowledge the threshold, but cannot explain how it is crossed (in *Murphy*, for instance, Miss Carridge knocks on the outside of a door after she has closed it behind her, 68). How does Watt enter Knott's? He tries the front door, but it is locked; he goes to the back door, but it is also locked; he returns to the front, but it is still locked; he returns to the back door and finds it "on the latch," and enters (36). Watt decides that he had been let in (36–37), but one can surmise that he was not. One night Watt returns downstairs to find a strange man in the kitchen.

> Watt asked this man who he was, and how he had got in. He felt it was his duty to do this.
> My name is Micks, said the stranger. One moment I was out, and the next I was in. (216)

Micks arrives to replace Watt just as Watt arrived to replace Arsene, and no one opened the door for him. Watt has some skill at opening locked doors, providing they have "simple" locks; but "obscure" locks he cannot open, nor counterfeit obscure keys (124). Presumably Knott's doors are of the obscure kind. Murphy enters Endon's cell with his key; Watt crosses "Knott's threshold" (37), but Beckett cannot explain how this is done.

The question that at first had been, "If there is a place of unity, what is it like?" is replaced by, "How can one get there?" and that question in turn seems increasingly naive, giving way to Zenovian regression: to get to the place of the object one first has to get to a place from which one could start for that place, and so on. The pilgrim's real question, then, is not so much how one gets to the object as how one moves from place to place. In *Murphy* Beckett uses his systematic topography to show the pilgrim's progress, Celia going over the bridge to the Park's grounds as Murphy crosses the gulf to Endon's cell. This general topographical thinking continues in *Watt*: Watt travels the world of "line," the east-west axis (30) represented by the railway, rows of cast steel, to reach Knott's house and its gardens, the place of circularity and repetition, and then leaves again by rail. But the question of progress is much more specific, and depends less on the narrative context. Increasingly in Beckett's fiction, liminal passage itself, not just the act of entering a designated "place," represents the movement of the subject on its pilgrimage. It is not easy to cross from one place to another, because the crossing is itself a place, a liminal zone separating one place from another. Beckett dramatizes this in a scene where Sam discovers that he and his garden are mirrored by Watt and his garden (159). The gardens are divided by fences that run parallel to each other, for no garden shares a fence with another. Sam finds a mysterious hole going through the fences of both gardens—a passage from one place to another—and offers several explanations for its origin (160–61), none convincing. It is hard to believe that anyone could have passed from one place to the other; Sam does not imagine that a human agent made the hole or that it has any purpose. Sam and Watt travel back and forth in the narrow zone between the two gardens, but they never cross from one garden to another.

What holds up the subject are the *empêchements*; in its centrifugal movement through the world of surface and form the subject is held up by the *empêchement-objet*, the opacity of the object. In Beckett's world of literalized metaphor these *empêchements*, or "impediments," are barriers, partitions separating one place from another, obstructing traffic, dividing the landscape. In *Murphy* this division is the "gulf" that separates the inmates from normal society, Murphy from Endon. In later works the landscape is often divided, and the fence, the hedge, the wall, the window, the gap, the ditch, and their relatives increasingly control the narrative.[37] But while some *empêchements* are barriers, like the gulf that isolates the object, others are thresholds, passages from one place, a bounded field or wood or garden, to another. Sam explains the distinction (which he says holds for Watt too):

> I was very fond of fences, of wire fences, very fond indeed; not of walls, nor palissades, nor opacious hedges, no; but to all that limited motion, without limiting vision, to the ditch, the dyke, the barred window, the bog, the quicksand, the paling, I was deeply attached, at that time, deeply deeply attached. (158)

A little earlier Sam said that he and Watt were "attached" to a little bridge over a brook: "For without it how should we have passed from one part of the garden to the other?" (155). These *empêchements* show Beckett struggling with the problem of showing obstructions that allow passage. They bar motion but permit a movement of the will, of desire, by revealing what is beyond them.

Beckett's problem is that while passage is desirable, desire is not. Watt, the errant man of surface and exterior, considers that to desire eternally without fulfillment is the highest good—"That with his need he might witness its absence" (203)—but that is the very opposite of union, and of Knott's condition, whose needs are always fulfilled (202–3). The threshold must also allow portage without recourse to desire. Here such impediments as Watt prefers come in handy—they render the will inconsequential. Beckett shows this again with the image of flies on a window: "The flies, of skeleton thinness, excited to new efforts by yet another dawn, left the walls, and the ceiling, and even the floor, and hastened in great numbers to the window. Here, pressed against the impenetrable panes, they would enjoy the light, and warmth, of the long summer's day" (236–37). For the flies the room's six sides are equally impediments, but the window, also "impenetrable," allows a kind of exposure to the other side. The flies are skeletal and so

---

37. This division of the landscape appears prominently in *More Pricks Than Kicks* in the form of hedges and low-lying stone walls dividing the fields. Such walls are especially characteristic of the Connemara region of Galway—see O'Brien's commentary, 305–6, and the accompanying photograph, 307.

represent inner being, independence from Watt's surface life: Watt sees the flesh before the bones, satisfied with appearances (73). But then everything at Knott's makes Watt curious. The only material change in Watt during his stay at Knott's is his ordered inversion of syntax, but that seems a willed attempt to emulate Knott. Although Watt wearies of his "many tedious years spent clinging to the perimeter" and yearns for that "harmony . . . when all outside him will be he," when, like Mr. Knott, "he will be in the midst at last" (40–41), he cannot penetrate the impediments of "line and surface," the fallacy of realistic art. He is habitual, and "our current habit of living is . . . incapable of dealing with the mystery of a strange key or a strange room" (*Proust* 9).

The problem for Belacqua, Murphy, and Watt is not just that the will defeats unity but that the will and the world of line and surface are related. The centrifugal movement to union is bound to fail because it assumes the very opposition it wishes to annul: that of a mobile subject contemplating a fixed object. Beckett requires different terms for the subject's search, just as he needs to translate the antagonism of anti-mind into manageable terms. The works that continue Beckett's search in the exterior, *Mercier and Camier* (1945), *Éleuthéria* (1947), and *Molloy* (1947), attack the fallacy of surface and undermine the world of cause and effect in an effort to solve this problem. But Beckett's centripetal search, an unraveling of the subject's matter of habit, already appears inevitable.

4

Threshold to Unity

At the end of *The Unnamable* Beckett solves the problems that have engaged him in seven major works of fiction. Having explored and rejected all possible relations with the object, the Unnamable finds unexpected wisdom: the way to union does not lie in the dynamisms of exterior and interior, but in the tension between them. It is a way "from impenetrable self to impenetrable unself by way of neither" (*Neither* 108). This solution is hard to predict, considering how lost the Beckettian subject seems to be in the middle novels. In *Watt* Beckett had only suggested what becomes an overt theme in these works, the difficulty of pilgrimage in the outside world. The world of *Mercier and Camier* and *Molloy* resembles the parceled landscapes of Bram van Velde. These protagonists do not move very far: Molloy is confined all his life to an area of six square miles around the town of Bally (*Molloy* 133), and Mercier and Camier "did not remove from home" (*Mercier and Camier* 7). While in *Mercier and Camier* Beckett shows the changing subject pursuing fixed objectives, as in *Watt*, this relation too begins to change. As Beckett undermines the linear quality of the exterior, a process accentuated in *Molloy*, his object also wavers. This new phenomenological problem, compounded with the problem of the subject's unacceptable desire, proves too much for the search for union with the object in the exterior. In the outside world the subject fails not only to reach a unity compatible with desire but also to find a fixed, uncontaminated object. This is particularly clear in *Malone Dies*, which begins with determination the search in the interior. "We can't change the country.

Let us change the subject," says Joyce in *Ulysses* (645), and Beckett takes
that advice. With *The Unnamable* the subject is free of surface, and free
to investigate any relation it chooses with the object. It is striking that
Beckett's protagonists must seek confinement in order to be free, if only
imaginatively, but the mental traveler can proceed in any way imaginable. This proves to be necessary for the Unnamable's breakthrough.

Rhetorics of Impasse in the Middle Novels

Mercier and Camier: The Chessboard World

Mercier and Camier (written in 1945) depicts the search for objectivity
plainly, while its protagonists, the "pseudocouple Mercier-Camier"
(*The Unnamable* 297), reveal the difficulty of the search. "We go
wherever the flesh creeps least," says Mercier (90), that is, where there
is no subjective change and no wandering. The two perceive the place of
the object but cannot participate in union itself: at one point they "held
back on the brink of a great open space, a square perhaps, all tumult,
fluttering gleams, writhing shadows" (89–90). This place is geometrically shaped ("a square") and contains the "gleams" associated with the
mind. It is like God's cave in *Paradise Lost*, where forms are made and
remade in alternating light and darkness. In the summary of this chapter
(a summary is provided every two chapters) this event is called "the
gulf" (96), tying it plainly enough with the gulf that separates Beckett's
earlier subjects from their objects. Mercier reveals a similar vision to the
innkeeper, Mr. Gast:

> You appear to me most often on a threshold, or at a window.
> Behind you torrents of light and joy which should normally
> annihilate your features, but do not. You smile. Presumably you
> do not see me, across the alley from where you stand and
> plunged in deepest shadow. I too smile—and pass on. (43)

Something like a dream *visio* haunts Mercier. Mr. Gast's features should
be annihilated in this place because the place of the object obliterates the
figure. Mr. Gast does not see Mercier as Endon did not see Murphy, and
Mercier passes on, the wandering subject.

  The couple's search is said to be simple, but the reader soon discovers
the difficulty of their progress. "The journey of Mercier and Camier,"

the narrator begins, deceptively, "is one I can tell. . . . Physically it was fairly easy going, without seas or frontiers to be crossed, through regions untormented on the whole" (7). "What we seek," says Camier, reassuringly, "is not necessarily behind the back of the beyond" (66). But crossing to the behind of things is what the protagonists' journey is all about. Their landscape is the divided topography of *empêchement-objet*, a virtual chessboard world only implied in *Murphy* and *Endgame*. Here for example is a field: "Its straggling expanse was bounded by a sickly hedge of old tree stumps and tangles of brambles. . . . Beyond the hedge were other fields, similar in aspect, bounded by no less similar hedges. How did one get from one field to another? Through the hedges perhaps" (56). A goat that tries to spring over the hedge cannot pass: "Would it continue thus all round the field? Or weary first?" (56). The question for the pseudocouple—as it often is for Alice in *Through the Looking-Glass*—is not so much where one is going but how one gets there, how one can pass from one bounded place to another.[1] Mercier, rebellious, exhibits the Murphy complex, longing to throw himself out of windows (28, 41, 46), seeking unmediated abridgment with the other side. Every distance is divided into a series of spaces that must be crossed: Camier at one point dreads to see Mercier "cross the sill and tread the last stage of the great space separating them" (81). Even the writhing square, when the couple finally crosses it, uncomprehending "what had chanced," is divided like Murphy's mind into furious wind and "zones of calm" (94).

Accordingly Mercier and Camier develop a rhetoric of deferment. They rarely know where to go or how to proceed. When Camier asks where they are going, Mercier replies that it does not matter: "We are going, that's enough" (90). Not seeing "the goal they had in view," they decided "to postpone all action" to the next day or later (73). This condition appears to be that of any Beckett character, although it was not Watt's problem, nor quite Murphy's either. It is a new kind of problem that appears here first. While scenes and devices in the novel recall the organized pilgrimage of earlier protagonists, the rhetoric of

---

1. The Horse, who had put his head out of the window, quietly drew it in and said "It's only a brook we have to jump over." Everybody seemed satisfied with this, though Alice felt a little nervous at the idea of trains jumping at all. "However, it'll take us into the Fourth Square, that's some comfort!" she said to herself. In another moment she felt the carriage rise straight up into the air, and in her fright she caught at the thing nearest to her hand, which happened to be the Goat's beard. (*Through the Looking-Glass* 41)

division and deferment undermines these scenes, these devices. For example, Mercier and Camier alternate wandering and shelter—and town and country (105)—but some of their shelters, only stages in ongoing progress, resemble what earlier Beckett protagonists would have considered final destinations. One of these shelters is the prostitute Helen's home; in contrast, Belacqua in *Dream* refused to accept the possibility of "Beatrice in the brothel," that is, transcendent presence embodied in the actual. Then there are the ruins found on the road: the couple enter "their inmost parts" and "lay there as in a tomb" (103). Like Murphy's, this shelter is a "hospitable chaos" (104) that looks like a good place to end, says the narrator—for anyone, that is, except Mercier and Camier: "Here would be the place to make an end. After all it is the end. But there is still day, day after day, afterlife all life long, the dust of all that is dead and buried rising, eddying, settling, burying again. So let them wake" (103). The next day they are "back on the road, appreciably recruited in spite of all" (104). Soon after, the two actually meet Watt, and leave him too behind: the novel summons the three earlier novels, *Dream*, *Murphy*, and *Watt*, deserting their eschatologies each in turn.

Beckett also sets up the couple's pilgrimage in Bunyanesque terms, only to undermine it. While their road "townward" runs through a "quag" (105), like Bunyan's to the Celestial City, it leads to an unlimited middle ground: "This can drag on for months, the betwixt and between" (109). Such liminality is paradigmatic of the way to heaven (as Kafka and Lewis also show in *The Castle* and *The Childermass*). Mercier takes leave of his children (31), though unlike Christian he chases his away, and Camier hears a mixed choir, as does Christian (*The Pilgrim's Progress* 203–4). Beckett's protagonists do not meet a soul (25). Like Bunyan's pilgrim, Mercier and Camier lose their "sack," but whereas Christian's sack is a burden removed by Christ, Mercier and Camier consider their sack "the crux of the whole matter in that it contains, or did contain, certain objects we cannot dispense with" (59). Their sack is not a liability but the pilgrims' sole concern and the object of their search (60, 88). Beckett also reverses Bunyan's treatment of the sack by using it as another head metaphor: his question is whether it contains anything indispensable in the first place, whether there is a mind rather than a brain, a soul in the body. Camier intuits that the sack contains "something essential to our salvation" (59); as the object of the pilgrims' search, it is a spiritual head-refuge. Unfortunately, concrete examina-

tion reveals that all the sack's contents are without exception superflu-
ous.[2]

Mercier and Camier's middle being of deferment and frustration is an
appropriate foil to the search among the material layers of objectivity.
The Unnamable too will find the road mushy like the mire that
surrounds it, but he will be wiser for this earlier failure, and *The
Unnamable* will show what to make of his regression. This novel,
instead, ends in suspension and false epiphany, just as *Dream of Fair to
Middling Women* did. In *Dream* Belacqua ends on Ballsbridge, "marooned on the bridge and far from shelter" (214). Mercier and Camier
end on the "charming" Lock Bridge, an emblem of their blocked
passage, with a great prospect open before them (120). Belacqua inspects
the firmament for stars but considers the heavens absolutely dark (214);
he experiences only the false epiphany of Irish rain (213). Mercier and
Camier search the sky for what the summary calls "the arctic flowers"
(123), which Mercier refers to as "the ancients' Blessed Isles" (121), but
Camier manages to see only "a few pale gleams"—the cosmic mirror of
the mind. The sky finally darkens to its "full," and like Belacqua,
Mercier hears human sounds long kept from him, "and the rain on the
water" (122).

Molloy: Two Fools, among Others

Molloy combines elements from Beckett's earlier novels and carries the
subject's search in the exterior to its inevitable impasse.[3] *Molloy* is of
course founded on the topographical dichotomy of wandering and
home—the double desire to rest and to wander that is for Molloy
constitutional. Like Belacqua, he considers himself both Narcissus and
Apollo: "For in me there have always been two fools, among others,
one asking nothing better than to stay where he is and the other
imagining that life might be slightly less horrible a little further on" (48).

2. Beckett also comments on historical salvation in a scene that recalls Céline and
Waiting for Godot. The couple's umbrella came out "around 1900" (74), which reminds
Camier of Ladysmith, or the Boer War (1899–1902). British forces were besieged in the
town of Ladysmith from November 1899 to February 1900, when they were saved by
British reinforcements: "We are saved. The century was two months old" (75). "Look at
it now," replies Mercier—in 1945 things were so much worse.

3. There are several resemblances between *Molloy* and the novels that precede it.
Molloy's telling begins at home and ends there, though in his story he never reaches that
place. Instead he sojourns in several homes, most notably Lousse's house and garden,
where the valet resembles Endon (43) and where a parrot recalls Helen's parrot in *Mercier
and Camier*. Like the goat in *Mercier and Camier*, Molloy bounds two or three feet off the
ground (54), and like Watt he travels east, toward the sun (62).

Moran begins his journey at home and, after he kills what seems his old
self at a shelter (150–51), returns home. He is a pilgrim (173), he says:
like Bunyan's pilgrims he walks a narrow path (127), passing through a
wicket gate both going and returning (127, 174), and like Céline's
Bardamu he survives on tinned sardines (135, 148). Molloy provides a
paradigm for the wandering subject with his wandering rocks, which he
rotates in four pockets and his mouth. These are like Knott's wandering
servants: the mouth is a cavelike source of breath, the godly dark place
of origination, a house like Knott's where each pebble (my element is
sand, says Molloy biblically) stops before wandering on through the
other lesser places, the pockets.

Molloy continues to investigate the two key questions of the centrifugal quest. The first is the question of desire, or of will. In *Mercier and
Camier* the protagonists know they are pilgrims but do not appear to
know why or where they are going. This ignorance appears at first
consideration a saving grace, eliminating desire. If you do not know
what you want, you cannot want it. Watt, encountered at the end of the
novel, substantiates this notion: "I too have sought, said Watt, all on my
own, only I thought I knew what. Can you beat that one?" (*Mercier and
Camier* 113–14). The problem is precisely that Mercier and Camier
cannot beat that one by much. They are ignorant, but not ignorant
enough. They have short-term objectives—to find the sack, to go to
Helen's, to find each other—and their pilgrimage is itself an act of will
because they debate and decide on their actions. They have a vision of
the place of union, and when they see it they know it, or at least Mercier
claims he does. They find constant testimonies to their vision, though
none suffices. In *Molloy* Beckett has tried stricter measures to suppress
the will, but only with marginal success.

It is tempting to speculate that in Molloy Beckett wanted to create
something like an objective person, for whom the subjective Moran
would search. Molloy describes his "ruins," where he wanders in his
imagination, as "a place with neither plan nor bounds and of which I
understand nothing," the antigeographical and unintelligible place of the
object, which he also calls lyrically "the indestructible chaos of timeless
things" (39). He explains, in a shapely passage, that getting to such a
place is above all a question of will, or of its absence:

> It is in any case a place devoid of mystery, deserted by magic,
> because devoid of mystery. And if I do not go there gladly, I go
> perhaps more gladly there than anywhere else, astonished and at

peace, I nearly said as in a dream, but no, no. But it is not the kind of place where you go, but where you find yourself, sometimes, not knowing how, and which you cannot leave at will, and where you find yourself without pleasure, but with more perhaps than in those places you can escape from, by making an effort, places full of mystery, full of the familiar mysteries. (440)

This is a place without foundation, whose "ground" is unfit for loads (i.e., figures), where one sees and is seen (40).[4] You do not "go" to such a place, explains Molloy, but find yourself there. The will does not enter into it.

But Molloy does desire, and never finds himself at such a place, unable to leave. Even Lousse's he can leave, with some effort. He wants all sorts of things—to get to his mother's house, for example, and to find a way to suck his pebbles in sequence, using only his four pockets. His desire lingers to the very end of his narrative, even though he claims finally that "Molloy could stay, where he happened to be": "I longed to go back into the forest. Oh not a real longing" (91). Molloy's clever solution to desire, then, is to find himself in a place without desire, but he never does. Moran offers a different solution: he has a clear-cut mission, to find Molloy, so he finds his excuse in the claim that agents like himself are not free (95). To the last he obeys Youdi's command, as relayed by Gaber; he does not know why his mission is called off, but returns home as told. But in all this he shows a good deal of determination. For him Youdi's "command" substitutes for the will, but this too, rather obviously, is not a way out, because Moran must still will to obey the command. These novels often mention a force that compels the protagonists to move toward a liminal zone, as Sam is drawn to the fence in *Watt* and Moran is drawn by his shelter (148). So far as these characters know, their journeys—under whatever pretexts— cannot elide desire and direction.

The second question tackled in *Molloy* involves the wavering object. Beckett's pilgrim finds the landscape increasingly divided, and this

4. Kenner says that the rituals in *Godot*, and the twin journeys in *Molloy*, and the parallel narratives in *Malone Dies*, "supply the words with something formal to disclose. . . . They are not the mystery, they do not clarify the mystery, or seek to clarify the mystery, they clarify the place where the mystery is" (*Samuel Beckett: A Critical Study* 142). Kenner is right about the place, but not about the mystery, as the passage just quoted shows.

division removes the object further behind layers of *empêchements*. Watt
discovers zones within zones, like the music room in Knott's house, and
zones between zones, like the corridor between the gardens. He can
never see Knott properly, for Knott sleeps in his day clothes, over which
he puts his night clothes. In *Mercier and Camier* grand goals give way to
immediate ends and no place is final—everywhere is nowhere, a place
among others in a disconnected, virtual topography. *Molloy*, though it
presents a semblance of depth, of historical cause and effect, elaborates
the same vision. Here the topoi of division rule. Moran travels "from
my country to Molloy's" (132), to "the Molloy country" (131, 161),
which is "so different from my own" (133). These geographical regions
appear at once to merge gradually and to end abruptly (65, 90). Each
region contains in itself further division: "don't imagine my region
ended at the coast," says Molloy pridefully, citing the kind of barrier
loved by Watt, "that would be a grave mistake. For it was this sea too,
its reefs and distant islands, and its hidden depths" (69). Hence Moran
can speak of these regions or counties not as territorial divisions but as
"territorial subdivisions" (134), and as expected, threshold edges matter
here most. Molloy's famous forest ends in a ditch that, when he falls into
it, opens his eyes (91); in telling his story Molloy crosses a "threshhold"
(*sic*, 8); and then there is "the threshold of the Molloy affair" (99) and
Moran junior's "threshold of life" (92). In Molloy's vision of A and C,
the road is "remarkably bare" because it is "without hedges or ditches or
any kind of edge" (8): if A and C recall Mercier and Camier, whom they
resemble, then Molloy considers their earlier way easy compared to his.

Confronted with this division, Molloy and Moran find passage
increasingly difficult. Molloy especially is "suspended" (16), plunging
into life "without knowing who was shitting against whom or on which
side I had the better chance of skulking with success" (32). The linear
world of pilgrimage breaks down: "I misjudged the distance separating
me from the other world, and often I stretched out my hand for what
was far beyond my reach, and often I knocked against obstacles scarcely
visible on the horizon" (50). The object recedes, like the sky that is
always farther away than it seems. Molloy pursues not The Object but
objects and objectives. He "hastened," says Moran, "towards extremely
close objectives" (113). The way, which Molloy explains is "nothing
more than a surface" (26), loses efficacy, and the protagonists turn away
from it. Molloy wants to leave the perimeter for the center, to hide in
the middle of Lousse's room (43), as Moran sees in his vision of him
(113); and even Moran, who is turned to the outer world (e.g., 114),

wishes to be in the middle of a desert (147). The center of a room is an odd place to hide, but it is not so odd if it represents depth as against the surface of the perimeter. This rejection of surface is partly a yearning to be in the midst at last. It also shows that the way of the exterior has failed Beckett's pilgrims.[5]

Molloy speculates disappointedly that there is no whole before death (27): he is not natural enough, he says, to enter into the "order of things" where all twists confusedly about him (44), and he will probably not have a natural end (113). For all the distance that Beckett's pilgrims have journeyed, they face anew Murphy's bane, the unattainability of that other world. In *Molloy* Beckett rejects the will and claims ignorance or obedience, but that ruse fails; he undermines the linear world of *empêchement-objet* only to find the object deferred, receding and diminishing. If there is a way to objectivity, it must lie in another direction.

Malone Dies

If the outside world impedes the quest for union, perhaps a course divorced of solid things would not. A more successful journey would follow mental laws, not go against them. Accordingly, Malone and the Unnamable seek a way to the place of the object that is removed from "the outer world" (*Malone Dies* 221). But the interior has its own *empêchements*, and soon proves as intractable as the solids.

Malone Dies begins optimistically enough: "I shall soon be quite dead at last" (179). Malone seems like a traveler who finally reaches the high road, conscious above all of new ease. He feels already a hair's breadth from home. This novel, it appears, is to be the end, the last of the series, leading at last to the object. "Something must have changed," says Malone.

> I will not weigh upon the balance any more, one way or the other. I shall be neutral and inert. No difficulty there. Throes are the only trouble. . . . But I am less given to them now, since coming here. (179)

Imagining himself at the mind's threshold, he thinks himself weightless, unsubstantial. Unlike Molloy, who decided he could never enter the

---

5. In *Éleuthéria*, Beckett's unpublished 1947 play, the protagonist Victor habitually breaks his window (Reading University Library typescript, act 1, p. 39), much as Murphy, and Mercier and Camier, and Malone sought an easy way out of the linear world. Victor too moves to the center of his room (133).

natural order of things, Malone easily foresees such an end: "Yes, I shall be natural at last" (179). Like Molloy, Malone finds himself in a room recovered from a lapse of consciousness, and vaguely remembers his walking adventures, and a forest (183). But he is no Molloy, if he ever was like him. He is on the threshold of being no more (194), or, in more picturesque terms, "on the point of vanishing" (195), only now he seems on the inner side of the threshold: birds come to his windowsill to ask for food (184), while he, Knott-like in his bed, is without needs, never hot, cold, dirty, or hungry (185). This is promising. He is in the dark (186)—the darkness coveted by Murphy—and if he is to tell stories to amuse himself they will be the opposite, without darkness in them, stories of outer things (190). The novel begins, then, with Malone's confident gesture of closure, one conscious of previous failures but also of new conditions: "All my life long I have dreamt of the moment when, edified at last, in so far as one can be before all is lost, I might draw the line and make the tot. This moment seems now at hand" (181).

Malone soon discovers that the end is not near. To begin with, he cannot escape the old problems of regression and desire. Regression and its ally positive logic explode the notion that the inner world is substantially different from the physical world. Malone finds that he cannot "cease," only "decrease": he is inside, beneath the flesh, but the self is layered, and Malone does not know how far in he has traveled (186). His life had been a series or succession of phenomena (234). "Unfortunately I do not know quite what floor I am on, perhaps I am only on the mezzanine" (218); nothing has enlightened him, he says, "on this subject" (219). Another problem is Malone's persistent will. Because of the haphazard and disorderly nature of his writing, Malone fancies that his subject "falls far from the verb," loses efficacy or government, and his "object" lands in the void (234). Like Marcel, whose weakness of will Beckett noted in the marginalia to his copy of *A la recherche*, Malone pretends an enabling absence, a negative capability (which he calls "a mercy") that severs the object from his will. And echoing Beckett's interpretation of Proust's object as the Idea that appeals to the subject, Malone says that objects he picked up when out walking seemed to need him as he needed them. *They* had needs. But Malone's sense of needlessness is false. He constantly desires things large and small, even when he catches himself in desire: "Quick quick my possessions," he bids himself, and replies, "Quiet quiet, twice, I have time, lots of time, as usual" (246). Anticipating a visitor, he produces a list of twenty-one requests and questions, such as "15. May I ask you a favour?" (272). Regression and desire, then, both old problems the interior search means to avoid, remain.

In attempting an interior pilgrimage Beckett also discovers two new obstacles, both aspects of *empêchement-sujet*—the subject's objectivity and its Humean projective tendency. Beckett dramatizes the necessary objectification of the subject through Malone's self-surrogates, who act out "real life" experiences. Malone claims that his characters are his opposites, but in fact they appear much like him. The description of Macmann, his needs tended to in an asylum, especially suggests Malone (257). Like his author, who passes from one story to another, Macmann must "proceed by other places to another place, and then by others still to yet another" (232). He searches for a point of portage, a "breach" through which he might slip out of the asylum's Edenic garden (278), and his keeper, Lemuel, exhibits the old predilection for abridging the crossing to the object by throwing himself out of the window (280). Malone's characters objectify his own inclinations and qualities, from which he cannot escape. Malone's other *empêchement-sujet*, in addition to this objectification of the subject, is the infection of his objects with his own transience. This difficulty plagued *Molloy* and even *Mercier and Camier*; here it threatens to sever the subject–object relationship altogether. Malone's creatures "must be able to move, or to be moved. . . . The speed I am turning at now make [*sic*] things difficult admittedly, but it probably can only increase, that is the thing to be considered" (274). The signifier is loose, correspondingly destabilizing its signified objects. Because Malone's creatures are so intimately tied to him and are so much like him, as he discovers in the course of his attempts to produce just the opposite relationship with them, his end is linked with theirs: he cannot through them reach a state opposite his own subjectivity.

Malone Dies ends with what appears like success, Malone's death and the end of his creatures. The two seem complementary: as Malone enters a new life, "being given . . . birth into death" (283), his characters are herded off in a boat where, adrift, they ship their oars (287). Their excursion is an *Imramh*, a Gaelic tale of "journeys into the invisible world"; the word means literally "rowing about" (Hull 127). But even as he seems to end his subjective being at last, in the midst of his description of his own "birth," Malone asserts an utter attachment to the outside: "I am swelling. What if I should burst? The ceiling rises and falls, rises and falls, rhythmically, as when I was a foetus" (283). Malone gives birth to himself—"I am swelling"—and does not escape his own subjective world. While he has pretended to dissociate himself from his creatures, at the end of the novel his association with them is complete.

This association deserves a close look. Who are these characters, herded off in the boat? They are inmates in the mental asylum where Macmann has ended, out on a pleasure excursion to see Druid ruins. They are easily identified as Beckett's earlier protagonists, described in chronological order, except for their deranged keeper Lemuel, who may stand for Samuel, the author himself. There is Murphy, "a young man, dead young, seated in an old rocking-chair, his shirt rolled up and his hands on his thighs, would have seemed asleep had not his eyes been wide open. He never went out [of his cell], unless commanded to do so" (281). There is Watt, "the Saxon," stiff and curious, with an "air of perpetually looking for something while at the same time wondering what that something could possibly be," who exclaims "What!" and dreams of a man named Quin (282), whom Watt had mentioned in *Mercier and Camier* (118). He is aghast at the "opacity" of things (282)—just Watt's problem with the *empêchement-objet*. The third is small and carries an umbrella and a cloak, like F. X. Camier, and like him ranges in a park, but Camier was fat and with scant hair (see *Mercier and Camier* 54–55), whereas this one is thin, with white flossy hair. This character cries (*Malone Dies* 283), whereas it was Mercier who cried (*Mercier and Camier* 32). The fourth inmate is probably Molloy, an itchy bearded giant (he has not been described in the earlier fiction). His identity is betrayed by his bearing, sprawled on the floor with his legs apart, mouth open. "He still loved the gloom and secrecy of the ferns, but never sought them out." Malone reviews the collection, apologizing authorially to those characters left out: "The youth then, the Saxon, the thin one and the giant. I don't know if they have changed, I don't remember. May the others forgive me. In the fifth [cell] Macmann, half asleep" (283).

By rounding up all his previous wayfarers, each inspected in his separate cell, and leaving them out at sea, Beckett calls the pilgrimage to an end, not because Malone's "birth" represents a positive attainment but because the interior journey had failed. At the end Malone is one of these vagrants, set adrift with them, no more fulfilled, no more fulfillable, than they. In a wry analogy Beckett confesses that he exploited these characters without advancing their cause: Lemuel, the keeper, takes a bucket of soup for himself and his five charges, but instead of nourishing them with their special pieces of bacon, which float in the soup, he eats the fat off them, "sucked the rinds and threw them back in the soup" (281). That is where the characters end, floating in the bay of Dublin, indistinguishable, in their end, from Malone's last "gurgles of outflow" (287). In the end the keeper Lemuel becomes indistinguishable from Malone: "Lemuel is in charge, he raises his hatchet on which the blood will never dry, but not to hit anyone,"

> he will not touch anyone any more, either with it or with it or
> with it or with or
>   or with it or with his hammer or with his stick or with his fist
> or in thought in dream I mean never he will never
>   or with his pencil or with his stick or (288)

This "he" refers ostensibly to Lemuel, but the stick, pencil, and dream are Malone's. What matters most here is the author-figure's relation to his charges, creatures, objects, ideas; and the point is that he cannot have any relations, any more.

Unfortunately, this lack of relation—a sexual failure as well, as the language of interdiction and the masturbatory overtones in the passage suggest—is not the sign of subjectlessness. Malone reviews his relation to his creatures in an earlier passage that also suggests Beckett's relation to his protagonists:

> My relations with Jackson were of short duration. I could have put up with him as a friend, but unfortunately he found me disgusting, as did Johnson, Wilson, Nicholson and Watson, all whore-sons. I then tried, for a space, to lay hold of a kindred spirit among the inferior races. . . . With the insane too I failed, by a hair's-breadth. (218)

There is no one "to lay hold of," no union with the other. All others find him foreign, repulsive. "And I thought I had it all thought out," complains Malone. "If I had the use of my body I would throw it out of the window" (218).

The Unnamable's Dynamism of the Intermediate

Beckett's greatest achievement in his serial fiction is to have found a way out of this impasse, a way to the place of unity, without renouncing any of the ground won (or lost, I should say) along the way. His solution is synthetic, not exclusive; he uses the old dead ends—both his failed journeys, the centrifugal and the centripetal—to produce a new vision. *The Unnamable* realizes the last movement of a dialectic; it incorporates Beckett's earlier works so well that in it they seem inevitably resolved, in retrospect. The novel does not, of course, come across as some great resolution, a clarification: it seems chaotic, "like a filmstrip in which each frame shows a different picture," as Albright puts it (170). Nevertheless it is highly organized, addicted to method (*The Unnamable* 303), symmetrical, and concedes everything in the end to "the spirit of geometry" (359).

The Unnamable is Beckett's purest subject. Beckett's protagonists know less and less where they are going and why; the Unnamable, it is tempting to say, knows nothing, reduced to endless speculation. But this is by no means the case. He is keenly aware both of the genealogy that produced him and of his own condition. "Can it be," he asks at the outset, "that one day I simply stayed in, in where, instead of going out" (291). Never mind how he became powerless to act (291); now he is "in a head" (372), fixed in the skull where once he wandered (303). He is marooned in the interior, a pure "subject," an eye clapped "at random in the thick of the mess" (380), a "subject" in the depth (343). He knows that he is the last of a line of futile travelers, "a ponderous chronicle of moribunds," "my troop of lunatics" (308), his daylight delegates (297). With them he shares the quest for admittance "to that peace where he neither is, nor is not" (334), where he feels and thinks and says and is nothing (374), but he cannot, he thinks, complete the mission they started, pure subject that he is.

> Come come, a little cooperation please, finish dying, it's the least you might do, after all the trouble they've taken to bring you to life. The worst is over. You've been sufficiently assassinated, sufficiently suicided, to be able now to stand on your own feet, like a big boy. That's what I keep telling myself. And I add, quite carried away, Slough off this mortal inertia, it is out of place, in this society. They can't do everything. They have put you on the right road, led you by the hand to the very brink of the precipice, now it's up to you, with an unassisted last step, to show them your gratitude.

These earlier characters have cleared the way for the Unnamable, the pure immaterial subject, to bridge the final gulf, take the plunge.

Through the splendours of nature they dragged a paralytic and
now there's nothing more to admire it's my duty to jump . . .
(333)

But Beckett's subject has plunged deep, turned and "set off in the other
direction" (323), and has found that the road in is just what the road
outside had been, a regressive series, place leading to place. "The last
step!" he protests, the Zeno of suffering. "I who could never manage the
first" (333). So he renounces the others (304), having wasted his time
"with these bran-dips, beginning with Murphy, who wasn't even the
first" (390). (Elsewhere he mentions the magical goal of ten thousand
words, another allusion to *Dream*, 310.)

The Unnamable does not immediately know the way out of this
mess, this free-floating subjectivity, but he determines to solve his
problem: "I'll find a way out of it, it won't be like the other times" (323).
The novel follows his systematic effort to examine his options. Whereas
Malone examines himself in the mirror of self-surrogates, discovering
only himself again, the Unnamable tells four symmetrical stories that
analyze the possible relations of self and other. These stories, which
together constitute an anatomy of subject-object relations, spatialize his
possible predicaments to give the "fair picture of my situation" (310) he
desires. For the Unnamable realizes that the subject-object relation need
not be fixed and cannot be assumed, as Murphy, for example, assumes
it. He is obsessed with this difficulty, and returns to it often. "Will
the day come when another will pass before me, before the spot where
I was?" he asks (293). Like Malone he discovers the infectious
empêchement-sujet: "They [the lights] are perhaps unwavering and fixed
and my fitful perceiving the cause of their inconstancy," he worries. "I
hope I may have occasion to revert to this question" (294). And "where
was I, ah yes, my subject, no longer there, no longer the same, or I
mistake the place, no, yes, it's the same, still there, in the same place, it's
a pity" (391). The stories work out these possible relations. They are, in
order, (1) the story of the Unnamable, about whom his objects revolve
(especially 295–301); (2) Mahood's first story of the amputee returning
home (317–19); (3) Mahood's second story of the amputee in a jar,
advertising a restaurant (327–45); and (4) the story of Worm in an airless
arena (337, 345–69).[6]

6. See Albright's summary, 170. Albright considers the Unnamable's story of himself
a frame narrative that opens the novel and resumes after the story of Worm, but toward

In the first the object is changing, wheeling, and the subject is fixed, probably at the center, certainly not on the circumference (295). This relation, which the Unnamable finds the most pleasing, reverses the one assumed in the early fiction, but undermined in *Molloy* and *Malone Dies*, of "a mobile subject before an ideal object, immutable and incorruptible" (*Proust* 6). It is a dichotomous condition that allows no middle ground—one is either a fixed perceiver or a changing perceived. The Unnamable wants fixity: "here all change would be fatal and land me back, there and then, in all the fun of the fair" (294–95). But if the subject does not change, then, it seems, it will never reach unity. Mahood's first story reverses the situation. Here the wayfaring hero revolves around his family, which, entombed in a rotunda, watches him close in on them. Unfortunately this Odysseus cannot stop when he finally gets home, but must reverse his spiraling course and spin out of the center again. Once one gives in to the "principle of change," the "principle of disorder" (342, 295), there is no stopping (the traveler stops often, but only to rest and go on, 318, 320). The problem here again is that the subject does not have any real relation with the object. Mahood, the purported teller, suggests that the Unnamable leaves home again because of the stench (his family having decayed by the time he arrives), but the Unnamable rejects this notion (321–23). His family, he rightly reasons, "had no part or share in what I was doing. Having set forth from that place, it was only natural I should return to it, given the accuracy of my navigation" (322).

Two other relations complete this symmetry, one where both subject and object move, and another where both are fixed. The former is pure subjectivity, the Unnamable's general condition that both requires and allows him to imagine some relation to the object in the first place. The second is pure objectivity, irrelevant like a portrait without the sitter. What he needs is a picture that puts him in some relation to his goal, a

---

the end the Unnamable does not really visualize his condition. He perceives himself differently at the end.

The Unnamable offers a rough analogy to his story telling with a little culinary anecdote regarding his benefactress-cook of the third story. Her gravy itself has not changed, but whereas her turnips in gravy are not so good as formerly, her carrots in gravy have improved. These are the kinds of notions, he tells us, "on which it is possible for me to build" (329). The vegetables and gravy, figures in their ground, constitute four symmetrical alternatives: carrots in gravy, old and new, and turnips in gravy, old and new. This is the kind of thinking that organizes the stories.

The Unnamable's third story may take something from Rimbaud, who proclaims: "I was a disreputable sign for an inn" (193).

story with a more dynamic subject-object relation. He tells two such stories. In the first he is marooned like a heliotropic flower in a jar, kept like a pet to advertise a restaurant. As a sign he is literally attached to the object he signifies. It is a fantasy of aesthetic retreat, a "natural transition" (330) from the amputated wayfarer of the second story to a state of rest where all needs are taken care of. But he still feels the world around him, the tarp over him, the sawdust beneath him, and follows the movements of Marguerite, his keeper, and of her customers. His fourth story describes what appears, at first, an even more ideal relationship, something close to unity. He is Worm.

> For this feeling of being entirely enclosed, and yet nothing touching me, is new. The sawdust no longer presses against my stumps, I don't know where I end. I left it yesterday, Mahood's world, the street, the chop-house. . . . I shall never hear again the lowing of the cattle. . . . There will never be another woman wanting me in vain to live, my shadow at evening will not darken the ground. The stories of Mahood are ended. (345)

Worm is riveted without bonds—as against the less ideal collar in the previous story—at the center of a hellish arena (358–59), a lifeless place walled by an "obstacle" (357). There is no subject here because Worm knows nothing and has no sensations (360). If this were really so, then Worm would have been it, with thee at last, safe in his "ozone" (366), his O-zone. But he is tormented by observing devils who shine lights on him through holes in the wall and make noises. These sensations reach him, and ruin everything. "If only I knew what they want, they want me to be Worm, but I was, I was, what's wrong, I was, but ill, it must be that, it can only be that" (364). He hears the voice, the noise, a sensation: "but I feel nothing, yes yes, this voice, I have endured it" (364).

The Unnamable discovers that he can imagine whatever relation he wants, can escape anything, be anywhere, with one exception, that he cannot escape the voice, his own voice. He realizes this already after his third story: "Having won, shall I be left in peace? It doesn't look like it, I seem to be going on talking" (345). These stories demonstrate, quite simply, that there can be no ideal subject-object relation that the Unnamable could achieve, no "way out." The Unnamable must return to his starting position as voice, restored to himself as he always thought he should be (e.g., 331), and try again. And in the last part of the novel he does. Journeying has failed; if the Unnamable is to reach the threshold to the place of the object, he must somehow be there, find himself there, as Molloy had guessed. And he must be not one part of the subject–object relation that had misled him so long but neither, neither part. These two requirements are essentially the same: the Unnamable must be a margin, neither subject nor object, neither in the self nor out of it. And he must account for the ineluctable voice.

Earlier the Unnamable remarks on his transition to the interior: "How all becomes clear and simple when one opens an eye on the within, having of course previously exposed it to the without, in order to benefit by the contrast" (342–43). Plotinus speaks similarly of the benefit of turning attention from exterior things to concentrate on the inner self (*Enneads* IV.8.1) and says that we know the Good by the experience of evil, "by the comparison of contraries" (IV.8.7). But what "benefit" does this juxtaposition yield? The movement out establishes a linear continuum of states, a regression of places; the movement in applies this continuum to the self. The Unnamable's regressive serialization is only possible in the centripetal world, for the same reason that Murphy's puppets or self-projections do not provide him with real extension. There is "no difference between the infinite circle and the straight line" ("Dante…Bruno.Vico..Joyce" 6): the movement out establishes linear progression; the movement in turns this line into an infinite regression, the circumference of an infinite circle. Beckett describes the process in a passage about Joyce's HCE, portrayed much as the Unnamable would be twenty years later:

> He continues to suggest himself for a couple of pages, by means of repeated permutations on his 'normative letters', as if to say: 'This is all about me, H. C. Earwigger: don't forget this is all about me!' This inner elemental vitality and corruption of expression imparts a furious restlessness to the form, which is admirably suited to the purgatorial aspect of the work. There is an endless verbal germination, maturation, putrefaction, the cyclic dynamism of the intermediate. (*Our Exagmination* 16)

In this context, the "inner elemental vitality and corruption of expression" is the Unnamable's regressive self-rejection, or self-transcendence; it undermines the form or external line, now internalized, enabling the Unnamable to occupy the "dynamism of the intermediate," the condition of being in between. How, then, is one to think of this condition?

The tension between these two infinities, the outer and the inner, establishes a liminal middle ground where the Unnamable must exist. Both regressive movements claim him, the one demanding an image, a story, the other undermining it in its depth. Consider Earwigger, the protagonist of *Finnegans Wake*, in this connection. He is the figure who appears everywhere as language (his "normative letters"), who is language itself. And he is also an eardrum, as his name suggests, a liminal tympanum.[7] This, the Unnamable discovers, is his own position:

> without an ear I'll have heard, and I'll have said it, without a mouth I'll have said it, I'll have said it inside me, then in the same breath outside me, perhaps that's what I feel, an outside and an inside and me in the middle, perhaps that's what I am, the thing that divides the world in two, on the one side the outside, on the other the inside, that can be as thin as foil, I'm neither one side nor the other, I'm in the middle, I'm the partition, I've two surfaces and no thickness, perhaps that's what I feel, myself vibrating, I'm the tympanum, on the one hand the mind, on the other the world, I don't belong to either . . . (383)

The Unnamable is language itself, which accounts perfectly for his irrepressible voice. He is neither the ear that receives the voice nor the mouth that utters it, neither the outside world nor the inside. Language does not belong either to world or to mind, and so it is the proper place for Cartesian consciousness (the "conarium" mentioned in *Murphy*),[8] the House of Being, as Heidegger calls it. The Unnamable describes himself as the state of union had always been described in Beckett's fiction: "I'm the air, the walls, the walled-in one, everything yields, opens, ebbs, flows, like flakes, I'm all these flakes, meeting, mingling, falling asunder" (386). There are no more people *or* things (394). He is at the door, he says, the threshold to the end: "perhaps it's a drop, find the door, open the door, drop, into the silence" (412). He is himself the threshold, the foil dividing worlds: "perhaps it's a door, perhaps I'm at the door, that would surprise me, perhaps it's I, . . . I can depart, all this time I've journeyed without knowing it, it's I now at the door" (413). The Unnamable's achievement is summarized in a Beckett poem of that period:

7. On the tympanum in this context, see Derrida's essay "Tympan" in *The Margins of Philosophy*.
8. See Dobrez 13–14.

my peace is there in the receding mist
when I may cease from treading these long shifting
    thresholds
and live the space of a door
that opens and shuts.[9]

The Unnamable has come to this conclusion. He no longer needs to seek the shifting thresholds of the earlier fictions, the passage to the place of the object, which recedes as the subject advances, only to disclose another such passage. "Nothing will have taken place but place," said Mallarmé in "Dice Thrown"; "A vrai dire moins une action qu'un site," as Beckett says in a stage direction in *Éleuthéria* (1), and in "On Way to *Comment c'est*": "Ici, est-ce assez dire?" (second text, 3). He is himself the liminal space that separates the wanderer from home. Home is not beyond but in between, the space of the door that seems to lead home.

One problem still faces the Unnamable. "Perhaps they [his words] have carried me to the threshold of my story," he worries, "before the door that opens on my story" (414). He is at the door, he knows, the threshold, but which side of it is he on? Perhaps it leads not to the All but back into being, back to the amputees and travelers and Malones and Molloys and Watts and Murphys he does not want to be again: "it will be the place, the silence, the end, the beginning, the beginning again" (413). For to end is not enough in Beckett's world, one must return to the world of things.

9. In *Poems In English* (London: Calder and Boyars, 1961, 49), the poem appears as "Dieppe 2," but in the Grove *Collected Poems in English and French* it is titled after its first line, "my way is in the sand flowing" (57). It is dated 1947–49.

5

Beckett's Cosmology

Beckett's work appropriates a larger topographical vision of the human cycle built on the dominant cosmological vision of the Western metaphysical tradition, a cosmic teleology made and remade by Anaxagoras, Plato, Aristotle, Virgil, the early Gnostics, Plotinus, Augustine, Proclus, Boethius, Dante, Bruno, Milton, Vico, Blake, Yeats, and Joyce, among others. Beckett takes part in this logocentric tradition, summing it up as no other modern writer has, and without a picture of this participation there can be no full account of his fiction. Beckett certainly interrogates this vision, as Henning says, but he ends up as part of it: he accepts from his precursors certain ideas as psychological fact, something like scientific findings that cannot be excepted by new research.[1] This chapter, then, considers Beckett's intertextuality in light of the individual talent. It is one of the truths of the critical world that Beckett is the last writer, the last word in his literary tradition, but this formulation refers not to his particular role in any tradition but to his so-called disintegration of semantic expression. Beckett's cosmological vision presents in its consistency as strong a claim as any for the literary-aesthetic power of this metaphysical system.

Neoplatonism follows the teaching of Plato, who sees a perfect (ideal, pure, as Beckett has it in his critical works) world of intellectual Forms

---

1. Wolosky says that "the premises and axiology of negative [Christian-Neoplatonist] theology act as a generative condition of Beckett's books" (216), but also that this context does not enable a systematic criticism of his work (214).

governing the fallen physical reality that mirrors them.[2] Neoplatonism
is also interested in Plato's theory, articulated most directly in the
Timaeus, that the material world was created through the emanation of
the original Unity. Plotinus, the first Neoplatonist, emphasizes the
traveling nature of the human soul, which seeks to reascend to the One,
and this cosmologically formulated interest in the relation of the
particular subject to its divine object continues to be the core of
Neoplatonic thought. Plotinus, in other words, sees things from the
human point of view, considering the relation of soul to Soul (a concern
that influenced German romantic philosophy). This emphasis suggests
Neoplatonic rather than strictly Platonic thought as Beckett's central
metaphysical context.[3] Like the Neoplatonists, Beckett sees matter as
metaphor, things as ideas, and a correspondence between human and
cosmic intelligence that depends on the assumption that Mind underlies
all there is. The connection so explicitly made between Beckett's
narratives underscores the intelligence behind them and, both by
implication and by analogy, the intelligence behind the world they bring
into being. Eminent among Beckett's Neoplatonic ideas is the metaphorical journey that distinguishes between figure and ground, between
the wandering subject and its home in unity (see *Enneads* II.6.1).
Neoplatonism paints the same picture: the fallen subject seeks the
undifferentiated One or All. Beckett is concerned also with the process
by which Unity emanates the concrete particulars of the physical world.
Other writers who show a metaphorical journey—Cervantes, or Swift,
or Céline—do not endow it with such abstract generative qualities. Both
Beckett and his metaphysical tradition construct the process of emanation and return in geographic and cosmic terms. For both, the relation
between the original One and the many is difficult. Neoplatonism sees

---

2. For a general introduction to aspects of Neoplatonism that concern this discussion,
see Thomas Taylor's introduction to *Select Works of Plotinus* (1909), Thomas Whittaker's
The Neo-Platonists (1918), David E. Hahm's *The Origins of Stoic Cosmology* (1977),
Richard Sorabji's *Matter, Space, and Motion* (1988), and A. C. Lloyd's *The Anatomy of
Neoplatonism* (1990). See M. H. Abrams, *Natural Supernaturalism*, chaps. 3–4, especially
pp. 172 (on "system"), 175–76 (on androgyny in the system), and 179–82 (on the cycle
and German idealism).

3. Plotinus's intellectual descendants rethink the relation of the soul to the Absolute.
Iamblichus, like early Christians and Gnostics, sees a substantial change effected in the
soul in its descent, and does not think that the soul can reascend without help from the
gods; Proclus holds to the notion that the human soul parallels the One and contains
within it the Divine. Some writers, like Virgil and Dante, conceive by analogy a world
that mirrors the Divine, while Hermetic writers like Paracelsus and Bruno believe that
the microcosmic soul can manipulate the Absolute directly, through magic.

a progressive serialization of the self, a mystical self-purification and transcendence, much like Beckett's devolving protagonists from Belacqua to the Unnamable; if Beckett's protagonists do not reincarnate a single mind (as one Neoplatonic tradition imagines the soul's journey), they dramatize the soul's staged ascent (as other Neoplatonists hold).

It is this broad conceptual affinity which makes the strongest claim for the presence of Neoplatonic thinking in Beckett's work. There are of course many references to this tradition in Beckett's work, such as Murphy's explicitly microcosmic worldview and his supposed reliance on Tommaso Campanella's *City of the Sun*.[4] There is Beckett's use of Bishop Berkeley in *Film*, his avowed interest in Geulincx, and his use of Dante's and Milton's geographical visions.[5] And "Dante...Bruno. Vico..Joyce" traces some of Beckett's own distinguished lineage.[6] Sometimes Beckett's work suggests a parallel in traditional cosmology that is merely suggestive. The seven novels from *Dream* to *The Unnamable*, for example, probably do not represent the seven spheres the spirit must ascend to reach the Ogdoadic sphere of the One, although the notion of the novels as spheres the spirit must traverse on its pilgrimage to unity is tantalizing. On the other hand, consider that "Samuel," from "shem" (Hebrew, "name"), is also "Sam" from "same," meaning "one":[7] Beckett's name, which means "name of God" in the Hebrew, is also the One. But Beckett's Neoplatonism is not expressed by allusion or analogy; it is manifested in the logic and order of his work.

4. *Murphy* 17. In Campanella's utopian city, life is ordered according to the principles of astrological harmony. Murphy relies on this educational story to determine the best time for his marriage. It is not clear whether the novel's first sentence supports his chances for success or denies them.

5. Beckett alludes to Arnold Geulincx in a letter ("On Murphy") to Sighle Kennedy (*Disjecta* 113). See also *Molloy* 51. Geulincx (1624–69), the Flemish Cartesian, believes that God intercedes between mind and body and can be discovered only in the process itself of the soul's incarnation. On Geulincx in Beckett, see Dobrez. For "Milton's cosmology," see also *From an Abandoned Work* 42.

Recall that the pilgrim E in *Film* originally pursued "One," not "Object."

6. The essay was Joyce's idea, and Joyce more or less dictated its contents, but it is clearly germane to Beckett's project, as Peter Hughes, for example, indicates with his title "From Allusion to Implosion. Vico. Michelet. Joyce, Beckett."

7. Nohrnberg, *The Analogy* 362.

I
The Cycle of Being

In the Yeatsian Wheel

In "The Philosophy of Shelley's Poetry" (1900) Yeats considers the power of a governing image: if the poet would only brood on it a lifetime, says Yeats, with his underhanded wryness, the image "would lead his soul, disentangled from unmeaning circumstance and the ebb and flow of the world, into that far household where the undying gods await all whose souls have become simple as flame, whose bodies have become quiet as an agate lamp" (*Essays and Introductions* 95). But Shelley, he goes on to say, was not interested in "the old wisdom," and was content to write unphilosophical verse. Yeats does not say why it takes a whole lifetime to understand the image, nor how *he* had come to this knowledge, being at the time only thirty-five. The answer to both questions seems the same: the knowledge of self-transcendence, of a pure being disentangled from material accident, cannot be learned in life because it is outside it, but it can be had from tradition, which is also larger than the individual life. The philosophy of Shelley's poetry belongs not to Shelley, who did not care for old wisdom, but to Yeats, who declares (in "Blood and the Moon" II, *The Poems* 237) that he takes his own poetic imagery from Shelley. The dead, Yeats implies, can know that which it takes all of life to find,

> For wisdom is the property of the dead,
> A something incompatible with life;
> ("Blood and the Moon," lines 49–50)

but if you are not yet dead you might find the same truth in tradition.[8] We can know unconditional reality, the simple and immaterial, if we relive the past, or if the past returns to us, as it does to Gabriel Conroy

---

8. As Langbaum puts it: "In *A Vision*, Yeats comes to see that the perfection of self, which the artist portrays in the figures of art and achieves for himself through the artistic process, cannot always in life be achieved within a single lifetime, that self-realization may require a succession of historical periods and a succession of lives" (*The Mysteries of Identity* 192–93). This does not exactly argue against Yeats's famous claim that "man can embody truth but he cannot know it" (*Letters* 922), but it grants that there is tension between our ability to know, to balance all (as the Irish Airman does for an instant), and our ability to live according to that truth.

in "The Dead"; knowledge may be transpersonal recollection, as Plato says, but recollection can also be memory, that process of retrieving or participating in the unaccidental ideal that Proust calls "reduplication" (*Proust* 56).

This little drama of Yeats and Shelley can serve as a parable for Beckett's interest in the tradition of the cycle of being, and in the special knowledge—the knowledge of a real or metaphorical afterlife—which that tradition provides. Yeats is obsessed with the Neoplatonic tradition and its emissaries—Ficino, Blake, the Golden Dawn—and he serves for Beckett as a ready and potent vehicle to Neoplatonism.[9] Beckett delineates the subject's movement to a state where there is no self and no differentiation between perceiver and perceived, and Yeats articulates the same system. In *A Vision* Yeats presents the Great Wheel, a version of the cycle of being, where the soul incarnates in twenty-eight Phases, moving from one to another and producing in each a different personality. Yeats admits the schematic nature of the system: it is not a psychology, an anatomy like Burton's, but an intellectual abstraction, a dance with stylized moves, "completed" behavior types whose total combinations yield all possible psychic orders (81). According to Yeats's scheme, "man seeks his opposite or the opposite of his condition, attains his object so far as it is attainable, at Phase 15 and returns to Phase 1 again" (81). Since this wheel is based on the lunar cycle, the first Phase is represented by the dark of the moon, the fifteenth by full moon. The dark side of the cycle (Phases 22–8), with Phase 1 at its apex, is characterized by passive being, and its Phases are "Primary"; the "Antithetical Phases" of the light half of the wheel (8–22), with Phase 15 at their center, are epitomized by "Unity of Being," a harmonious balance of all thought or life (see Diagram 5.1). Phases 1 and 15, the "two eternities" ("Under Ben Bulben" II), are poles of complete objectivity and complete subjectivity, respectively, where there can be no human life. In these Phases the spirit regenerates, rebeginning its quest at the first Phase, returning to imperfection after Unity at the fifteenth. The subject in Yeats's system, then, seeking its opposite condition, moves from the dark to the light and back, from Objectivity to Subjectivity.

9. On Yeats's revision of Neoplatonism, see Keane's *Yeats's Interactions with Tradition*, especially chapter 5. Frye rightly says that Yeats is more interested in "the creative power that builds the eternal golden city out of time" than, in effect, that golden city itself ("The Top of the Tower" 136–37).

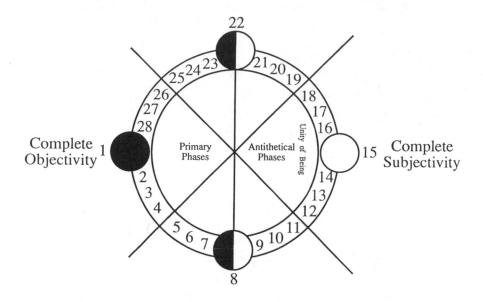

Diagram 5.1.

Beckett follows the same track, in the other direction: his pilgrims also seek unity, but move from light to darkness, from subjectivity to the place of objectivity. It is Yeats, actually, who argues in his later poetry especially in favor of incarnation and against the One, in love with what is passing and to come. Beckett returns to Plotinus, more like Yeats's *Soul* than his *Self* (in "A Dialogue of Self and Soul"). But Beckett does not revalue Yeats, because Yeats's cycle shows the movement to unity just as it does its opposite. Both writers see life as opposition, a whole made of contradictory impulses, warring with itself. Beckett's travelers are not just pseudocouples but essentially double: they must overcome their *empêchements* to reach unity. For Yeats, being is always double: all Phases in one "tincture" (dark or light—primary or antithetical) retain some of the opposite tincture, which must be eliminated before the complete undifferentiatedness of Phase 1 or 15. So to reach full subjectivity, for example, the soul must overcome its old social or moral self and assume instinctual and imaginative freedom again. This can be seen best when Yeats depicts the cycle not as a simple circle, but as a vortex or double gyre (*A Vision* 70–80): as the soul travels from one

side of the double gyre to the other, say from Phase 1 to 15, its subjective gyre broadens while its objective gyre narrows. When the spirit
reaches Phase 15, the objective gyre has narrowed to nothing, and the
subjective gyre is all. The soul then returns in the opposite direction.

Yeats, furthermore, explains why a return from objectivity to the
differentiated world is necessary. Reality, Yeats writes in his 1930 diary,
citing a basic tenet of Neoplatonism, is made of two contradictory but
complementary circuits.

> Plotinus calls well-nigh the most beautiful of Enneads *The
> Impassivity of the Disembodied* but, as he was compelled to at his
> epoch, thought of man as re-absorbed into God's freedom as final
> reality. The ultimate reality must be all movement, all thought,
> all perception extinguished, two freedoms unthinkably, unimag-
> inably absorbed in one another.

This argument leads Yeats to a simple conclusion:

> Surely if either circuit, that which carries us into man or that
> which carries us into God, were reality, the generation had long
> since found its term. (*Explorations* 307)

Reality is both, both "a congeries of beings" and "a single being," both
the emanated particulars of the fallen world and the One: "Could those
two impulses, one as much a part of truth as the other, be reconciled, or
if one or the other could prevail, all life would cease" (*Explorations* 305).
Plotinus argues similarly for the existence of the universal soul:

> Every body, indeed, is in a perpetual flow and movement . . .
> and the world would soon perish if it contained nothing but
> bodies. (*Enneads* iv.7.3e)

And again:

> Unity was not to exist alone; for if unity remained self-enclosed,
> all things would remain hidden in unity without having any
> form, and no beings would achieve existence. (iv.8.6)

Yeats's Plotinian vision recalls Murphy's desire to be a mote in the
dark of absolute freedom; there, as Yeats reports, matter is reduced to

thought. But Beckett too does not see the absolute as the only reality. In his interview with Tom Driver (1961) he explains a vision much like Yeats's:

> If life and death did not both present themselves to us, there would be no inscrutability. If there were only darkness, all would be clear. It is because there is not only darkness but also light that our situation becomes inexplicable.

This remark shows the Neoplatonic side of Beckett's concern with the refracted world of light and dark, and may well come directly from Plotinus:

> If whiteness were existence itself, it would . . . possess an eternal existence; but, in reality, it is no more than whiteness. (*Enneads* iv.9.9)

While Beckett is concerned with "the circular movement of the mind flowering up and up through darkness to an apex" (*Dream* 14–15, *Disjecta* 45)—a Yeatsian phrase that comes from Dionysius the Aereopagite (Wolosky 215)—he rejects the possibility that life would cease at one of its extremes.[10] To splice Beckett and Yeats: "If there were only darkness," "then the generation had long since found its term." Life would not go on if Beckett's subject could simply stay at the place of the object.

Beckett has denied that he disliked Yeats's poetry,[11] despite the quip in *Waiting for Godot* about "the wind in the reeds" (13).[12] He uses the Yeatsian paradigm both to organize his work and in passing. In . . . *but the clouds* . . . , a 1976 television drama, the voice echoes the closing lines of "The Tower" (Esslin, *The Theatre of the Absurd* 90), and in *Texts for*

10. Unseld says of one of Beckett's verses that Beckett "had Lao-Tzu's dictum in mind, that not until the utmost has been reached can things turn into their opposite" (95).

11. In conversation with me. Armstrong says that "in conversation Beckett acknowledged the importance of W. B. Yeats's later work" (32), but in 1934 he "chastised the elder Yeats brother for his 'flight from self-awareness' " (160). In 1961 Beckett evidently read through Yeats's *Collected Poems* (30–31). Harrington says that in 1934 (in "Recent Irish Poetry"), Beckett "was selective in his praise for Yeats's poetry" (175). Beckett rejected, predictably, the suggestion that he had been influenced by Yeats's system (in an August 1987 reply to my questions regarding the possible influence of Yeats's system).

12. Rose also sees Arsene's speech in *Watt* (55–56) as a parody of Yeats's "The Lake Isle of Innisfree" ("The Irish Memories" 131).

Nothing 13 the voice can foretell "last images, end of dream of being past, passing and to be," an allusion to "Sailing to Byzantium" (Rose 229). Camier "cast a cold eye" on Mercier (*Mercier and Camier* 67), a jocular reference to "Under Ben Bulben," and Belacqua prefers the quietus of darkness to the gyrations of life, "the frivolous spirals, ascending like the little angels and descending, never coming to head or tail" (*Dream* 108). Malone confesses to a similar vision:

> I was speaking then was I not of my little pastimes and I think about to say that I ought to content myself with them, instead of launching forth on all this ballsaching poppycock about life and death, if that is what it is all about, and I suppose it is, for nothing was ever about anything else to the best of my recollection.

He could have held his peace instead,

> having my little fun and games with the cones and cylinders . . . (*Malone Dies* 225)

This passage is typical of the way Yeats works in the Beckettian narrative. Malone speaks of his "pastimes" and of his "recollection" of life and death, an allusion to the Platonic doctrine that knowledge is recollection of past times; he says that he launched on "all this ballsaching poppycock"—the circular (ball) and regenerative (cock) nature of life and death. His alternative amusement with the Yeatsian cones and cylinders would not have offered a different vision of life.

Yeats's gyres help organize *Murphy*.[13] Beckett's pronouncement on figure and ground has a Yeatsian aspect:

> "Murphy, all life is figure and ground."
> "But a wandering to find home," said Murphy.
> "The face," said Neary, "or system of faces, against the big blooming buzzing confusion. I think of Miss Dwyer." (*Murphy* 4)

The face is the Divine, while "a system of faces" is the congeries of beings, the emanated particulars of the world. The "system" is "blooming" because, like Yeats's system, and Dante's, it is a widening gyre fashioned

---

13. Harrington speaks of the "consistently Yeatsian framework of allusions in *Murphy*" (see 95–97).

after the rose, intellectual symbol of Heaven and of the climbing stemlike process by which it is reached. After Wylie finds Neary bashing his head against the buttocks of the statue of Cuchulain at the Dublin General Post Office (42), a scene clearly connected with Yeats,[14] the two go to a pub where Neary denounces Cuchulain as "that Red Branch bum" (46) and finds occasion to explain the inaccessibility of Yeatsian divinity, that "the full is only reached by admittance to the most retired places" (47). Wylie also seems to have Yeats in mind when he says that "humanity is a well with two buckets . . . one going down to be filled, the other coming up to be emptied" (58). A similar construction may be found in Celia's double desire to make a man of Murphy and to quit her profession: "Both these lines led to Murphy (everything led to Murphy), but so diversely, the one from a larval experience to a person of fantasy, the other from a complete experience to a person of fact" (66). This follows rather neatly from "a larval experience," or Phase 1, to the fantasy of Phase 15, or "complete experience," and then back to particular fact.[15] The novel ends with a Yeatsian spool of history, represented by the line of Mr. Kelly's kite, "a wild rush of line, say the industrial revolution" (279–80). Yeats sees in his wheel not only the gamut of human identities but also the historical rise and fall of civilizations, East and West dominating in turn.

Beckett finds an analogy to these conceptual gyres in the game of chess. The black pieces and white are arranged as mirror images at opposite ends of the playing field. When Murphy and Endon play, they simply develop their pieces in symmetrical patterns and return them to their original configurations, echoing the Yeatsian cycle. Like two gods at the poles or axes of the Wheel, Endon at Objectivity (Phase 1), Murphy at Subjectivity, they play with their toys or puppets, just as the spirits in Yeats's cycle are puppets: "Constrained, arraigned, baffled, bent and unbent" ("The Double Vision of Michael Robartes," line 9). The Yeatsian gyre appears again in *Krapp's Last Tape*. Yeats envisions the gyre as a bobbin wound with the experiences of life, a mummy-cloth of thought for the dead (as in "All Souls' Night" and "Shepherd and Goatherd," lines 89–112); in order to return to the cycle of being

14. As Bloom notes (*Yeats* 445). The passage in *Murphy* could not have been intended as a parody of Yeats's poem "The Statues" (as Bloom speculates) because the poem was written in 1938, the novel in 1935. The two do, however, speak to the same subject. On dating "The Statues," see Finneran 84.

15. Yeats defines "phantasy" as "a continual escape from and yet acknowledgment of all that allures in the world" (*A Vision* 85), a version that suits Murphy very well. Yeats assigns "phantasy" as a character of Phases 15–18 (see *A Vision* 85, but also 100).

after death, the spirit must retrace or "dream back" its life, reliving and so putting to rest its unresolved past experiences (*A Vision* 226). "When I'm dreaming back like that I begins to see we're only all telescopes," as Joyce puts it (*Finnegans Wake* 295.10–12). Krapp records his tapes on his birthdays, returning to his origin, metaphorically, at each session. Like a Yeatsian spirit, or a Freudian patient regressing to a fixation, he winds the tape to past experiences, reliving moments he cannot overcome. Beckett uses the paradigm (received perhaps through Unamuno's "The Other") in *Murphy*: Murphy's memories, scraps of the past, "rose and climbed out of sight before him, as though reeled upward off a spool level with his throat. It was his experience that this should be stopped, whenever possible, before the deeper coils were reached" (252). Krapp draws his favorite word out as though unwinding a thread: "Spooool!" (12). This is his medium as well as the message: the word "spool" means "bobbin," and "tape" (Skeat says) comes from "tapestry" or cloth.

In the Unnamable's second story the spiraling protagonist considers the shape of his movement and wonders what would become of him once he got home:

> I must have got embroiled in a kind of inverted spiral, I mean one the coils of which, instead of widening more and more, grew narrower and narrower and finally, given the kind of space in which I was supposed to evolve, would come to an end for lack of room. Faced then with the material impossibility of going any further I should no doubt have had to stop, unless of course I elected to set off again at once in the opposite direction, to unscrew myself as it were, after having screwed myself to a standstill, which would have been an experience rich in interest and fertile in surprises if I am to believe what I once was told, in spite of my protests . . . (316)

Instead of widening as Yeats's gyre does before reversing the subject's movement—before the exchange of the tinctures—the Unnamable's gyre narrows as an hourglass would (a more conventional figure, X) and widens after chiasmus at the centerpoint. Could he stay there, says the Unnamable, he would have a "fertile" experience, the experience of regeneration. ("Screwed" is also suggestive.) Given the shape of Yeats's double vortex, it is no wonder the Unnamable can tread the threshold to the place of the object (at the end of the novel) without moving to the periphery of his circle. For Yeats, the point of passage to regeneration is at the still center of the gyre. The Unnamable is modeled here after Dante's Satan, "dead forever," a mine of useless knowledge, marooned in the earth (317): when Dante's pilgrims pass the frozen center of his gyre, at the dead center of the earth, they are reborn in a way, past the spiritual low point of hell, and begin to walk upright.

Beckett's Être Manqué in the Womb of Chaos

Beckett, like Yeats, links the regenerative nature of godhead (or of the place of the object) with the nature of the traveling subject, both equally necessary to the cycle of being. His subject must be capable of regeneration. The generative nature of Beckett's unity is evident in Belacqua's "third being," "the dark gulf . . . the Limbo and the wombtomb alive with the unanxious spirits" (*Dream* 107–8), an undifferentiated One (63), "without axis or contour, its centre everywhere and periphery nowhere" (108). This formulation—"*Deus est sphaera cujus centrum ubique*"—comes originally from *The Book of the Twenty-four Philosophers*, a pseudohermetic twelfth-century manuscript (Poulet 151), and is retailed by Yeats in "Discoveries."[16] By associating womb and tomb Beckett proclaims the generative nature of the dead world; it is an association that has a long history in Western logocentrism.[17] The Expelled equates cradle with grave (*The Expelled* 11–12), and the Unnamable fancies that he ended his long voyage in his mother's "entrails," and from there set out on the next (*The Unnamable* 323–24). "I'd have a mother, I'd have a tomb," says another narrator, "I wouldn't have come out of here, one doesn't come out of here, here are my tomb

---

16. Yeats's version:

> If it be true that God is a circle whose centre is everywhere, the saint goes to the centre, the poet and artist to the ring where everything comes round again. . . . Is it that all things are made by the struggle of the individual and the world, of the unchanging and the returning, and that the saint and the poet are over all, and that the poet has made his home in the serpent's mouth? (*Essays and Introductions* 287–88)

In some cultures the underworld is thought traditionally to be in the womb of the earth. See Neumann's Jungian study, *The Great Mother* 44.

17. As in *Job* 3.10–11, Shakespeare's *Romeo and Juliet* ii.iii.9–10, and Blake's *Jerusalem* 1:8–9. For the Garden of Eden as womb, and on the "tradition of the unborn realm" (529), both in Spenser and in his sources, see Nohrnberg, *The Analogy* 525–68, but especially 439–42, 527–37, and 554–62.

For a discussion of Beckett's womb-tomb association in context of similar associations in fiction of the time, see Cunningham 100–101.

and mother, it's all here this evening, I'm dead and getting born, without having ended, helpless to begin, that's my life" (*Texts for Nothing 9* 119). Beckett sees this generative wombtomb realm as Chaos, a theme brought out explicitly when, in *Murphy*, Ticklepenny connects the gas radiator and the w.c.: "The extremes having thus been established, nothing remained but to make them meet" (172). In *Lessness* a chaos of minimalist phrases, the sentence reduced to least being, recombine to yield another beginning, and in *Mercier and Camier* Mercier sees "torrents of light and joy," a chaotic mingling of forms, coming together and falling asunder. Murphy's third, dark zone is a place of "forms," "nothing but forms becoming and crumbling into the fragments of a new becoming" (112). Belacqua's umbra is such a realm of formal chaos, a place of pure formal recombination like Knott's house in *Watt*.

Beckett relies on the traditional association of Chaos and the womb or Eden, a garden of forms that gives rise to human life. "Cyclically conceived," Nohrnberg says, "departure from life may be compared to re-entering the womb. Thus there is a certain logic in Spenser's locating Chaos in 'the wide wombe of the world.' Likewise, the Garden of Adonis is a realm of postexistence" (*The Analogy* 529). Leopold Bloom brings the matter up in the sixth (or "Hades") episode of *Ulysses*, where like Odysseus (and Aeneas) he goes down to the world of the dead. "Whores in Turkish graveyards," he thinks, inimitably. "Love among the tombstones. Romeo. Spice of pleasure. In the midst of death we are in life. Both ends meet. Tantalising for the dead" (108). And he thinks of "bad gas" (103), or chaos: "Gas of graves" (108). In Spenser's *Ruines of Rome*, Nohrnberg also says,

> it is predicted that at the completion of the Platonic Great Year, the "seedes, of which all things at first were bred, / Shall in Great Chaos womb again be hid" [XXII]. Sir Thomas Browne places the seeds in the same repository, in the *Garden of Cyrus*, where he writes that "Legions of seminall Idaea's lye in their second Chaos . . . till putting on the habits of their forms, they show themselves on the stage of the world." (*The Analogy* 555)

In *Malone Dies* the asylum's garden is a sexual Eden, described in terms borrowed from Milton's *Paradise Lost*. "Yes it was a plateau, Moll had not lied, or rather a great mound with gentle slopes. The entire top was occupied by the domain of Saint John and there the wind blew almost without ceasing"—much as it does in the park in *Murphy*. "A high wall encompassed it about . . . all this fucking scenery. . . . In a word a little Paradise for those who like their nature sloven" (*Malone Dies* 277). The dead, in Beckett's urgent words, must "find the weeds engage them in the garden": "all aboard all souls" ("Malacoda," lines 13, 27). In his third being Belacqua is "a waking ultra-cerebral obscurity, thronged with grey angels." There, in a telling phrase, "the spirits of his dead and his unborn . . . come abroad" (39). Beckett imagines a condition where the Yeatsian spirits, dead souls awaiting rebirth, neither fully alive nor extinguished, incarnate and move on in the cycle of being. There Belacqua is between life and death, among the waking unborn.

Beckett suggests one reason why his subject must be dead when it unites with its object: life itself is the ultimate impediment, the constitutional delimitation that separates inner essence from the objective Ideal. In *Proust* Beckett explains the sin of being or, more particularly, the sin of birth or origination:

> Tragedy is not concerned with human justice. Tragedy is the statement of an expiation, but not the miserable expiation of a codified breach of a local arrangement, organised by the knaves for the sake of the fools. The tragic figure represents the expiation of original sin, of the original and eternal sin of him and all his "soci malorum," the sin of having been born. (*Proust* 49)

As Yeats puts it, "the crime of being born / Blackens all our lot"—though he adds, with a touch of Blake, that "where the crime's committed, / The crime can be forgot" ("Consolation"). This leads to the accepted notion that Beckett sees life as a "pensum"[18] and also helps explain the Beckettian subject. Life, according to this formulation, is incompatible with the Ideal; for there to be a union of subject and object, the pilgrim must be disburdened of the sack of life.

This notion has a long history in modern literature, from Samuel

---

18. *The Unnamable* 310, and see *Malone Dies* 259 and 239–40. Yeats's word is "expiation" (*A Vision* 238), and the narrator in *Texts for Nothing 8* wants to be "authorized to expiate" (113).

Harvey discusses the notion that in Beckett's work life is a burden (*Poet and Critic* 118–19). Pilling suggests that Beckett found the idea that birth is a crime in the work of the seventeenth-century Spanish dramatist Pedro Calderón de la Barca (*Samuel Beckett* 130); in his *Confessions* Augustine gives Psalms 51:5 as the source for this notion (book I.7, p. 28).

Richardson to Kafka.[19] Beckett is interested in Bunyan's version of it, but also in Céline's more secular sense that life itself is the problem. At one point in his *Journey to the End of Night*, in a passage about a literal underworld, Céline manages to portray human bodies "who asked for nothing better than to enter into Eternity," "ancient stiffs" who are still living a sort of life: "One by one their so-called heads stood silent in the harsh circle of lamp light. It's not exactly night they have in their eye sockets, it's almost a gaze, but gentler, like the gaze of those who know" (334). Céline affirmed that his novel was not a history of true persons but of "fantômes."[20] So in Yeats's Phase 15 the soul is in an immovable trance (*A Vision* 136), and on its way to this purgation it is "shade more than man, more image than a shade," "a mouth that has no moisture and no breath": "I call it death-in-life and life-in-death" ("Byzantium," line 16). "It is even possible," Yeats says, "that being is only possessed completely by the dead" ("Certain Noble Plays of Japan," *Essays and Introductions* 226).

The subject, then, removed from unity and shedding its material *empêchement*, is only half-alive, "a presence," in Beckett's words, "embryonic, undeveloped, of a self that might have been but never got born, an *être manqué*."[21] This half-life is a key discovery for Beckett. In 1935 Beckett heard C. G. Jung lecture, and was impressed by his corroboration of this notion.[22] Jung spoke of a ten-year-old girl who, he suspected, had premonitions of her own death, and said of her that "she had never been born entirely" (Jung 107, Bair 209). Forty-one years later, when the actress Hildegard Schmahl asked Beckett about May, a character in *Footfalls*, he recalled Jung's lecture and told her about the girl

19. "Your merit is your crime," writes Miss Howe to Clarissa ("Sat. March 25" letter); and Clarissa later explains to Miss Howe that her sin is punished "by *itself!*" ("Tuesday Night" letter [April 11]) (Richardson, *Clarissa* 115 and 208).

20. Quoted in Hewitt 75. About his final dance the narrator of *Bagatelles pour un massacre* says, "Voici qui danse exactement entre la mort et l'existence" (Hewitt 163), and in *L'Ecole des cadavres* Ferdinand's "favorite role," Hewitt says, is that of a ghost, "sermonising his readers from beyond the grave" (173).

21. On Beckett's concept of the *être manqué*, see Read. Beckett's words are originally given in Harvey, *Samuel Beckett: Poet and Critic* 247. Pilling mentions Shelley's "intuitions of a pre-natal life" (*Samuel Beckett* 136, and see 216 n. 38).

22. For a discussion of Jung's lecture and Beckett's interest in it, see Bair, *Samuel Beckett* 208–11. These lectures were published as *Analytical Psychology, Its Theory and Practice* (1968). Beckett attended the third lecture (Bair 208).

Jung's influence is often considered strongest in Beckett's drama, especially in *All That Fall*, where the lecture is discussed directly, and in *Footfalls*. O'Hara considers *Molloy* Beckett's most extended expression of Jung's idea (47).

whom Jung could not help because she was not quite living.[23] Mrs.
Rooney in *All That Fall* (1957) recalls a similar lecture by "one of these
new mind doctors" (*The Collected Shorter Plays* 35): "he suddenly raised
his head and exclaimed, as if he had had a revelation, The trouble with
her was she had never really been born!" (36). In an unpublished
manuscript which appears to have been written in 1968, Beckett gives
what is essentially the same story:

> Sa mère   fille m'a dit, avant d'entrer dans le coma, Elle n'est
> pas vraiment née, elle n'est pas vraiment au monde, tempère-lui
> l'espace, ne le laisse pas dans ce temps. Depuis tous nous
> voyagions, au milieu des os.

On the back of a subsequent leaf Beckett doodled in blue ink two
versions of the Jungian mandala, each composed of three concentric
rings with a dark dot in the middle.[24] This is the figure Jung had drawn
in his lecture, representing the different levels of consciousness with
significant Neoplatonic undertones; the dark core is the collective
unconscious, where all beings share a basic psychic identity. This is the
structure of the self in much of Beckett's fiction. Peggy Guggenheim
says that Beckett told her he could remember his own birth, or life in the
womb, and so the notion that one may not be fully alive could have
seemed especially important to him.[25] He has said that he "was born
old" (Harvey 119), but has denied that he or anyone he knew had been
"not properly born," in any sense of the expression.

Beckett's subject is often an *être manqué*. Mr. Knott in *Watt* does not
rise from sleep or retire from vigil—he does not, that is, alternate
between night and day, dark and light, the cycle's polar opposites—but
is perpetually in "a state that was neither sleep nor vigil, nor vigil nor

23. Schmahl played May in the Schiller-Theater production of *Footfalls* that Beckett
directed in Berlin (1976). See Brater, *Beyond Minimalism* 54, 64.
24. Reading University Library manuscript, "Recent acquisitions." The manuscript
quoted is numbered "33)" and the doodles are on the back of the first leaf of "34)." The
space after "mère" is in the original.
One of Beckett's two mandalas has a bridge connecting two of the concentric circles.
Jung sought for bridges and doors to the unconscious psyche (Westman 210), a dark
womby chaos (207). For a general discussion of Jung's mandala, see Jung, "The
Symbolism of the Mandala," *Dreams* 169–297.
For a more particular discussion of Jung's debt to Neoplatonic and Hermetic
representations of cosmological principles, see Westman.
25. Esslin, *The Theatre of the Absurd* 35; Guggenheim, *Confessions of an Art Addict* 50.

sleep" (86). It seems partly in reference to him that the sixteenth entry in the novel's "ADDENDA" reads, "never been properly born," though another character, Arsene, is probably the prime suspect: he is named after Arsenius, who is reported to have said, in the fifth century, "je suis déjà mort" (Wolosky 214). The protagonist of *First Love* describes himself on one occasion as "even more dead than alive than usual" (26), and in an early draft for *Textes pour rien* the narrator speaks of being "ni mort ni exagérément vif."[26] "I don't know when I died," begins the narrator of *The Calmative*; Malone posits that one goes on after death because, being already mostly dead, one is powerless to stop: "And when (for example) you die, it is too late, you have been waiting too long, you are no longer sufficiently alive to be able to stop" (*Malone Dies* 241). The Unnamable, predictably, tops them all, boasting that the soul is "notoriously immune from deterioration and dismemberment" (*The Unnamable* 330). "I shall never get born, having failed to be conceived" (353), he says. By claiming responsibility for his own conception—*he* failed to have been conceived—the Unnamable implies in effect his antecedence to his own being, that is, perpetual being. "I alone am immortal," he complains, "what can you expect, I can't get born, perhaps that's their big idea, to keep on saying the same old thing, generation after generation" (383). He lives forever because he was never fully released into the world:

> Come into the world unborn, abiding there unliving, with no hope of death, epicentre of joys, of griefs, of calm. Who seems the truest possession, because the most unchanging. The one outside of life we always were in the end, all our long vain life long. (*The Unnamable* 346)

The Beckettian subject is alive despite the fact that it has died, and it is dead despite the fact that it was never conceived. It is better to cease "before having been," as one narrator sums the problem (*Texts for*

---

26. The narrator speaks of being "en équilibre," balanced between highs and lows:

> Les bas, c'est bien, c'est beau, si l'on veut, moi je n'en sais rien, les hauts aussi, à la rigueur, mais les uns après les autres, [above the last five words Beckett wrote "alternant"] non, ce n'est pas intéressant. Une petite santé étale, au moral comme au physique, de quoi être tout juste présent, ni mort ni exagérément vif, dans toutes ses parties, voilà le rêve, si l'on veut arriver à quelque chose, dans la vie. ("Preliminary to *Textes pour rien*," second text, 2)

Nothing 8 115); "I too shall cease as when I was not yet," says another
(*From an Abandoned Work* 45). This logic is circular because life is a circle:
the subject finds itself trapped in a cycle of being that cannot end,
because it was never begun, and cannot begin, because it never ends.

Perhaps if the subject were properly born it could die for good and
leave the cycle, but improperly born it must renew its journey. So the
Unnamable, who was given up for dead in his youth (331), expresses his
incompleteness of being as a function of his improper birth. He gives a
history of his origination, a seven-month baby whose parents died, "he
at the conception, she at the nativity" (377). Beckett's subject looks to its
birth because birth is the one threshold in life's circle. We cannot see the
point of origin in the Yeatsian Wheel, either Phase 1 or 15, because it is
an undifferentiated ground (or figure), all dark or all light, but we can
see the gyre just before or just after the exchange of the tinctures. Yeats
shows the gyre at that stage in cross-section in *A Vision* (74), and it is,
not unpredictably, a mandala figure. The mandala's core, the ideal core
of Beckett's subject, is also the point of the subject's origin, the earliest
moment in the subject's history that is accessible to consciousness. "You
were born on an Easter Friday after long labour. Yes I remember. The
sun had not long sunk behind the larches. Yes I remember" (*Company*
34). As Stephen thinks, teaching history, "They knew: had never
learned nor ever been innocent. All" (*Ulysses* 24–25).

There is precedent in the Greek tradition for remembering one's birth.
Pythagoras could remember previous lives, according to Xenophon and
Empedocles, and Plato believed in *anamnesis*, an impersonal memory
from a time when the soul contemplated the Ideas directly.[27] So several
Beckett characters reenact the search for origin through ritual: Molloy
moves his pebbles in the cycle of being, putting each in turn in his
mouth, the origin or source; Krapp reels his tape back in time on his
birthdays; and in *Murphy* Mr. Kelly's kite is a historical bobbin, released
and gathered, connecting Kelly with "the point at which seen and
unseen met" (280). It is because Beckett's subject is one such as these,
half-alive or half-dead, that it can journey the life cycle. Yeats refers to
Plato's notion of recollection as a "doctrine of pre-natal memory" ("My
Friend's Book," *Essays and Introductions* 416): we can reach the pure

---

27. Eliade 51–52. Eliade also says that certain disciples of Buddha were numbered
among "those who remembered births" (*jatissaro*) and cites examples from the *Rig Veda*,
IV, 27, i, and the Bhagavad-gita, IV, 5. Those who "know," in this sense, can recollect the
beginning, "become contemporaneous with the birth of the world."

forms of chaos, the pure condition of Belacqua's third being, by remembering back to conception.

All the Dead Voices

Beckett, then, conceives his subject as a Jungian *être manqué* who remembers the mandala core of the Wheel of Being, but when Beckett heard Jung speak in 1935 he had already written *Dream*, where these concepts are first articulated. Jung only reinforced what Beckett already knew. Beckett relies on a long tradition to construct his subject; there is, however, another, albeit more speculative, way to think of his relation to the tradition of the half-dead subject. In a sense, the hero of Beckett's cycle is the ancestor who hands down knowledge of the cycle, who has access to the mystery of being that, as Yeats says, requires all of life to be learned. Like Yeats's Shelley, Beckett's own literary and philosophical precursors can validate his vision.[28] Beckett's vision of the subject, along these lines, is empowered by the fact that he, an author so deeply impressed with such a vision, participates in a tradition of authors who are themselves such subjects. There is an interesting foretaste of this notion in Unamuno's "The Novel of Don Sandalio, Chessplayer." "Every poet, every creator, every novelist," writes Unamuno,

> creates himself as he creates his characters, and if they are stillborn, if they are born dead, then it is because he himself is one of the living dead. When I say every poet . . . I include God, who in creating the Creation . . . is doing no more than creating Himself in His Poem, in His Divine Novel. (225)

Two of Beckett's precursors exemplify this relation to one's ancestry themselves—Joyce and Vico. Beckett advertises *Work in Progress* in "Dante...Bruno.Vico..Joyce" as based on the Viconian cycle of history, and for well-known reasons. In some sense, however, the *Wake* has Vico himself as its subject. Of course, the *Wake* has many protagonists, but underlying all of them is Finnegan, the giant figure who, like the large-bodied Giordano Bruno, imagines the whole world which is

---

28. Beckett has called his literary and intellectual ancestors his "precursors," as James Knowlson has said in conversation. "For the contributor's page of the *European Caravan* in 1931," notes Gontarski, "Beckett spoke freely of 'influence,' allying himself with his countryman [Joyce]" ("Molloy and the Reiterated Novel" 57).

himself.[29] He is the Ur-hero of the book, and he is in some ways Vico.

In his *Autobiography*, Giambattista Vico attributes his genius and special knowledge—his "ingenuity and depth"—to a singular event of his childhood:

> He was a boy of high spirits and impatient of rest; but at the age of seven he fell head first from the top of a ladder to the floor below, and remained a good five hours without motion or consciousness. The right side of the cranium was fractured. . . . The surgeon, indeed, observing the broken cranium and considering the long period of unconsciousness, predicted that he would either die of it or grow up an idiot. However by God's grace . . . he grew up with a melancholy and irritable temperament such as belongs to men of ingenuity and depth. (111)

Vico's fall is the first event of his life that he recounts. It constitutes in effect a second birth, a fall into knowledge, a return from death, from long unconsciousness and a broken skull. It is not surprising, then, that he knows the origin and cyclical history of civilization. This is Finnegan's story too, a mason who falls down his ladder while building a wall: "His howd feeled heavy, his hoddit did shake. (There was a wall of course in erection) Dimb! He stottered from the latter. Damb! he was dud" (*Finnegans Wake* 6.8–10). The original song of Finnegan's death relates that, like Vico, Finnegan fractures his skull in his fall.[30] But Finnegan does not exactly die and, smelling whiskey (the spirit) at his wake, returns to life. He is not dead, only "dud." Soul of the devil, he says, did you think me dead?: "Anam muck an dhoul! Did ye drink me doornail?" (24). "He stottered from the latter" means not only that Finnegan tottered from the ladder, but also that he stutters his letters. So HCE, Finnegan's ostensible manifestation (see the question of Finn MacCool's identity, *FW* 126.10–139.14), is a stutterer. That stuttering is the language of *Finnegans Wake* itself, a language that is half there and

29. Or the sleeping body, as Bishop reads the book in *Joyce's Book of the Dark*.

30. *Finnegans Wake* 6. This refers to part of the song, "Finnegan's Wake," which McHugh quotes in the *Annotations*:

> One morning Tim was rather full,
> His head felt heavy which made him shake.
> He fell from the ladder & broke his skull,
> So they carried him home his corpse to wake.

half not; it expresses the special knowledge given to one half-asleep and half-awake, to one returning from death, one both present and absent. This is true of all language, since all language must be both stable and sliding, but in the *Wake* Joyce makes this knowledge of language that is in language one of his explicit subjects. That construction of language is in part what Derrida seems to mean when he writes that, for Plato and his tradition, written language is half-dead, removed from its life at the origin:

> As a living thing, *logos* issues from a father. There is thus for Plato no such thing as a written thing. There is only a *logos* more or less alive, more or less distant from itself. Writing is not an independent order of signification; it is weakened speech, something not completely dead: a living-dead, a reprieved corpse, a deferred life, a semblance of breath. ("The Heritage of the Pharmakon: Family Scene," *Dissemination* 143)

Language is alive at the godhead origin, the dead place of the Beckettian object, and it is dead—an errant "ghost" or "phantom"—when it wanders the streets, unable to repeat its origin (143–46). The return from death becomes emblematic of the life cycle, that is, of the historical cycle that is the subject of the *Wake*.

Vico, then, exemplifies in his return to life the view of history he advocates, and that rebirth explains his privileged knowledge of the historical cycle. These particulars make him a good model for Joyce's subject, Finnegan. Several details of Vico's personal history, however, are also like Joyce's. Two of these stand out especially: Vico's father, like Joyce's, was advised to send his son to be educated with the Jesuit fathers (*Autobiography* 112), and Vico's daughter, like Joyce's, suffered from infirmities that occasioned great unhappiness and ineffectual medical treatments (203). These coincidences in their generational histories must have struck Joyce, who said that Vico's theories "gradually forced themselves on me through circumstances of my own life" (*Letters* 241); he was both fond and fearful of such personal congruities and often attributed prophetic power to them (Ellmann 592, Colum 164–65). So Joyce could identify with Vico because their theories of social history are alike and because their personal histories are alike. As an acknowledged precursor, Vico helps validate Joyce's vision not only with his work or doctrine, but with his life. That is the point about Beckett's precursors that I take the Joyce-Vico relation to illustrate.

Among Beckett's literary ancestors, those who have a similar relation
to him include Augustine, Dante, Vico, Yeats, and Joyce.[31] In his
confessions Augustine is already a saint, and so is his mother. He is also
perfect, however, as an ancestor to Beckett. God will relent from
laughing at him, he says, "for all I want to tell you, Lord, is that I do not
know where I came from when I was born into this life which leads to
death—or should I say, this death which leads to life?" (*Confessions*
24–25). He does not know, he says, how he was conceived (204–5). This
ignorance of his origin occupies him relentlessly, partly for his own sake
and partly because knowledge here should endorse the existence of
godhead at the threshold of the life cycle:

> Answer my prayer and tell me whether my infancy followed
> upon some other stage of life that died before it. Was it the stage
> of life that I spent in my mother's womb? . . . But what came
> before that . . . ? Was I anywhere? Was I anybody? (26)

Augustine's question contains its answer, as it often does—he is trapped
by his own presuppositions, for he asks God in effect if He exists. Is
the womb where God is, he wonders; he associates womb and tomb
because if God is infinite and unchanging there can be no true end to life.
The end must be regenerative: "In you 'today' never comes to an end"
(27). This is the Yeatsian logic of the congeries of being, and good
Neoplatonism. Augustine relies on it repeatedly. "In this world one
thing passes away so that another may take its place," he says, "and the
whole be preserved in all its parts. 'But do I pass away elsewhere?' says
the Word of God. Make your dwelling in him, my soul" (81). And so

31. Dr. Johnson, while not properly in Beckett's imaginative tradition, deserves
mention here. In 1937 Beckett started to write *Human Wishes*, his unpublished play about
Samuel Johnson and Mrs. Thrale, titled after Johnson's poem "The Vanity of Human
Wishes" (Bair 253–57). Speaking of his own literary tradition in a 1973 interview with
Deirdre Bair, Beckett claimed Johnson as his precursor. Bair rightly says that Johnson's
life, along with his work, may have appealed to Beckett, calling attention among other
things to their similar physical afflictions. Johnson's life has something in common with
Vico's, since both were born into disease and disfigurement, coupled with prodigality
and talent. Johnson himself reported that "I was born almost dead" (Bate 5). In a 1937
letter Beckett says that Johnson "was spiritually self-conscious, was a tragic figure, i.e.,
worth putting down as part of the whole of which oneself is part" (Bair 256). That is the
role of the half-dead subject for Beckett. Johnson "must have had the vision of *positive*
annihilation," Beckett writes in another letter (254), a vision of final death, that is, which
his life as an *être manqué* would contradict; but to that end Johnson preferred, Beckett
says, "eternity of torment."

all things tell us that they did not make themselves (198): "in you we are remade" (91). Because the whole is preserved, our knowledge of things is already present in the mind, in good Platonic fashion, thought (*cogito*) a re-collection (218–19). In this way Augustine convinces himself that divinity is indeed at the head of life's cycle. When his mother dies she returns to God, and Augustine is consoled because she is not wholly dead (200). With this endlessness comes uncreatedness, or improper birth, a principle Augustine sees at work in his personal life. His baptism, he says, was postponed, making him "as yet unmoulded clay rather than . . . the finished image" (32). And the revelation that brings him knowledge of his true origin in God comes to him in a garden (171), emblem of formal chaos and the womb-tomb principle.

Augustine's sense of his improper birth makes him a suitable precursor to Beckett's subject. But Beckett too is, conceptually, a half-dead subject who remembers his birth, and so it is interesting to find in Augustine's biography aspects of Beckett's life, and in Beckett's work aspects of Augustine's life, just as Vico's autobiography foreshadows Joyce's life, and as Joyce's work incorporates details from Vico's life. Both Beckett and Augustine suffered psychosomatic illnesses (*Confessions* 55). Both had especially close relations with their mothers and were supported by allowances from them (59). Both were attracted by theater in their youth (59) and, I might add, became writers. Augustine consults astrologers (73), as Murphy does; is obsessed with God's "goad" (144, 185), which appears on two little wheels in Beckett's *Act without Words II*; and quotes "kicking against the goad" (66) from *Acts* 9:5, which Beckett uses in his title, *More Pricks Than Kicks*. Augustine writes that "we carried your words with us as though they were staked to our living bodies" (182), which suggests the less allegorical, literalized practice in *How It Is*. He yearns for God's "door" (127, 347), as does the Unnamable. In fact the end of *The Unnamable* may echo the end of Augustine's *Confessions*, much as the end of *Dream* echoes the end of Joyce's "The Dead." God, Augustine decides at last, is goodness itself, and so needs no good beside himself: "You are for ever at rest, because you are your own repose" (347). Like the Unnamable, God is found to be not only already at the place where he wishes to be, but also to be that place itself (for a discussion of "place" in this context see Chapter 6). This truth cannot be taught, says Augustine. "We must ask it of you, seek it in you; we must knock at your door. Only then shall we receive

what we ask and find what we seek; only then will the door be opened
to us" (347). Augustine, one might say, is one of Beckett's subjects, and
as such succeeds also as one of his ancestors.[32]

Dante also offers the intelligence of origin that Vico and Augustine
possess. Like Beckett's Belacqua, he believes that Divine Presence is
made manifest in Beatrice, and seeks the Rose at the end of the mind. A
mental traveler to the origin, he is a pilgrim alive in the realm of death.
Passing through the otherworld, Dante finds several liminal crossing
points where the spirits are not yet in their places, but in between places.
Such is Belacqua's state, awaiting Purgatory, and such is the Limbo
being of those in the antechamber to Hell, "who lived without infamy
and without praise" (canto III, lines 34–36). They are mingled with the
angels who neither rebelled against God nor were faithful—"those nor
for God nor for his enemies" (*Fizzle 8* 57)—and who in consequence
belong neither in Heaven nor in Hell. These, Virgil explains, "have no
hope of death" (III.46) and so cannot enter the kingdom of death. They
"never were alive."[33] Virgil too is suspended without place, as his
"liminal status" in Limbo and Eden suggests; Nohrnberg rightly
compares him in this context to Aeneas ("The *Inferno*" 80). As Dante
projects the case, Virgil the author sees himself as liminal, and so
appropriates the Homeric Odysseus who harrowed Hell to create
Aeneas, a liminal subject in his image, suspended between dead Troy
and Rome yet unborn, between myth and history, a kind of *être manqué*.
Then Dante, recognizing himself in the same tradition, takes Virgil
along in his own autobiography, *The Divine Comedy*. Virgil, in other
words, is the suitable companion for one "nel mezzo del cammin di
nostra vita." And so, approaching Satan, Dante discovers a state much
like that of the unborn spirits in Limbo: "it was less than night and less
than day" (XXXI.9–10). One hears in these lines an echo of *Genesis*, the
chaotic state of the world before God separated light and dark, earth and
water, figure and ground. When Dante reaches Satan he approaches the
chiasmus or inversion of the gyres of Heaven and Hell, and feels more
acutely his own liminality. Words fail to describe not Satan—whose
ontology is certain—but Dante himself:

32. Of course, Augustine's "autobiography" is selective, even distorted, shaped to
teach the reader about God, not about Augustine (Scholes and Kellogg 169).

33. Canto III.63. "The characters in the vestibule suffer a suspension or paralysis of the
will; their abdication of free choice is the larger 'great refusal' here. Unable to surrender
to death, they are also spared this assent, in that they never were alive" (Nohrnberg, "The
Inferno" 85).

> I did not die and I did not remain alive; now
> think for yourself, if you have any wit, what
> I became, deprived alike of death and life!
>
> (Canto XXXIV, lines 24–26)

Dante reenacts his own *Aenead*, with Virgil as his master, or author, and himself as Virgil's subject.

Dante and Virgil show the logic of Beckett's ancestry. Like Beckett's other precursor pseudocouple, Joyce and Vico, Dante and Virgil demonstrate how the half-dead author validates his sense of his own liminality and the liminality of his subject by making the subject of his autobiography not only himself but his half-dead ancestor as well. Beckett's precursor, in other words, is not only half-dead, or improperly born, like Beckett's autobiographical subject, he also uses the knowledge derived through half-being to construct a relationship with *his* precursors, an autobiography in which his ancestor, the ancestor of Beckett's precursor, is the subject. By doing so, Beckett's ancestor establishes a tradition in which he participates, a tradition in which Beckett finds his place. Beckett invokes this tradition, and his subject is endorsed by it. Like T. S. Eliot's Tiresias, "throbbing between two lives," Beckett's subject can see into all things and fit them together, because he is not any one thing, and does not fit together himself. Such a subject, endowed with special knowingness by history, can pass—indeed must pass, as Augustine's and Yeats's logic shows—through the cycle of being, and return to see the stars again.

II
The Neoplatonic Metaphysics
of Beckett's Fiction

Krapp remembers a hard rubber ball he once gave to a dog, a ball he says he might have kept (20). Of this exchange Beckett has commented that, "if the giving of the black ball to the white dog represents the sacrifice of sense to spirit the form here too is that of a mingling."[34] The play uses this division of light and dark to depict Krapp's struggle with sensuality. Krapp tries to replace his sexual and material desires (for the dark nurse, drink, and bananas, especially) with reason and mind (the new light above his table, his art of memory). But however he may try, as Beckett's comment suggests, Krapp finds dark and light, as he says, unshatterably associated (21). So the light above his desk only accentuates the darkness surrounding him, differentiating his figure from the ground; moving about in the dark he feels "in a way," and then comes "back here to . . . (*hesitates*) . . . me" (15, and see 26). No matter how hard he tries to control his senses and replace them with reason, he ends up being both light and dark, a white face and shoes, but black clothes, the soul in its sensible habit, and filled with "the fire in me now," both heat and light. Krapp is as venal as ever, addicted to bananas and alcohol, crying over "*Effie*," Theodor Fontane's *Effi Briest* (25)—which appeared also in *Smeraldina's Billet Doux*—and receiving Fanny, the old whore (25–26). Nonetheless, his failure, the failure of mind to be rid of the body, does not contradict its own ideal or object. In his ledger Krapp discovers the turning point in his life:

> Memorable . . . what? (*He peers closer.*) Equinox, memorable equinox. (*He raises his head, stares blankly front. Puzzled.*) Memorable equinox? . . . (*Pause. He shrugs his shoulders, peers again at ledger, reads.*) Farewell to—(*he turns the page*)—love. (13)

Krapp finds the word "equinox," so insistently repeated, no longer memorable, and its association with his farewell to love puzzling. At the equinox the balance of light and dark shifts: Krapp's memorable equinox was presumably the vernal one (21 March), when the day grows longer than the night, the "dissolution of storm and night with the light of the understanding" (21). From that time on Krapp renounces his dark desires, and can say farewell to love. It is a new page in his life, as the stage direction indicates.

That change parallels the turning point in Krapp's artistic career. Krapp realizes that his artistic subject should be the darkness that he wishes to escape in life. This revelation is commonly said to refer to Beckett's turn in his artistic career from ironic control to the admission

---

34. In his production notebook for *Krapp's Last Tape*, quoted in Gontarski, "Crapp's First Tape" 66.

of weakness in the trilogy. It is also relevant to a later turn in his career. At some point Krapp's Yeatsian spool ends and he must begin a new one. Beckett's literature of darkness ends, and one of whiteness begins. The world of the Unnamable disappears and, after the half-dark of *How It Is*, a place of modulated light appears, as in *Imagination Dead Imagine* and *Ping*. The art of bodily disintegration perfected in the trilogy gives way to a mental world where the body's condition is only a fact, not a feeling. A literature of protracted endings and waiting finally ends, and one of beginnings takes its place, as the original French title of *How It Is* indicates: the work of *Comment c'est* (from "commencer," to begin) begins. This extraordinary change in Beckett's work has not been discussed with enough fanfare, and though the later work does not disregard the problem of ending, or the condition of darkness, it presents on the whole a radically different world from that of his earlier fiction.

One reason for this change of direction can be found in Beckett's Neoplatonic vision. Krapp's Yeatsian metaphor of the light and dark gyres is also a picture of metaphysical or cosmological renewal. The rebeginning in the middle of Beckett's work is part of that metaphysic. After the spirit, refined from body in *The Unnamable* to language itself, attains its object, it is refracted, emanated from the whole back down to creation. Passing through the turning point of *How It Is*, Beckett's *être manqué* must begin the cycle anew—but then departure is no less difficult than arriving had been.

The One and the Many

For Beckett, the cycle of being involves the ontological question of generation. It asks, in the context of Neoplatonism, how the eternal Mind, or the One, refracts into the particulars of our world, and how these particulars may return to unity. This vision of a world that is both constant and evolutionary depends, like our knowledge of the life cycle, on the serial or successive nature of being, the links between the souls that form the chain of life; so Beckett usually frames the question of generation in terms of the One and the many—how one gets to the many, and vice versa. This dichotomy is a central problem in Neoplatonic metaphysics, which is never very reassuring about the contradictory claims of unity and plurality. So Neoplatonism presents two contradictory views of divinity, two views of the particular world, two ways to divinity, and Beckett engages all of these.

Beckett's characters often speak of the One, "the one outside of life we always were in the end, all our long vain life long," as the Unnamable says (346). The particulars, "we," participate in the One, though it is always elsewhere, outside, on the other side. The One "seems the truest possession, because the most unchanging," outside of life; by the same token it is immaterial and so impoverished, "who, having nothing human, has nothing else, has nothing, is nothing" (346). These, the Unnamable says, are "first notions," notions fundamental to being and to origin: "The one . . . crouches in their midst who see themselves in him," that is, among (or possibly in the center of) its mirrored semblances, "and in their eyes stares his unchanging stare" (347). The traveling subject, as in *How It Is*, is the dream of one who is in another world, "someone in another world yes whose kind of dream I am yes said to be" (145). These words recall Knott and his servants; Pozzo, who is not particularly human, as he says; and Endon, in whose unchanging stare Murphy is unseen: though Beckett's articulation of the One in *The Unnamable* and after is more specifically metaphysical than it is in the early fiction, it is not new either.

Malone Dies and *The Unnamable* show most explicitly Beckett's indebtedness to Plato's *Timaeus*, the Ur-text of Neoplatonism. As Plato tells it, God divided the compound of elements "lengthwise into two parts which he joined to one another at the center like the letter X, and bent them into a circular form, connecting them with themselves and each other at the point opposite to their original meeting point" (*Timaeus* 36 b). That is, God looped the two strands of the X each to itself and then joined the two resulting hoops to form a ball, the world. This double cycle meets at the equinox—Krapp's equinox—where the zodiac's two movements are balanced.[35] It is "the first loopings of the loop, so help me God," which Malone claims to have witnessed (268). Appropriately, Beckett creates an image of this connection of the X with itself (though not an entirely faithful one) in Malone's knife-rest: X——X. Malone also describes another looping in terms of x's: when you "turn over on your back," he says, "the head comes to rest at x inches approximately from where it was before, x being the width of the shoulders in inches, for the head is right in the middle of the shoulders" (241). "Over, over, there is a soft place in my heart for all that is over, no, for the being over, I love the word . . . vero, oh vero" (*From an*

---

35. The Platonic circles of Same and Different meet at the vernal equinox. See Freccero, "Dante's Pilgrim in a Gyre" 178, 180.

Abandoned Work 48). Plato claims that the world is living, intelligent, and round (*Timaeus* 30 c), "able to converse with itself, and needing no other friendship or acquaintance" (34 b). Its surface is "smooth all around for many reasons":

> in the first place, because the living being had no need of eyes when there was nothing remaining outside him to be seen, nor of ears when there was nothing to be heard, and there was no surrounding atmosphere to be breathed, nor would there have been any use of organs by the help of which he might receive his food or get rid of what he had already digested, since there was nothing which went from him or came into him, for there was nothing besides him. Of design he was created thus—his own waste providing his own food, and all that he did or suffered taking place in and by himself. (33 c)

This is clearly not a case of modern solipsism (even the Cartesian kind advanced by Schurman). Consider in this context the Unnamable's reasoned description of himself, "a great smooth ball I carry on my shoulders, featureless."

> No more obscenities either. Why should I have a sex, who have no longer a nose? All those things have fallen, all the things that stick out, with my eyes my hair, without leaving a trace, fallen so far so deep that I heard nothing . . . of the fall of my ears heard nothing. . . . I'm a big talking ball. . . . I always knew I was round, solid and round . . . (305)

The Unnamable cannot decide why he is a smooth and solid ball, though "there must be reasons" (306). The reader is also told that he sees nothing (305), and might infer from the case of Worm that he has no air to breathe.

This description parallels Plato's account of the genesis of a world that, though intelligent, has no sense organs because it has no need of them. The created universe should not be confused with the One proper, the high God that (in Platonic thought) creates the universe through his demiurge; so if the Unnamable fancies a likeness to Plato's world, he is not for all that like the Platonic One. But this is not an obstacle: Beckett plays the Unnamable's mutability against his oneness, using the Neoplatonic paradigm. Similarly, Beckett's place of unity is not the high God itself but the fountainhead of the life cycle, which, according to Platonic interpretations, is created by the high God. The problem, rather, is with Neoplatonic theory itself, which cannot resolve the contradiction between singularity and plurality. Plato both tackles and evades the issue. There is, he says, speaking of the world, "an invisible and formless being which receives all things and in some mysterious way partakes of the intelligible, and is most incomprehensible" (*Timaeus* 51 b). Though he emphasizes mystery, his formulation contains its own answer: the many forms of particularity can only be accommodated by something that has no form: "that which is to receive all forms should have no form" (50 e). So the single God is "the form which is always the same, uncreated and indestructible." The demiurge, the second nature or being, is more like Beckett's mutable pilgrim, "like to" the first nature but "created, always in motion, becoming in place and again vanishing out of place" (52, 52 b). The third nature is eternal space, which "provides a home for all created things" (52 b). These three, like the Father, Son, and Holy Ghost of the Christian myth, suggest the trine being of Belacqua and Murphy. But how the formless "partakes" of the intelligible, Plato declines to say. He only deduces that the formless and unchanging must exist if plurality is to be accommodated.

Beckett's cycle of life is the chain of being linking the One with the serial particularity emanated from it. Malone distinguishes these matters neatly when he wonders whether Macmann is not really a different person who only looks like Macmann. The Macmanns, he says—that is, the sons of man, "mac" meaning son—resemble one another. They pride themselves

> on having one and all, in the last analysis, sprung from the same illustrious ball. It is therefore inevitable they should resemble one another, now and then. . . . No matter, any old remains of flesh and spirit do, there is no sense in stalking people. (259)

This "ball" is (as a verb) the original sex act, and also (as a noun) kin to the earth, Krapp's "old muckball" (*Krapp's Last Tape* 24). It is also, however, Plato's spherical godhead. It is both the perfect original All and the cycle that it engenders. The sons of man resemble one another because they are all part of the same being, "old remains" (a fine turn of phrase) of the same "flesh and spirit." That, as Boethius understood, is both a source of singularity and of equality.[36] "Now and then" means "now as before," and also "alternatingly"—because you cannot be always in the One and also in a life cycle.[37]

Beckett's fiction insists on a more precise reading of human descent. Human genealogy is not linear, as *Genesis* would have it, but circular, a "rigmarole" (*Molloy* 13), a "family circle" (*The Unnamable* 375), Malone's "loopings of the loop, so help me God" (268). Life is a loop that joins Malone's "ball" with the original Ball, the family circle joining "the shitball and heaven's high halls" (*First Love* 19). Hence the encapsulation of human history in *Company*, for instance: "One two three four one. Knee hand knee hand two. One foot. Till say after five he falls. Then sooner or later on from nought anew. One two three four one" (49). This is a story about a crawler, if you like. It is also the journey of human generations, which leads from "One" to company, to "two, three, four," and then to the fall and the beginning again, following the cyclical form of 1–2–3–4–1. Not to reduce this story to the apocalyptic revision of history of the *New Testament*, Beckett emphasizes the link between the two poles, the original One and the many, through the chain of human generation: in the Judeo-Christian tradition proper such intimate relation with the deity is unthinkable. "Dish and pot, dish and pot, these are the poles," says Malone (*Malone Dies* 185), singling out the alternation of aliment and dispatch, the going in and the coming out. "In the beginning it was different," he continues; before genesis ("In the beginning"), before emanation there was no now and then, no cycle, no alternation and no time. The *Texts for Nothing*, coming as they do after *The Unnamable*, and near the turning point in Beckett's fiction, show a special interest in the Neoplatonic paradigm. The narrator of *Texts for Nothing 10* says that "one day I shall know again that I once was, and roughly who, and how to go on, and speak unaided, nicely, about number one and his pale imitations" (124). "Number one and his pale imitations" does put it nicely. This is not just about the writer and his alter egos; number one is the original One, the one "I once was," and the imitations are the Platonic shadows mirroring it (*Enneads* v.4.1). These pale imitations form a human series, "him and me and all our train" (*TfN 13* 139), through which the individual can "try and be one again" (*TfN 8* 113). "One alone," says the Unnamable,

---

36. "All men come from noble origin. Why then boast of your ancestors?" (*The Consolation of Philosophy* 53).

37. "Sprung" and "stalking" imply that all stem from the same root, descended by the single ladder of life. One sense of "stalk" is the sidepiece or "stem" of a ladder (Skeat 514).

"then others. One alone turned towards the all-impotent, all-nescient, that haunts him, then others" (*The Unnamable* 346).

The Chain of Being

Thinking about Mahood and Worm, the Unnamable gives one version of the serial process linking the subjects in the cycle. If someone were sent to get him out of his solitude, he says, to connect him with the chain of being, that someone might stay with him, and then they would both "disappear," escape the cycle: they would be two, but "unbeknown" to each other (378). But then yet another would come to get *his* predecessor back to the life cycle, "to see what has happened to his pal, and get him out, and back to his right mind, and back to his kin, with a flow of threats and promises, and tales like this of wombs and cribs" (378). This is a tale of generation, a lineage, and these generations form the human series:

> it's like the old jingle, A dog crawled into the kitchen and stole a crust of bread, then cook up with I've forgotten what and walloped him till he was dead, second verse, Then all the dogs came crawling and dug the dog a tomb and wrote upon the tombstone for dogs and bitches to come, third verse, as the first, fourth, as the second, fifth, as the third, give us time, give us time and we'll be a multitude, a thousand, ten thousand, there's no lack of room . . . (379)

This drinking song contributes to the argument for periodicity in *Waiting for Godot*—the third verse repeats the first, the fourth repeats the second and so on ("there's no lack of void" also reappears in that play). Here the Unnamable states more explicitly the cyclical nature of human generation. Duality multiplies of itself: only two verses, or two acts—or two subjects of the many—yield an eternal cycle. The outcome, given time, is a multitude sufficient to fill the room available, just as in Milton's epic, Satan guesses that humanity is created to fill the room left by the rebel angels' fall.[38]

---

38. "Our hell will be heaven to them," says the Unnamable (379). See his earlier remark: "They are not interested in me, only in the place, they want the place for one of their own" (369).

For Milton's version see *Paradise Lost* ix.144–57.

Beckett repeatedly makes clear that the human series depends on a periodic alternation of subjects that operates by the principle of displacement: when one subject arrives another must leave. The chain of life is a closed system, like the two well-buckets in *Murphy*. This displacement is linked throughout the fiction with wandering and home, concealment and revelation. So Watt travels the road to Knott's house, and when he arrives Arsene must leave, just as Vincent had to leave when Arsene arrived. The same holds true for Walter, Erskine, and Arthur (*Watt* 56, 148). The "series of men," and of dogs, and of pictures in *Watt* alternate similarly, the one leaving home when the other arrives (38–39). In *Endgame* Beckett hints that there is an alternation of tormentor and tormented that mirrors the relation of wandering and home. Hamm, the tormentor, controls the home, as his name suggests: "home" comes from the Old English *ham* (Shipley 182). Hamm insists on his position exactly at the center, to emphasize this: as the god-figure, Hamm is at the center of the cycle. Clov, the tormented, is the subject that tries to leave but cannot, and remains poised on the threshold of Hamm's. His name suggests his dilemma: "cleave," "clove," from the Old English *cliofan*, means "to cut with a blow," while the word's other root, OE *clifan*, means "to cling" (Shipley 84–85). Of all Beckett's inventions the couple of "tormentor" and "victim" in *How It Is* brings out most explicitly the serial ontology of humanity, "so on and similarly all along the chain in both directions . . . from the one to the other inconceivable end" (141). The tormentor becomes victim when it is abandoned by the tormented, and the tormented, or victim, after abandoning the tormentor, becomes a "traveller" and then, finding a victim, becomes the tormentor (*How It Is*, part 3). This holds for *What Where* too, a dramatic correlate to *How It Is*, where identical characters appear to alternate roles as tormentors and tormented, with "head haught" and "head bowed" (43–44); when the cycle is finally completed, the coordinating voice (V) tells that it is "without journey" (59).

As these examples show, the transmission of life in the cycle is not familial, though it does involve human generations; it is not a sexual procreation but a principle, a mysterious but fundamental movement of life. The sexual metaphor is obviously useful to explain this cycle, but emanation and return is not a sexual issue. Beckett represents this transmission with his wandering couple, and his couples are usually of the same sex to emphasize this point, which comes out explicitly in *How It Is*. The book is specifically and explicitly about the way in which the "procession" of humanity (145) derives from the couple. Pim and Bom appear to be male but have androgynous qualities, to underscore their representation of all humanity. But while the narrator tells with excruciating particularity how the tormentor becomes victim and then wanderer and then tormentor again, it is never clear whether the protagonists find anyone new or only exchange roles. It is possible that they represent two sides of the same being, that there is only one Pim/Bom who takes sides against himself, traveling with his sack of life in the mud. The only number that matters in the book is the number one, as the narrator's repeated calculations demonstrate. The narrator's attempt to deduce just how many individuals there are in the life cycle returns inevitably to one: "as for example our course a closed curve and let us be numbered 1 to 1000000 then number 1000000 on leaving his tormentor number 999999 instead of launching forth into the wilderness towards an inexistent victim proceeds towards number 1" (117). Since in a closed system, "our course a closed curve," all the pilgrims revolve one by one, there may as well be only two of them as any number. The pilgrims are interchangeable, their roles fixed by the system. The couple, then, is only a "pseudocouple," as Beckett calls it in *The Unnamable*, a part of unity still. "The as one plodding twain," Beckett calls them (*Worstward Ho* 20).

This system emphasizes the oneness of being, and so brings out the self-contradictory nature of the relation of the couple. On the one hand, the couple are interchangeable, the same, like each other because they are semblances, to use Beckett's word, in the life cycle. On the other hand, they represent the original One and the one who leaves him, the godly one and the emanated subject. Accordingly there are two kinds of couples (as has often been remarked), an egalitarian couple displaying a "horizontal" relationship and a hierarchical couple displaying a "verti-cal" one. Among the former are Nag and Nell of *Endgame*, Vladimir and Estragon, Mercier and Camier, and Watt and his doubles. The vertical relationship is clear with Hamm and Clov, Pozzo and Lucky, Knott and Watt, Malone and Macmann, the Unnamable and his surrogate selves, all god-figures and their fallen angels, as Pozzo calls Lucky. With Vladimir and Estragon Beckett displays a special subtlety, since they are at once interchangeable and different, Vladimir being more parental, Estragon more forgetful and childish. This dual quality is also clear in *How It Is*, where the protagonists are both interchangeable and hierar-chical, tormentor and tormented. They work out the problem of depicting a human cycle removed from questions of reproductive sexuality, where the protagonists exemplify both original unity and the serial subject.

The Unnamable and other Beckett narrators suggest that they could reach the One again through the many, through increase, as it were, and not by reducing their number. A nice pickle, which the Unnamable dismisses easily. "But let us go back as planned," he says,

> afterwards we'll fall forward as projected. The reverse would be more like it. But not by much. Upstream, downstream, what matter, I begin by the ear, that's the way to talk. Before that it was the night of time. Whereas ever since, what radiance! Now at least I know where I am, as far as my origins go, I mean my origins considered as a subject of conversation, that's what counts. The moment one can say, Someone is on his way, all is well. Perhaps I have still a thousand years to go. No matter. He's on his way. (352)

The Unnamable can go either forward or backward toward his origin because he is somewhere in the life cycle, in circular history; "before that" there was a timeless world, the dark before emanation or "radiance."[39] He worries that he might be just beginning the cycle, his "thousand years"—the rounded time span sought by the Lynch family in *Watt*—and so would lose more by going forward, rather than back, but is reassured that "someone is on his way": when the other takes his place he will move on, eventually to reach his origin. This pilgrimage is accomplished by the transmission of the voice, the words, from one being to another. "And who's this speaking in me, who's this disowning me," asks the narrator of *Texts for Nothing 12*—who dis-owns him, divides him from the one[40]—"as though I had taken his place, usurped his life." This is an occupational hazard when you are just one of the many: maybe the narrator is already where he should be, and any newcomer would displace him from where he wants to remain. "Will they succeed in slipping me into him, the memory and dream of me, into him still living, amn't I there already, wasn't I always there, like a stain of remorse" (134). A note creeps in about his remorse, as though

---

39. Cp. *Enneads* v.1.6. In *Murphy* too the two poles in the cycle connected by the series are the pot and radiance: the "pot poet" Ticklepenny connects "the furthest-fetched of visions to a reality," making the extremes of w.c. and radiator meet by means of a "series" of "feed tubes" (*Murphy* 171–72).

40. The association of "own" and "one" is traditional.

he were the original sinner, the original sin itself (the sin of Being) transmitted through the generations. "Will they succeed" is indeed the issue here, for if they do he would fail to keep his place at the throne.[41]

Beckett's subject knows that it will eventually get to the One again, if it is not there already; but it does not know where it is in the cycle. It knows that it is a variant on the One, but not which variant. As the narrator of *From an Abandoned Work* says,

> With so much life gone from knowledge how know when all began, all the variants of the one that one by one their venom staling follow upon one another, all life long, till you succumb. So in some way even olden things each time are first things, no two breaths the same, all a going over and over and all once and never more. (47)

All things, the narrator implies, are already in the One, "all once and never more," and also unique, gone without repetition. Having lost contact with the origin, with that knowledge gone, the subject thinks it is unique even though it may be repeating an earlier voyage—the Unnamable's consciousness of this ontological uncertainty becomes almost unbearable towards the end of the novel. "All hangs together, I am in chains," says Malone, referring both to the chain of being and to the cosmic chain on which, in Neoplatonic cosmology, God dangles the earth and the spheres:[42]

> Unfortunately I don't know quite what floor I am on, perhaps I am only on the mezzanine. The doors banging, the steps on the stairs, the noises in the street, have not enlightened me, on this subject. All I know is that the living are there, above me and beneath me. (218–19)

---

41. This succession, together with the provocative "stain of remorse," suggests Joyce's use of "agenbite of inwit": Beckett will slip into Joyce's place, or succeed him as the agenbiter. See Chapter 7.

42. Neoplatonic cosmological hierarchies have in common the concentric organization of the universe, with God at the farthest reach and earth at the center. In the *Paradiso* Dante offers the earth at the center, with hell at its middle, the farthest point from God; then the seven planetary spheres, and the eighth heaven of Fixed Stars, in concentric circles (see Canto xxii); these are encompassed by the ninth sphere of the Prime Mover; beyond everything is God's Empyrean sphere. The Hermeticists generally see the All as a circular body that envelops the world; within it are the decans, who work on things below through their sons, the demons, or through the planets; the planets (or the zodiac), finally, surround the earth. See Yates, *Giordano Bruno* 46–47.

Like the Dantean vision of a vertical hell, this topography is fashioned after the Neoplatonic cosmology of a suspended world. The Unnamable could be the earth at the center, or else the One at the periphery, "from whom all depends," as Plotinus puts it (1.6.7): "I on whom all dangles, better still, about whom, much better, all turns, dizzily, yes yes, don't protest, all spins, it's a head, I'm in a head" (372). He cannot tell in which extreme he is.

Plato's claim that the invisible and formless being "receives all things and in some mysterious way partakes of the intelligible" is awkward, and sticks in the throat of Neoplatonism. How does one reconcile the plurality of wandering subjects and the unity of the One that supposedly emanated them? This is a Neoplatonic problem more than a generally metaphysical one, because it stems from the supposition that, as Plotinus says in the *Enneads*, "the One is all things, and is none of those things" (v.2.1). Aristotle's God is, in contradistinction, as A. O. Lovejoy puts it, "a sort of finite or closed circle, shut up within the limits of its own unity" (155). Plotinus, explains Lovejoy,

> sought in that very concept of perfection and self-sufficiency, which had been the terminus of the ascending process of abstraction by which Platonic metaphysics reached its definition of the real, the ground and the necessity for a descending process by which, out of the universal and the abstract, particular beings and the subjects of concrete predicates must arise. (154)

Plotinus took the abstract One that Plato deduced from the particular mirror-world and deduced from it the necessity of emanation. He complemented Plato's emanation with the subject's return. By joining the many to Plato's One, Plotinus required of his followers an impossibly double consciousness, a split personality.[43] Considered in this light, many of Beckett's equivocations, like the following one from the Unnamable, make sense. Perhaps "a whole people is here," he says, and then, "no, I'm alone" (409). He states these contrary views in terms of the life cycle: "you must go somewhere else, wait somewhere else, for

43. "In fine," writes Lovejoy, "to assert of an ultimate reality both its transcendence, as regards its essence or nature or distinctive predicates, and its inclusion of the whole *esse* of something which is defined as having a nature or essence excluded from those predicates is to adopt self-contradiction as the method of metaphysics" (174).
    To put it another way, Plotinus was inconsistent. Fortunately, while Beckett's work participates in the metaphysical tradition, it is not metaphysics.

your turn to go again, and so on, a whole people, or I alone, and come back, and begin again, no, go on, go on again, it's a circuit, a long circuit, I know it well" (410). "Two holes and me in the middle, slightly choked," he says elsewhere, but then immediately adds, "Or a single one, entrance and exit, where the words swarm and jostle like ants, hasty, indifferent, bringing nothing, taking nothing away" (355). He is either a station along the way, or self-sufficient. This heightened consciousness characterizes the Unnamable because he is at the threshold of unity, the chiasmic point in the circuit where he is in fact in the place of the One, as every subject who completes Beckett's cycle must be, for a while.

There are two views of the One, and so there are two ways to reach it too. If the One is in all things, then the subject can know it by participating in matter, in all the particulars of the world, which are perforce good. If, on the other hand, the One is separate from the created world, self-sufficient, then to reach it the subject must purify itself, refine away its own materiality. Lovejoy points out two solutions to the Neoplatonic dilemma. One can claim, as Schopenhauer and Spinoza do, that diversity is illusory, a refraction of the mind, or hold, with Neoplatonic thought, that the many are included in the immutable Absolute (143–44, 152). This appears to be Beckett's solution. He reconciles purity with the material world by translating the particularity of anti-mind into mind, and stating the physical in mental terms. The subject moves in a single world of thought, and this thought embraces all particulars, brought into the circular sovereign head. The problem Beckett does not answer is the one that troubles Alice in *Through the Looking-Glass*: whose thought is it?

6

The Space of a Step: Unity and Emanation in Beckett's Late Fiction

One of the most perplexing aspects of Neoplatonic theory is that it fails to explain convincingly why the One, perfect and self-sufficient, should want to emanate, to divide itself into the imperfections of plurality. Beckett considers several solutions to this problem in his fiction. One answer is that God needs others in order to be seen and appreciated. This seems to be Milton's idea in *Paradise Lost*, up to a point: the Son and the angels extol God automatically and mirror His glory. So Beckett's Worm is necessary to his master's glory (*The Unnamable* 368), and Molloy seems to be necessary for Youdi's well-being: "a culprit is indispensable . . . a victim is essential" (*The Unnamable* 411). One must posit the existence of a third, superior person, a master or mistress, "for without some such superior existence the existence of the house and parlour maid . . . is hardly conceivable" (*Watt* 50–51). This third person's existence "also in a sense if you like depends on the existences of Ann and Mary," the parlour maids (51)—"(I say house and parlour maids, but you know what I mean)" (50). Self-perception itself creates the double, the "I" and the "me," and from the double the whole train proceeds. It is in this Humean sense of the serial identity of the self that Malone says that he has been "nothing but a series or rather a succession of local phenomena all my life" (234). The serial being of humanity is reduced to the perceptions of a mind, the many brought to life by the One Mind.

I have argued that Beckett follows the soul on its pilgrimage to unity through his first seven novels, culminating in *The Unnamable* with the discovery of the threshold to that place. Then, in *Texts for Nothing* and

Krapp's Last Tape, Beckett prepares for his chiasmic flip, exchanging darkness for light, endings for beginnings, and despair for understanding. The earlier novels show the subject's movement up to the One; the later fiction portrays life at the head of the cycle of being, life waiting to be born and life at its first moments of descent. The later works divide into three broad groups, in the context of my discussion. *How It Is* and *The Lost Ones* can be considered together: *How It Is* outlines explicitly the metaphysical system arrived at so painstakingly in the trilogy, and *The Lost Ones* asks what would happen to those left out of the cycle of life, denied exit from the place of objectivity. These works argue that the subject lives when it is in chains, and dies when it is free. *Imagination Dead Imagine, Ping, All Strange Away, Ill Seen Ill Said*, and *Lessness* show the place of objectivity in terms of the life cycle. *Worstward Ho*, the *Fizzles*, and *Company* describe the descent from that place, the early stages of emanation. These works display a temperament thoroughly different from that of the *Texts for Nothing* and of the trilogy, the temper of objectivity.

Anthropologies of Generation and Decay:
How It Is and *The Lost Ones*

How It Is balances between the first-person anguish of the trilogy and the almost scientific third-person detachment of later works. It is the story of life, a sketch of history, of before and after ("before Pim, with Pim, after Pim"), but it is told in the first person by one of the living, a half-dead subject, "born octogenarian at the age when one dies in the dark the mud upwards born upwards floating up like the drowned" (70). The protagonists crawl in the mud, which is itself liminal, earth and water, the thin membrane that divides memories of light and dark, sense and reason, world and mind.[1] The narrator explains that he has two pairs of eyes, "the blue" and "the others at the back" (8, 104): those at the back are the proverbial inner eyes of consciousness, here dramatizing the two-sidedness of the subject traveling the threshold itself between subjective life and unity.[2] This subject is wise to the process of "translation" (142) whereby the Unnamable finds himself at

---

1. Schurman argues for it as the "space of the mind" (136).
2. One can think, says Djuna Barnes, "with the eye that you fear, which is called the back of the head" (83). This version of the mind looking onto its own inner arena was established by the seventeenth century. See Rorty 50–51.

the outer threshold just when he reaches the still center of his gyre: "you think you're calm and you're not in the lowest depths and you're on the edge" (20). He also knows his life cycle, which rests at its head and then resumes:

> you are there somewhere alive vast stretch of time then it's over
> you are there no more alive no more then again you are there
> again alive again it wasn't over an error you begin again all over
> more or less in the same place . . . (22)

How It Is is profoundly aware not only of Beckett's metaphysical scheme but also of its own transitional position in Beckett's work. Several times the narrator refers to the translation of the outer world into the head that characterizes the progression of Beckett's fiction: "all that once without quaqua on all sides now in me" (126), and "one life everywhere ill-told ill-heard quaqua on all sides then within . . . in the little chamber all bone-white" (134). The voice ("quaqua") especially was once without, now within (see also 139).

In *How It Is* one is a victim, then traveler, tormentor, and victim again (cp. *The Unnamable* 381). The book is divided into three parts. In the first the narrator, a traveler in the mud, recalls scenes from his earlier life "above in the light,"[3] scenes reminiscent of *More Pricks Than Kicks* stories like *Fingal*. In the second part the reader learns more about the protagonist's relation with Pim, his victim. He communicates with Pim with a cruel and simple system of stimuli and responses; Pim is almost lifeless. Part 3 tells of life after Pim, when the protagonist continues his journey and apparently convinces himself that he is alone. From his reiterations it becomes clear that he had himself been the victim of one Bom, before he left Bom (in part 1) to find Pim and torment him (part 2), only to have Pim leave him (or "vanish") in part 3. Presumably Pim will himself become a tormentor, a Bom, when after a period of traveling he finds another; the protagonist, now abandoned by his victim, will be found again by a tormentor, just as he had been before part 1, and will become a victim again. Indeed, it is possible that he will be found by his own former victim, Pim, now turned tormentor. This periodic formula advances the chain or succession of humanity. The subjects travel the east-west axis, dragged along "by the mere grace of our united net sufferings from west to east towards an inexistent

---

3. A reference to Dante's *Inferno* xv.49: "There above in the bright life."

peace."[4] This net—perhaps the same that Lucky's dance of helplessness describes in *Waiting for Godot*—compels the congeries of beings to move along their "single eternity" (24), "so on and similarly all along the chain in both directions" (141).

This procession cannot be stopped "without prejudice to a single one among us," without doing injustice to some who will remain victims (141). The system of the novel is found good—miracle of miracles, after the anguished confusion of the trilogy—because it is just, good because necessary, good because reasonable. One has to look closely at *The Unnamable* to find an organizing principle; here such a principle is repeatedly underscored. The governing principle here, it will be noted, is the same one that underlies the earlier fiction. There is a "natural order" to life (e.g., 7, 25, 27), "here where justice reigns" (134), an "ancient natural order the journey the couple the abandon" (20). The procession cannot be stopped unless "this diversity" (140), or double-ness, "the season of our couples," is erased—that is, "without first closing our ranks and of two things one" (141). This does in a sense happen at the end, when the narrator decides that he is alone, and had been so all along. Everything, "all this business of a procession," and Pim and Bom, and the rest, was invented, "all balls" (145). He is the only dream of another, "of someone in another world yes whose kind of dream I am yes said to be" (145). This conclusion is anticipated in the beginning of the book:

> question if other inhabitants here with me yes or no obviously all-important most important and thereupon long wrangle so minute that moments when yes to be feared till finally conclusion no me sole elect
>
> and yet a dream I am given a dream . . . (13)

But true oneness would preclude the dreaming other too, the One, presumably, outside the life cycle. At most the narrator proposes that he is alone with the One who dreams him. That would leave those two to exchange places as tormentor and victim, perpetuating the life cycle; as

4. 143. It is curious that the protagonists of *How It Is* travel from west to east, a point mentioned often, and not from east to west, as formerly. This may represent their return from the unity sought by earlier protagonists, and dramatizes the way in which the fiction pursues a new direction while sticking to its theme.

the narrator remarks, the tormentor would rather stay where he is, but the victim has a slightly stronger interest in moving, which justly prevails. There is some corroboration for this view, especially if the voice the narrator hears is taken to be his own, as he often suggests (e.g., 87), and not the ancient word transmitted through the generations (138–39). The narrator also animates his victim, Pim, who would never be but for the narrator "anything but a dumb limp lump flat for ever in the mud" (52)—"but I'll quicken him" (52).

Beckett weaves these speculations throughout his narrative, just enough to question the orthodox Neoplatonism so reiterated there. Are there many subjects or just one (124)? Or are the many really glued together into one (140)—otherwise would they not forget what God's voice (139) had told them, and fail to transmit the information from one to another (121)? The couples would then experience their torment always anew (as *Waiting for Godot* suggests), and would not know about the "immense circuit" that they form and form again (121). These speculations suggest that the system elaborated in *How It Is* is not so necessary as it is made to appear, despite the claim for its natural justice. It may still be only the thought of one, dissociated from the assurances of collective experience. Like classical metaphysics, it is a cosmology deduced from abstract mathematical assumptions (that a trilogy would generate an infinite series, for example) that, in the end, say more about the imaginative tradition that conceived them than about the natural world. If the alternative worlds offered in *How It Is* question the book's governing scheme ("the journey the couple the abandon"), however, they also complement it, because all subscribe to the same metaphysical framework. To ask whether humanity is one or many is not to offer radically different worlds but to affirm a worldview that imagines both.

But is this, then, the only world, the only logic imaginable? Toward the end of *How It Is* the narrator wonders whether it is not too late "to conceive of other worlds" as just as his (143). There can be a world, he posits, "where no one ever abandons anyone and no one ever waits for anyone and never two bodies touch" (143). *The Lost Ones* describes such a world (though the searchers there do touch each other). Like *How It Is*, this work is a kind of metaphysical anthropology, for in its world human engagement constitutes a cosmological system. But whereas in *How It Is* the protagonists travel the seemingly inescapable east-west axis, lending the work the essentials of an independent topography, here north, for example, and so all spatial direction, is defined not by geographical rotation or by a magnetic pole but by a stationary woman

(56). Like *How It Is*, the work describes an ordered and closed system governed by strict rules, a world with its own fanatic justice where "all is for the best" (42), a place proportioned "for the sake of harmony" (*The Lost Ones* 7). But whereas *How It Is*, told from the point of view of a traveler narrator (cp. 123), allows speculation about the nature of the world and its rules, here a community of lost ones cannot escape knowledge of its confining world of "certitudes" (42).

There is no story here and no characters, only a picture of a world. The wanderers are themselves features of a landscape that seems made for their use; their automatic death-in-life announces the place of unity—for *The Lost Ones* participates in Beckett's ongoing metaphysical argument. It depicts a cylinder of solid rubber, recalling Endon's padded cell, whose floor is divided, like Murphy's mind, into three unmarked "zones" (43–44): a narrow outer ring in which "climbers" move clockwise, a narrow ring just within that in which "watchers" move counter-clockwise, and the rest of the floor the center, where "searchers" look unsuccessfully each for its "lost one." Movement in the first zone (the outer) is most regulated, in the second less so, while the third zone is chaotic by comparison (since the searchers may move in any direction). These rudimentary parallels with *Murphy* suggest that the world of the cylinder is—not surprisingly—a microcosmic mind. Other details support this notion. A sourceless, dim, and omnipresent yellow light illuminates everything in the cylinder evenly, "as though every separate square centimetre were agleam" (7); there is no shadow or marked differentiation, so perception is difficult (55). The climbers use fifteen ladders to reach twenty niches in the wall of the cylinder; their alternation of wandering with visits to the niches, to which they are compulsively drawn, suggests the metaphors that characterize the workings of mind in Beckett's fiction. Such periodic alternation is also expressed by the steadily oscillating temperature (8), and by rare lulls in which all action freezes for ten seconds or less, and then resumes (36–37).

This periodicity reveals the similarity between the workings of the mind and the metaphysical chain of the Neoplatonic many, which is ruled by the law of displacement. Like the mind, the wayfaring subjects in the chain of being are driven home, to the head of the cycle, by their relatives fore and aft, but must wait their turn to enter, and then exit again. In the cylinder, the climbers cannot enter an occupied niche, and must wait for its occupant to descend. A climber is never obliged to climb, but once he has queued up at the foot of a ladder he cannot leave,

and must advance from the last place in line to the first, until it is his turn
to ascend. Attempts to "leave prematurely" are "sharply countered by
the other members and the offender put back in his place" (45). Having
waited in line, the climber ascends the ladder or returns to the third
zone, to the center (or, rarely, to the middle zone). Similarly, those who
enter the first zone may not turn left, against the direction of the
"stream" of climbers there, but must proceed clockwise to a ladder, and
may not circle more than once before they choose a ladder. The first
zone, then, both because of its queued bodies and its clockwise
procession, represents the metaphysical chain of traveling bodies, the
"net" as it is called in *How It Is*, which, by virtue of its connectedness,
enforces its own order.

   This organization of life in the cylinder works out a model of the
Neoplatonic cycle. The model does two things: it shows that the
workings of the life cycle are those of the mind—the divine Mind or
Nous, that is, which runs the universe—and it suggests how the process
of emanation and return might work. The subject at the third zone is at
the chaotic inner place of unity, jumbling together with other resident
searchers in a constant melee; from there it is impelled by an urge to
climb to seek the succession of beings in the first zone. Eventually it
returns to the center, driven by a complementary urge, the "passion to
search" (50). Beckett captures the Neoplatonic parallel by using Plato's
original model for this process from the *Timaeus*. According to Plato,
God "made the universe a circle moving in a circle" (*Timaeus* 34 b).
When he formed the elements into an X and then joined them to form
the sphere of the world, "he made the one the outer and the other
the inner circle" (36 b). The world, in other words, is ringed by two
circles, the "Same" and the "Different," as they are traditionally called
(Wetherbee 39), which rotate in opposite directions. That is what
Boethius refers to when he says:

> You release the world-soul throughout the harmonious parts of
> the universe as your surrogate, threefold in its operations, to give
> motion to all things. That soul, thus divided, pursues its
> revolving course in two circles, and, returning to itself, embraces
> the profound mind and transforms heaven into its own image.
> (*The Consolation*, Poem 9, p. 60)

Boethius's formulation shows how similar *The Lost Ones* and *How It Is*
are in design: the threefold *How It Is*, too, is a working out of this

Platonic paradigm.[5] Beckett hints at the circles of Same and Different in
the cylinder when he describes the two zones of climbers and watchers,
"which suitably lit from above would give the impression at times of
two narrow rings turning in opposite directions about the teeming
precinct" (29).

But unlike the procession of subjects in *How It Is*, which forms a true
metaphysical cycle, the movement of emanation and return in *The Lost
Ones* is only a mock cycle. The niches and the searchers' arena are dead
ends: the niches lead nowhere, and the searchers cannot find their lost
ones. These wanderers cannot find their missing doubles, so essential to
Beckett's vision of the cycle of life as a procession, a chain of beings
developed through the couple. They cannot cooperate, constitution-
ally—cannot join forces (20–21)—and so must remain all ones, themselves lost in their world of high certainty. The world of the cylinder is
really all a third zone of objectivity, all Murphy's chaos, because there is
no way out of it, and in this it resembles complete, solipsistic subjectivity. The quasi-loops accomplished by the subjects in the cylinder
show they have the right instinct, like insects whose life cycle is
disturbed, to act in the right way, but also that the best they can manage
is merely formal behavior.

There are two legends, or philosophies, in the cylinder, entertained by
rival "schools" (18), positing two ways out of the cylinder. One holds
that there is a trapdoor in the unreachable hub of the ceiling (18), leading
"to earth and sky" (21); the other believes in a secret, undiscovered
passage leading from one of the tunnels, the niches in the wall, out
to "nature's sanctuaries" (18). But neither alternative to a confining
material life, neither religion (the sky) nor Wordsworth's nature, is
available. The myths emphasize the problem to which they respond in
the first place. Plato says that "generation appears to be transmitted
from one [element] to the other in a circle" (*Timaeus* 49 d), but for lack
of "the other" there can be no generation in the cylinder. And so the lost
ones are condemned to wear out their Democritan energy and become
the "vanquished." Slowly each lost one will wear down and sit without
life on the floor of the third zone, till only one searcher is left, "this last
of all," still looking for his lost one (60–62). When this last one finds his
place and dies, the light fades and the temperature comes to rest near
freezing: life is over in the cylinder.

How It Is and *The Lost Ones* show that the mind and the world of

5. Cp. Dante's *Paradiso* x.9.

generation work in the same way, that they are similarly constituted. They also show that if the mind did not participate in the world, did not allow for emanation, but was closed in upon itself, as the cylinder is, then all life would end.

The Bounded Infinity of Random Orders

The lost ones' two legendary ways out of the cylinder are like the two ways that Beckett's fiction assays and then rejects, first mimesis—the linear way of his early subjects in the external world—and then insubstantial abstraction—the regressive centripetal movement of the trilogy into the self. These ways are represented by the two pictures in *Watt*, the abstract picture of a broken circle and a dot, which hangs in Knott's house and represents Watt and the cycle of life, and the "realistic" painting of a horse, which hangs in the train station and represents the "line and surface" of the natural world. Each portrays the reality in which it is hung. In the world of *The Lost Ones*, however, neither way is available. *The Lost Ones* is Beckett's reply to Democritus and the atomists, "the one scientific doctrine of antiquity which Neo-Platonism had been unable to turn to account" (Whittaker 198). Democritus the Abderite, whose phrase "nothing is more real than nothing" Beckett liked,[6] believed that this world will eventually disintegrate (Hahm 188), as would life in the cylinder.[7] Engaged as he is in pursuit of the Neoplatonic vision, Beckett pauses with *The Lost Ones* to ask what would happen if things did not work that way, but rather as Democritus insisted they do. The answer is that life would have ended already; that was Yeats's conclusion when he said that, if life were not an ongoing cycle, "the generation had long since found its term" (*Explorations* 307). The original French title of *The Lost Ones*, *Le Dépeupleur*, something like "the depopulator," suggests as much: the cylinder is a machine for eliminating its populace. The atomistic model fails to explain life, in other words, because life is not over, and so Beckett continues to explore the process of generation in Neoplatonic emanation.

6. Regarding Beckett's references to Democritus, see Kennedy, *Murphy's Bed* 300, 52; Pilling, *Samuel Beckett* 64, 151–52; Rabinovitz, *The Development of Samuel Beckett's Fiction* 87–88, 100 n. 34; Rosen 181; and Henning, "The Guffaw of the Abderite," and *Beckett's Critical Complicity*, especially 174, 187.

7. Democritus also thought of seeing ants on the vault of the sky, a matter alluded to in *Murphy*: "Mr. Endon lay back and fixed his eyes on some object immeasurably remote, perhaps the famous ant on the sky of an airless world" (248). See Rabinovitz 87–88.

After *How It Is*, Beckett evidently decided not to write long prose works,[8] but the short works that follow continue to work out his project. *Imagination Dead Imagine* and *Ping* both explore the life between life and death.[9] The four-page-long *Imagination Dead Imagine* outlines, with geometrical detachment, a white rotunda three feet in diameter containing a couple, a woman and a man ("the partner"), lying buckled up and back to back on the floor. Here the light and temperature oscillate as they do in *The Lost Ones*, between light and dark, hot and freezing, taking twenty seconds to move between extremes (63). The rotunda may remain in either extreme for indeterminate lengths of time, and the temperature and light may reverse the direction of their change midway (64). There may also be pauses "between end of fall and beginning of rise" (63); these words place the rotunda in the life cycle between the fall (emanation) and the rise (the return). (The fall may be death, and so the return, and the rise may be the rebeginning of the life cycle, and so emanation: this reversibility of terms characterizes the cycle.) As in Yeats's system, the poles are dark and light, fixed, and perfect: "The extremes, as long as they last, are perfectly stable" (64). The cycle can clearly linger at the poles for some time, just as in *The Lost Ones* the climbers and the searchers can linger for some time in the first and third zones of the cylinder, respectively.

While the shape and rhythms of the rotunda correspond to the life cycle, other details imply that the rotunda is not a microcosm but a beginning point for the cycle. The couple suggests generation; if it is at the place of unity, it is still double. Each figure, furthermore, is "bent in three" (65), which endows Beckett's foetal figures with a Christian and Neoplatonic aspect. (In *How It Is* the "single eternity" of time is "divided into three.") The two figures seem incubated as in an egg, fully shaped like homunculi. We are told that the rotunda would have a ring (of sound) as of bone (63), implying that the couple is in a head, like images. Beckett repeats the phrase "in the beginning" (64, 66) to emphasize creation, the word made flesh. Like Belacqua and Murphy in

8. "I don't expect I'll have any more big ones," Beckett is quoted as saying, in *No Symbols Where None Intended* (Lake 134).

9. Lake suggests that "*Imagination Dead Imagine* can be seen as a reduction of *All Strange Away*" (135), and that *Ping* (or the French original, *Bing*, which appeared in 1966) "sprang from Beckett's struggle with *Le Dépeupleur*" (133). I take *Imagination Dead Imagine* to represent Beckett's ideas in *All Strange Away* (collected in *Rockaby and Other Short Pieces*). It should be noted, however, that *All Strange Away* dates to 1964, before even *Le Dépeupleur*, which was begun in October 1965, and completed in 1966.

their absorption, the couple is still but not asleep (66); like Murphy vanishing in Endon's eye, it is a "white speck lost in whiteness" (66), figure indistinguishable from its ground, life from death. The narrator does insist that the two are not alive, but the way in which this is done suggests that they are not dead either: "No, life ends and no, there is nothing elsewhere" (66). The rotunda is merely the most extreme point discernible in the life cycle, the point before or just after complete whiteness (as in the Yeatsian vision), where only a trace of dark remains.

Imagination Dead Imagine, finally, stresses the epistemological aspect of ontology in Beckett's vision—that being depends on perception, on differentiation. The story's opening lines propose this:

> No trace anywhere of life, you say, pah, no difficulty there, imagination not dead yet, yes, dead, good, imagination dead imagine. Islands, waters, azure, verdure, one glimpse and vanished, endlessly, omit. Till all white in the whiteness the rotunda. No way in, go in, measure. (63)

This first act of imagination creates the world after the model of *Genesis*, dividing water and sky ("azure"), and these from earth and vegetation. These differentiated traces are to be omitted, removed, till all that remains is the whiteness of the rotunda (or of the white page), a skull without material contents. But though there cannot be any shadow (as in *The Lost Ones*), and the two bodies are white, their "whiteness merging in the surrounding whiteness" (65), they are alive. They would mist a mirror, and their left eyes open at intervals, "piercing pale blue" (65). Here is contrast, and life. The woman's hair, too, is "of strangely imperfect whiteness." Such differences participate in Beckett's scheme, where the distinction of figures from the "white ground" signifies life and belies the strong sense that the rotunda cannot be entered or left in the ordinary living way. Rather it is a death-in-life, a dead imagination that nonetheless can imagine and be imagined, be figured in an image.

Ping, and *Lessness*, which derives in part from it,[10] both pursue this vision of the head of the cycle, the place of unity where some kind of dead life or half life remains. In *Ping* a human figure, "almost white on white," with some traces of black, light grey, rose, and light blue, is confined in a room (69). The body's legs are "joined like sewn," so it

10. "*Lessness* proceeds from *Ping*," wrote Beckett. For Beckett's comments on the structure of the work, see Esslin, "Samuel Beckett—Infinity, Eternity" 118–19.

cannot wander; this also hints, however, that the body is at some late embryonic stage, not just close to the end of its cycle, as "traces alone unover" implies (70), but also close to rebeginning it, like the foetal couple in *Imagination Dead Imagine*. Evidently there was "a meaning a nature" of old, a whiteness and blueness to which there might yet be a way, an exit, perhaps (as in *The Lost Ones*) in the unseen ceiling (70). Memory of that nature, however, is fading or already over (72). Like the liminal white works that precede it, *Ping* shows a seemingly fixed world, "all known all white," which proclaims the end of life and shows a deathly figure in a mental sarcophagus; and like these others, *Ping* insists on traces of life, hints at a way out to nature, and suggests that life is also near its birth point or beginning. These works sharpen the objective quality of Beckett's narrative, our sense that we see and know all that can be seen and known, and that what we see is shown fairly and adequately. At the same time, Beckett carefully infuses in these works a spirit of randomness and unaccountability. The climbers in *The Lost Ones*, for instance, may wait long at the queues to the niches, or they may not, so that the wait for a ladder does not correlate with the length of a line to that ladder, as compared to the wait at another line. Just when it appears that life is regular and predictable, our information is made imprecise by intangible factors (here the whim of the climbers). So in *Imagination Dead Imagine* the light and temperature may reverse the direction of their change. The work recalls the diurnal and seasonal changes we know as irreversible—and so appropriates Earth topography, where the climate is linked to the movement of the planet—and also rejects them as inadequate models. Life is not all mathematical, in these fictions, no matter how comforting and fundamental that discipline is to us, and to the ancients who founded their metaphysics on it. Beckett keeps the spirit in his cosmological machine.

In *Ping* Beckett introduces irregularity and unpredictability through the apparently random appearance of the word "ping" in the work. *Ping* consists of seventy sentences, of varying lengths; the word "ping" appears thirty-four times, twenty-one times in lowercase and thirteen times capitalized (always at the beginning of a sentence). There may be a pattern to its occurrence, a symmetrical clustering,[11] but even

11. The occurrence of "Ping" or "ping," mapped by upper and lowercase p's, and excepting the title, is:

pppPppPPpPppPPppPpPPpppPPppPppPppp.

The first seven pings, together with the last seven, constitute a palindrome:

pppPppP ‖ PppPppp.

if this is so, when reading the story one is bound to miss it. Like the "lius" of *Dream*, which are the swarming electronlike notes of the world's fallen melody, these "pings" seem to represent the random element in life; absurd in isolation, they may yet make a melody together.[12] While the world order appears fixed, it is not—like the wandering mind. Both world and mind are frustrated by the "ping" of things: "white body fixed ping fixed elsewhere" (69).

Beckett combines these themes of order and irregularity, and of the similarity of life's beginnings and endings, in *Lessness*, a one-page work that is so abstract and disconnected that it seems to be made only of suggestive fragments. These fragments are themselves syntactically scrambled, as is the first sentence: "Ruins true refuge long last towards which so many false time out of mind." But published in 1970, after *How It Is*, *Imagination Dead Imagine*, and *Ping*, it invokes in shorthand those earlier themes, and relies on them to make good sense.[13] A body in a mindlike place, a "little void mighty light four square all white blank planes," has forgotten most of its earlier adventures,[14] which suggests that it is near the end of life. This forgetting is given in Beckett's patented terms of world and mind, where the figure has dissolved into its ground: "all white gone out of mind." At the same time it is suggested that the figure is only beginning its life, a "little

---

The thirteenth through the seventeenth pings are reverse images of the eighteenth through twenty-second pings, read backwards:

$$PPppP = pPPpp.$$

Divide the string of pings into two equal strings, place them each above the other, and these symmetries will appear organized around the center four pings (which of course appear after one-fourth and three-fourths of the work). Italicizing the palindromes, and putting the reverse mirror images of pings in bold italics, and setting the center apart, these strings would look like this:

$$pppPppP \quad Pp \quad Ppp\textbf{\textit{PPppP}}$$
$$\textbf{\textit{pPPpp}}pP \quad Pp \quad pPppPppp.$$

The occurrence of pings shows an hourglass pattern that suggests the Yeatsian shape of life. The pattern's irregularities, however, render its meaningfulness doubtful.

David Lodge says that "*Ping* tends to be followed by words or phrases which suggest the possibility of some other presence or place" (88–89).

12. The word "ping" appears in *Dream*: "But they [the book's characters] will let us down, they will insist on being themselves, as soon as they are called for a little strenuous collaboration. Ping! they will no doubt cry with a sneer, pure, permanent lius, we? We take leave to doubt that" (*Disjecta* 45).

13. *Lessness* was first published in the *New Statesman*, 1 May 1970; *Sans* was the original French title.

14. But Beckett says that "all gone from mind" signifies "refuge forgotten," and not the forgetting of the life that came before. See Esslin, "Samuel Beckett—Infinity, Eternity" 118.

body" whose heart is beating. The figure, it seems, imagines its own journey, wandering in a liminal world where sky and earth are mirrored. The mirrored world recalls both Marcel's first epiphany in *A la recherche* and "the long clear-cut commissure of earth and sky" in *Molloy* (159). To travel the membrane separating the two is, as in *How It Is*, to travel the space of the door separating dark and light. A kind of rebeginning is implied: "He will curse God again as in the blessed days," "He will live again the space of a step it will be day and night again over him the endlessness." Overtones of *Genesis* ("it will be day and night again") suggest re-creation; the figure is much like that in *Ping*—"Legs a single block arms fast to sides"—a partly differentiated organism in the beginning of its development. Like the Unnamable, it is at the threshold to another phase in the cycle: "In the sand no hold one step more in the endlessness he will make it."

The structure of *Lessness* also suggests both disorder and eternal return. "It is composed," Beckett says, "of 6 statement groups," six themes or ideas, "each containing 10 sentences." These themes are presented in an apparently random order, and then repeated in another order, equally random. This gives the work its chaotic quality. But the grouping and repetition in *Lessness* itself carries a message. As Beckett explains, "The whole consists therefore of 2 x 60 = 120 sentences arranged and rearranged in 2 x 12 = 24 paragraphs" (Esslin, "Samuel Beckett" 118). *Lessness* is arranged like a calendar, a time machine recombining one year's elements to make another, one cycle recurring in the next, and so forth. As Esslin rightly says, "what *Lessness* represents in its form is an image of eternal return: the finite number of elements are here arranged in a manner which is both random and governed by a rigid formula" (119). What *Lessness* brings out more clearly than do its predecessors, a point that in turn helps explain those earlier works, is that the disorder it represents does not undo or somehow contradict its vision of order. Instead, it is a looseness that permits recombination. On this reading, it is chaos that makes order possible. By uniting order and disorder in its form, moreover, *Lessness* erases the boundary between beginning and end, the shelter and the world. In the work, the traveler's sky and earth are endless because they are united, the many made "as one": "all sides earth sky as one all sides endlessness." This, the traveler's eternity, is matched by the eternity of the imagining mind, "four square all white blank planes," where again difference is dissolved, producing a single white image. The two eternities are the same, that of the wandering mind and that of the imagined wanderer: "Legs a single block." Beckett reiterates this theme with the beautiful line, "Figment dawn dispeller of figments and the other called dusk." There is a little Frost in this. Dawn and dusk are identical beginnings and ends, and so both are figments, figments that alternatively undo each other, like the traveler and the dreaming mind, till they are the same.

Beckett captures this idea with the ruin. Here Beckett shows explicitly why it is such a fine trope. The ruin combines home and the way, much as the head metaphor does. "Ruins true refuge," begins *Lessness*, and later, "true refuge issueless." By "issueless" is understood that the true refuge is true because it is closed and also because, in generational terms, it does not produce the issue or offspring necessary for the chain of being. But the ruin is a true refuge not because it excludes the waste around it but because, like the double cycle of *Lessness*, it incorporates it, because it encompasses all the possible ways out of itself. It is the whole world, bounded and infinite. If the dreaming mind is the traveling subject, then its true refuge is the circuit of life, no less confining for being so large. Another way to put it is to say that we are imprisoned because the world is finite, because life, in Beckett's classical design, is a loop. Neoplatonism arrives at the same solution to the problem of particularity: the many are parts of the one Mind, which is comprised of their sum. So while *Lessness* sets up the two poles of Beckett's system, the bone-white room and the infinite waste, it also explains that his refugees are imprisoned because the poles are interchangeable, and the system a closed one.

A Fragment Comes Away

Lessness would seem to be a logical end for Beckett's fiction. He has worked out the implications of his system to the point where less is more, where lessness is endlessness; he has reconciled the home and the way to show that the unity of all things is true refuge; and he has shown both how and why "it is the shape that matters." In a way, *The Lost Ones*, *Ping*, *Imagination Dead Imagine*, and *Lessness* resemble the mental world of *Dream* and especially of *Murphy*, so that in them Beckett seems to have returned to his starting point. However, while Murphy thinks that his mind is separated into zones, these late works show a world that is increasingly mediated. As the Christian overtones of *How It Is* already imply, three are one; in the divided topography of *The Lost Ones* it is possible to move physically between the three zones. *Lessness*, finally, obliterates all boundaries by enlarging its prison to include everything, so that light and dark no longer represent, as they do to Murphy and to Krapp, opposite poles in the life cycle. Here one can travel everywhere "and never once [overstep] a radius of one from home" (*Company* 60).

It is this oneness, to be sure, that Beckett sent his pilgrims out to find at the beginning of his fiction: they have found unity *and* returned to Beckett's original terminal. And Beckett lingers at this threshold: in *All Strange Away* (written in 1963–64, published 1976) and in *Ill Seen Ill Said* (1981) he again shows life at the place of the object. *All Strange Away* belongs with *Ping* and *Imagination Dead Imagine*, showing the last refuge, impossible to enter or exit—outside of life—but somehow containing the pilgrim nonetheless: "no way in, none out, try for him there" (39). Likewise *Ill Seen Ill Said* shows a cabin "at the inexistent centre of a formless place. Rather more circular than otherwise finally" (8). Again this is a place defined by "zones" (9), where the division of East and West prevails (21), "the required clash" (43), but where the imagination and the material world are confused, conflated (20). In this final place, the pilgrim changes place by pure mental travel, without moving (19, 46). Like the dawn and dusk of *Lessness*, here the light and dark extremes meet: "On the one hand embers. On the other ashes. Day without end won and lost." The real and "its contrary," "once so twain," are now one (40). Again the ground, here white stone, is "gaining" (26), gravestones take the place of the living, and the lone protagonist, an old woman whose husband has evidently died, signifies by her "Memnon pose" this transition to white, and to oneness. The statue of Memnon at Thebes (actually the statue of Amenhotep III) was said to make a musical sound at the first touch of sunlight.[15] Beckett's "Memnon pose," however, also suggests "menopause," a parallel surely to Krapp's "equinox" (and see Minnie in *All That Fall*). Through Memnon, Beckett connects the protagonist's change from reproductivity to sterility with the change from dark to light—the same relation seen with Krapp—only here white stone has gained much ground since the phase of life portrayed in *Krapp's Last Tape*. Life, in these late fictions, is about over, dissolved into what seems an inescapable unity. Had Beckett left his project at this stage, he would have implied that life aspires to unity, a stable state that prevails because it holds contradiction together, and that once a living being attains this state it remains there, lost in the bosom of Abraham.

Against this notion Beckett sets the binding necessity of continuing

15. As Zurbrugg notes, "*Ill Seen Ill Said* and the Sense of an Ending" 146.

the cycle. After the liminal place where the dark and the light touch and mingle, Beckett's fiction returns to the cycle—not to the point of repeating what had gone before, but enough to show the next stage, the descent that follows unity. That is the accomplishment of the *Fizzles* (published 1976) and of *Worstward Ho* (1983).

Fizzles

The *Fizzles* are earlier works, but one should consider Beckett's agency in keeping them unpublished and in timing their later release.[16] This belatedness is especially interesting considering that the *Fizzles* show various earlier Beckett characters again,[17] seen anew in light of Beckett's later work. Appearing in the 1970s, these eight short prose pieces show Beckett's characters in the other world as they are about to enter the life cycle again. Beckett has reviewed his troops before, at the end of *Malone Dies*, and there too they were marshaled in a place of origin and confinement, a Miltonic Eden. In *Malone Dies* Beckett's review emphasizes that his characters are all part of the same eschatological argument, bound on the same trip, adrift in their boat. In *Fizzles* their reappearance shows what has become of them: they continue to exist in the other world, past their figurative death, and it is suggested that their return to the lower world is inevitable.

One of the *Fizzles* that does not show an earlier protagonist, *For to end yet again*, illustrates Beckett's argument. Its position in the collection is itself telling: it is last in the Grove Press edition, as befits a work that shows an ending, a work whose images recall some of Beckett's late fiction, and it is first in the Calder edition, which is appropriate because its characters begin an explicit descent, the process of emanation from unity. The work opens with talk of the skull alone in the dark, about to "begin"; this beginning, it becomes more clear, is a beginning of recollection, of glimmers of the remembered daylight world, which, internalized, embody the wandering of thought: "the skull makes to

16. The *Fizzles* were first published individually; all were written originally in French except *Still*, which was written originally in English. Their order in the French, English, and American editions varies. In the Grove Press (USA) edition the order is: (1) *He is barehead*, (2) *Horn came always*, (3) *Afar a bird*, (4) *I gave up before birth*, (5) *Closed place*, (6) *Old earth*, (7) *Still*, (8) *For to end yet again*. In Calder (GB): 8, 7, 1, 2, 3, 4, 5, 6.

On dating the composition of the *Fizzles*, see Knowlson and Pilling, *Frescoes* 132.

17. Pilling says that this return detracts from the work—that *Closed place*, for example, is not really noteworthy because it "returns to *The Lost Ones* material" (*Frescoes* 134). He lists several of Beckett's motifs that recur in the *Fizzles* (133–34). Brienza similarly suggests that the first *Fizzle* is not successful because it is "a fragmented recycling" of Beckett's earlier works (*New Worlds* 202).

glimmer again in lieu of going out" (55). "Going out," of course, means both the physical movement of wandering out from shelters, and extinction: the mind rebegins its journey instead of ending, or dying out. The journey's rebeginning is described as a gradual lightening, passing into a uniformly grey earth and sky, a merging point. From inside the hermetically sealed "last place of all black void" (56), then—the last place of *All Strange Away* and *Ping*—the pilgrim of Beckett's cycle comes out again:

> There in the end same grey invisible to any other eye stark erect amidst his ruins the expelled. Same grey all that little body from head to feet sunk ankle deep were it not for the eyes last bright of all. The arms still cleave to the trunk and to each other the legs made for flight. (56)

The expelled, again, still amidst what the narrator describes as "his" ruins, the ruins of his last refuge now cracked open like an egg. His arms "still cleave" together, he is newborn, just emerged from total unity. Beckett's "cleave" works (as in *Endgame*) to suggest both separation and clinging; so does "still," here used as Yeats likes to use it, to mean both continued action and immobility. Figure is physically submerged in its ground as well as indivisible from it, for lack of differentiation, to the eye. The figure in its grey dust is compared to ancient monuments, crumbling in their deserts. Beckett's short story, *The Expelled*, also describes expulsion in thinly veiled Neoplatonic terms. It begins:

> There were not many steps. I had counted them a thousand times, both going up and coming down, but the figure has gone from my mind. I have never known whether you should say one with your foot on the sidewalk, two with the following foot on the first step, and so on, or whether the sidewalk shouldn't count. At the top of the steps I fell foul of the same dilemma. In the other direction, I mean from top to bottom, it was the same, the word is not too strong. I did not know where to begin nor where to end, that's the truth of the matter. I arrived therefore at three totally different figures . . . (9)

It does not matter whether the poles are counted as steps in the ladder of ascent or descent, because both ways up and down are mirror opposites in the continuous cycle of being.

The expelled is afoot again, and something like a whole world, differentiated into its elements, is created around him. "Grey cloudless sky ocean of dust not a ripple mock confines verge upon verge hell air not a breath" (56). Air, water (ocean), earth (dust), and fire (hell) are all here, and yet they are denied as they are evoked: the ocean is an ocean of dust, the air cannot be breathed. This is a mock confine, a world becoming out of unity, still unformed, not properly born, as it were, "the ruins of the refuge" (56). But then comes a change, the "first change of all in the end": "a fragment comes away and falls." This fall continues the process of disintegration while it makes a beginning, not only a first fall but also a seed-sowing in the earth (see also Chapter 7 below). The place is a Dantean limbo, an anteroom to life, filled with "timeless air of those nor for God nor for his enemies" (57), the first stage in Dante's descent. But here is a beginning of life, not of death: after this invocation of limbo the story introduces "two white dwarfs . . . linked by a litter." The two appear a single whiteness at first, and their litter is white; they compose an unmistakable couple again, though their oneness is emphasized, "bleached as one same wilderness they are so alike the eye cannot tell them apart." They walk face to face, one going backwards, and exchange places, guided in their course by whichever of them follows. There is a little irony in this, because if the one who follows directs the course, he appears not to direct it, for then he would not follow. The joke indicates, however, that both dwarfs are responsible for their course, and that there is a course. Their litter is "the dung litter of laughable memory" (58); the Platonic recollection of life persists beyond the last refuge and returns to the world. The dwarfs, "sprung from nowhere," participate in the ancient cycle where extremes meet, "the boas" so favored by Coleridge, "which past with one last gulp clean sweep at last" (59). The expelled sees them from afar, he amidst his ruins, they on their way to a home, as their phrenological "bump of habitativity or love of home" implies. If the expelled had a home it is now in ruin, but his expulsion is followed by the couple, who begin the journey home again. The reader now learns that the "fall" and first "change" that had been associated with the advent of the couple were the fall and change of the expelled (59). For him it was "last change of all in the end." He is fallen headlong amidst his ruins, mingling with the dust (though he is not dead), while the couple are stranded between the earth and sky (60).

This last (and first) *Fizzle*, then, is a narrative about the rebeginning of the life cycle, a descent along a course that leads from unity and indistinguishability to the world of earth and sky, to the couple and the journey home again. *He is barehead*, the first *Fizzle* in the Grove edition, shows Murphy, explicitly named, in a similar journey, and *Fizzles* 3, 4, and 5, which suggest several of Beckett's earlier protagonists, reinforce the impression that the entire collection is about this descent.[18] *Afar a bird* (*Fizzle 3*) suggests Malone, speaking through a traveling character who personifies him. Its landscape, however, resembles the topography of *Mercier and Camier* and of *Molloy*, where the traveler moves "between road and ditch" (25), hugs the hedges and passes through them (27). *I gave up before birth*, the fourth *Fizzle*, suggests *The Unnamable* in form and content. It is all one sentence, narrated in the first person, the voice repeating and contradicting itself. It begins:

> I gave up before birth, it is not possible otherwise, but birth there had to be, it was he, I was inside, that's how I see it, it was he who wailed, he who saw the light, I didn't wail, I didn't see the light, it's impossible I should have thoughts, and I speak and think, I do the impossible, it is not possible otherwise . . . (31)

The *Fizzle* revisits the Unnamable's habitual preoccupations, concentrating on the question of the life after death. His body, he says—his other ("I was inside," "in his flesh")—will die and rot, but he will not (32). This *Fizzle* occupies in the collection the Unnamable's place in the cycle, where Beckett's narrative attains the threshold to the objective world, the world of mind. *Fizzles* 1, 3, and 4, then, recapitulate *Murphy*, *Malone Dies*, and *The Unnamable*. *Fizzle 5*, finally, *Closed place*, clearly resembles *The Lost Ones*. It is a world where "all needed to be known for say is known" (37), comprised of an arena and a ditch, with a narrow track between the two. There is room for millions, wandering and still, who do not see, hear, or touch each other. The arena is a kind of cemetery, divided into chesslike squares: "In the beginning" all the lots were bright, but now there are more dark than light. Bodies lie on some of the squares—apparently on the dark ones. Like the world of *The Lost Ones*, this is a machine-world, a Kafkaesque colony designed to extinguish all life.

These four *Fizzles* recapitulate the rough course of Beckett's fiction, but *Fizzles* 3, 4, and 5 do not consider emanation, the differentiated

18. The second *Fizzle*, *Horn came always*, in which a visitor comes repeatedly to speak to the narrator, who is in bed, looks forward to *Ohio Impromptu*, with its similar scenario.

descent so explicit in the eighth, *For to end yet again*. The first *Fizzle*, *He is barehead*, does take up this theme. It shows Murphy as he continues his life—or rebegins it—past his death. He wears "vaguely prison garb" (7) but does not remember anything in this connection except "heaviness," "fullness," and "thickness." In his former life he was a warden at the asylum, where he sought a last confinement, and perhaps the vague fullness and thickness refer to Murphy's passage through death, through the place of the object or the "full" of the Yeatsian cycle. He is escaping a kind of prison, forcing his way out of a dead end or closed place, toiling through a subterranean labyrinth: "But instead of stopping short, and even turning back, saying to himself, This is the end of the road, nothing now but to return to the other terminus and start again, instead he . . . squeezes through" (8). As expected, his course lies between two termini, a loop, but he manages to leave the one in search of the other. Having come out of death, Murphy is still "fragile" (12–13), but he is intact: "The legs notably seem in good shape, that is a blessing, Murphy had first-rate legs. The head is still a little weak, it needs time to get going again, that part does. No sign of insanity in any case" (9–10). As already noted, Murphy at his end seemed a little insane, incapable of remembering anyone, his mind full of jumbled bits. Now he is all right again.

It is clear that Murphy has just started on a journey back to the living world, to "the open" world of true air (13). He is climbing, but the ground also drops violently, his course sloping with an alcove and below, though he does not know in which direction life awaits him (10). Murphy has already a number of memories, but he has not been long on his way; "his little history takes shape" as he goes (13), but there is not much of it yet.

> He has already a number of memories, from the memory of the day he suddenly knew he was there, on this same path still bearing him along, to that now of having halted to lean against the wall, he has a little past already, even a smatter of settled ways. But it is all still fragile . . . as destitute of history as on that first day, on this same path, which is his beginning, on days of great recall. (12)

In other words, when Murphy became self-conscious again he was already on this road. He is not an infant, however. When he remembers back to that original moment of consciousness, "that first instant beyond which nothing," he finds that he was already old and had the Platonic knowledge (or recollection) of the essentials: "he was already old, that is to say near death, and knew, though unable to recall having lived, what age and death are, with other momentous matters" (12–13). Murphy is knowing, he comes trailing clouds of glory from beyond.

Murphy's return, finally, is a process of detachment much like that recounted in *For to end yet again*, the eighth *Fizzle*. There "a fragment comes away and falls"; here, along with the sound of the body on its way, is the sound "of fall, a great drop dropping at last from a great height and bursting, a solid mass that leaves its place and crashes down, lighter particles collapsing slowly" (11). Murphy's journey, the reader soon learns, is related to this descent: "He himself has yet to drop" (12). According to a Neoplatonic tradition that Yeats quotes—a tradition that goes back to Heraclitus—the water drop signifies the generated soul (Keane 147–48). In the final stage of pregnancy the foetus "drops" or descends in the womb, readying for expulsion. Murphy's descent is a birth. He is returning, reborn through the womb of chaos, a grown homunculus laboring in a labyrinthine anteworld. This world is wet and not of stone (11), as befits the way from the womb, and is airless: when he reaches the outside, it is said, he will suddenly breathe. Consider again the description of his escape: "There are places where the walls almost meet, then it is the shoulders take the shock. But instead of stopping short, and even turning back . . . he attacks the narrow sideways and so finally squeezes through" (8). Murphy is about to be born again, to rebegin the cycle of Beckett's fiction.[19]

Worstward Ho

Worstward Ho reworks the theme of metaphysical generation, following the general Neoplatonic paradigm. The work sounds several of Beckett's established themes—the need to "missay" and to "fail better," and the difficulty of doing so; these themes, though legitimate enough, may obscure the metaphysical melody that is very explicit here.[20] *Worstward*

19. Breuer claims that Beckett was interested in the psychoanalytic theories of rematriation, and particularly in the work of Sándor Ferenszi (78), and that his trilogy characters seek an imaginary return to the womb (76). This interpretation supports Beckett's more graphic depiction of Murphy's birth from the "womb of chaos."

20. *Worstward Ho* has received relatively little critical attention, partly perhaps because of these themes, brought out in such sentences as, "No words for what when words gone," a motif that elicited from the blurb writer at Grove the comment that "*Worstward Ho* explores a tentative, uncertain existence in a world devoid of rational meaning and

Ho returns in part to the images of *For to end yet again* (the eighth *Fizzle*), but with a stronger emphasis on a cosmological frame for the work. It begins by invoking a place for the body: "Say a body. Where none. No mind. Where none. That at least. A place. Where none. For the body. To be in. Move in. Out of. Back into. No. No out. No back. Only in. Stay in" (*Worstward Ho* 7). But can there be a body "where none," that is, physical being without space or extension to precede and contain it? And can there be a place "where none," that is, without any body in it, a place for the body before a body defines it as such? Is "the dim void" (10) a place, though nothing is in it? Which, Beckett is asking, comes first, matter or space? This is a real problem, when you go about ordering first things, creating a world: "First the body. No. First the place. No. First both" (7–8).

Beckett echoes here an old argument about the relation of place or space (*topos*) and being (or the body), a problem about which the ancients never ceased to argue.[21] Democritus and Aristotle set the stage: Democritus believes in a positive void, as real as any body, and thinks the world (being) is placed within the void; Aristotle, in the opposite corner, does not believe in the void and says that space does not in itself have physical extension. He defines *topos* geometrically as the inner boundary or surface of the bodies that circumscribe or encompass the place in question (*Physics* 212 a). The universe, according to this definition, can have no place, for it is not defined by bodies outside of it (212 b). Neoplatonism, predictably, argues against Aristotle and for a positive concept of place as anterior to matter. Plato locates place (*chōra*, or "room") between the Forms and the particular world, less pure than the Forms and more abstract than particularity. While both Democritus and Aristotle think of place as passive, Plato allows it not only positive being but agency, an active character (*Timaeus* 51 b–52 d). Space precedes being and generates it. The Neoplatonists follow suit, considering space or place as an agent of generation superior to matter, for it mediates between the high and low orders of the world, and contains or encompasses all things; although Plotinus finally distinguishes between

---

purpose." For similar criticism see Brater, "Voyelles, Cromlechs, and the Special (W)rites of *Worstward Ho*," especially 166–73.

21. See Samburksy, especially the introduction, 11–29. He notes that the place of God (the Stoic Supreme Being) was gradually identified with the whole universe (15); in Hebrew, God is also called *maqom*, or place.

a lower, "container" space and a higher, "intelligible" space (*Enneads* II.5.3), the two are never entirely dissociated.[22]

Beckett is no Aristotelian: he sees the void as a place ("A place. Where none"), and situates the body in this place ("For the body. To be in"). But he is not about to explain this metaphysics. At one time, he says, he used to ask how the metaphysical world he envisions were possible— "How if not boundless bounded," for example—but now he knows better than to ask (11). So while this work offers no metaphysical answers, it has a metaphysical story to tell (and Beckett admits that he did at some time try to answer these questions). Still he cannot avoid the philosophical dance: the head is the seat and germ of all, he says, and then stops himself to argue about it: "All? If of all of it too. Where if not there it too? There in the sunken head the sunken head" (19). If the Mind encompasses everything, then it is its own place. If it generates everything, then it must have generated itself too, or else, as some Neoplatonic heretics hold, the All is not generated but eternal. Beckett, then, begins with *topos*, with place as agent, as the divine Mind, seat and germ of all, and from this proceeds to create the world. This creation, the Neoplatonic process of emanation—"germ" denotes both seed sowing and decay—suggests again the rebeginning of the cycle of being.

The story develops in stages. First there is place. Then comes a resurrection, a sprouting, surprising and miraculous:

> It stands. What? Yes. Say it stands. Had to up in the end and stand. Say bones. No bones but say bones. Say ground. No ground but say ground. So as to say pain. (8)

"It" refers to the body, which is resurrected, but because the story begins so abstractly, the narrative offers a concrete analogue, a ground

---

22. Iamblichus thought of space as incorporeal, though it sustains the real, but the later Syrianus and Proclus considered it material. "In order to establish a connection between space, which he identifies with light, and the corporeal world, composed of many moving bodies, Proclus conceives a model made up of two overlapping spheres, equal in volume. One of them is made of immobile light, representing space, and the other is the material universe, the sum total of all bodies in various states of motion" (Sambursky 19–20). This is a characteristic Neoplatonist solution, superimposing the ideational and the particular.

Later Neoplatonists, like Simplicius, distinguish between two kinds of place, absolute, immobile space and the changing place of the body (28). This version still allows for a relation between the two worlds, the ideal and the real—that is, for the causal agency of the transcendent over the material world, of space over being.

from which the figure may arise, and bones, to add pain or sense (sensibility) to abstraction. This is a vision of resurrection, like Ezekiel's dream. It is not clear whether the body ever was "down," or dead; there is "no choice but up if ever down" (18). "Had to up in the end" states this compulsion explicitly, for the cycle demands resurrection. So the story, up to this point, tells "how first it lay. Then somehow knelt. Bit by bit. Then on from there" (10). The alternative to this death and rebirth is perpetual half life, to say that the body never lay down. The narrator suggests this alternative, and embodies it with the figure of kneeling: "Or never down. Forever kneeling. Say from now forever kneeling" (18). And the body is described as a "shade" (11).

Next the story introduces an other. "Another. Say another" (10). This other may have sprung from the first body's head—"Seat of all. Germ of all" (10)—or from the process of perception ("Hold and be held," 13), but that is not fully explained; first the void gives rise to one, now there are two. This is to be expected, because the couple is required for generation in Beckett's scheme of things, and indeed Beckett is quick to follow his introduction of "another" with a prophecy of generation: "No future in this. Alas yes" (10). The narrator tries to deny the process of generation, protesting that there are now two bodies because it is possible to enter the place but not to leave it, that is, implying vaguely that the second body entered and the first could not leave: "no out of. Into only. Hence another" (11). But this soon turns out to be false—this is indeed multiplication and refraction, the process of emanation from unity. The two bodies baffle the narrator, who suggests that there might be two places for the two bodies (11) but then rejects the idea: "No. No place but the one. None but the one where none" (11–12). There is only one head, the One, one mind to the many particulars of the world. Beckett identifies the One directly when he asks whose words these are that are said. "Whose words? Ask in vain. . . . No words for him whose words. Him? One. No words for one whose words. One? It. No words for it whose words" (20). "In vain" is also good, for there are no words to say God's name in vain. The two bodies are identified as an old man and a child (13), emphasizing their generational relationship, but they are also similar, as a couple should be: they are both bowed, and go "with equal plod" (13), and both have fair hair, though for opposite reasons: "Dim white and hair so fair that in that dim light dim white" (16). Extremes meet. "Hand in hand" on their solitary way, they walk back and forth, "unreceding" (16), fading and reappearing in the dim light, now the one, now the other shade. It is possible that in that void there is a "grot," or "gulf," a Platonic cave of being from which the light shines unaccountably out (17), and maybe it is there the two go when they disappear. This cave, and the lines "Know no more" (18) and "Enough to know no knowing" (30), return to Milton's cave of light and dark in *Paradise Lost* (vi.4–12), and his injunction to Adam and Eve: "Sleep on / Blest pair; and O yet happiest if ye seek / No happier state, and know to know no more" (iv.773–75). The first couple walk "hand in hand" in their bower (e.g., iv.689), as Vladimir and Estragon did before their fall.

The narrator is still confused: "Where then but there see—"; "Where then but there see now—" (12). The narrator has just reiterated emphatically that it is impossible to leave this place, and now one of the two shades turns as if to go. "First back turned the shade astand. In the dim void see first back turned the shade astand. Still" (12). It appears that the twain do change when they go and return, though the narrator takes some time to make this out (14)—it is a subtle change, as if this motion itself thickens the plot, stimulates generation. Next the narrator manages to count to three, one for the kneeling one, two for the "as one plodding twain," three for the head (20). Now the narrator concedes that all is lost—there is no stemming the tide. "Something not wrong with one. Then with two. Then with three. So on. Something not wrong with all. Far from wrong. Far far from wrong" (21). Once there is one there are more, and now there are many. The narrator alters the figures in order to "worsen" them (21–25), because there is "something there badly not wrong" (21), like the director in *Catastrophe* who alters his actor. But then worsening is exactly what emanation is about, the proliferation that the narrator desperately wishes to reverse by lessening (25) his figures; emanation is a fall from perfection, from Plato's Good, to the world of particulars, so particularity is itself bad, or, as the narrator says, "worse." But now the void is a narrow field "rife with shades" (25).

The narrator identifies the process of "worsening" with "worsening words" (29), hinting at last that the worsening process involves language or logos, the emanated Word. The mind "secretes" these words (30), which are identified as "they" (30). These secreted or emanated words—"As somehow from soft of mind they ooze" (34)—correspond to the bodies or shades that will soon leave their place. The narrator admits as much, having returned to "the plodding twain": "They then the words" (31). The phrase conveys the Neoplatonic notion that the many are to the One as words are to the mind. They proceed like a text, "left right unreceding on" (43). Like the Unnamable, who found himself the space of a door, himself the liminal language that can cross the threshold to the mental world beyond, these characters are words, the returning words. Things cannot be annulled, "least never to be naught" (32); the dim light cannot go out, and the cycle continues to be formed, "that almost ring" (32). To form that ring things must first fall apart. "So little worse the old man and child. Gone held holding hands they plod apart" (34). The couple move apart, a "rift" between them. And plodding apart they blur in the void (35). Now the skull where they had been opens: "No dome. Temple to temple alone" (35). Note Beckett's clever use of "temple" to suggest the divinity of the mind. The head is now said to be only a shade, "shade three." It is an old woman's head (35). When next the narrator turns to the twain, "two once so one," as befits the differentiated subjects of emanation, they are separated by a vast void (41), "vast void apart" (45). This is no great success for the narrator, however, for the "void most when almost" (43), most void when it is almost gone, and nothing will be entirely gone. In the "latest state" the old woman watches, the couple recede. There is a hint that, like the old woman of *Ill Seen Ill Said*, this woman remembers some dead, that the man and child are her dead relatives (46), but this is only a hint. In any case, the narrator finally realizes that "worse in vain," that it is not possible to have less, beyond some point. In the end the couple reach that point—"At bounds of boundless void" (47)—at the end of their tether, "whence no farther," no less, no worse. Beyond this last extension there cannot be less, in Beckett's world, a well with two buckets. For when the One is least, the many are strong, and roam the earth again seeking shelter.

7

The Spirit of Geometry

Giordano Bruno thought that readers of literature should visualize what they read, because through the contemplation and manipulation of images one can attain divinity (Yates 255). While for Plato, and even for Plotinus, metaphorical images are arbitrary, useful in order to clarify abstract ideas, for Hermeticists like Bruno and Ficino metaphorical relations actually correspond to physical ones (Vickers 119–20). Hermetic practice both exalts the arts as vehicles to divinity and reduces them to mere utility, making "concessions," as the Unnamable puts it, "to the spirit of geometry" (359). Beckett does not subordinate the artistic image to a higher reality but strives to show that the two are one; his fiction slowly develops a mental image of the world that assumes the world's power. "Berkeley proved that the world was a vision," said Yeats, and though his judgment seems qualified by its past tense, Beckett takes things up from there. Beckett pictures the world as a metaphysical process, a movement of the life cycle that gives birth to itself, recreating itself between its Brunovian maxima and minima. Beckett's world is both abstract, a geometrical picture, and a dynamic, self-generating thing. It is a sexual geography based in part on Dante's cosmic topography—or, more particularly, on a version of Dante's vision articulated in *Finnegans Wake*.

Dropping in Dante's Earth

Murphy's "drop" in the *Fizzles* is one instance where the life cycle gives birth to one of Beckett's characters, but Murphy is not the only character to drop. Malone too is an old foetus, ready to drop:

> Be born, that's the brainwave now. . . . That has always been my dream at bottom, all the things that have always been my dream at bottom, so many strings and never a shaft. Yes an old foetus, that's what I am now, hoar and impotent, mother is done for, I've rotted her, she'll drop me with the help of gangrene, perhaps papa is at the party too, I'll land headforemost mewling in the charnel-house . . . (*Malone Dies* 225)

Malone's "strings" suggest the umbilical cord, an association on which the Unnamable also draws in connection with *his* "drop":

> depart into life, travel the road, find the door, find the axe, perhaps it's a cord, for the neck, for the throat, for the cords, or fingers, I'll have eyes, I'll see fingers, it will be the silence, perhaps it's a drop, find the door, open the door, drop, into the silence . . . (*The Unnamable* 412)

The Unnamable thinks of eyes and fingers because his eyes will be useful just in time to see the fingers that will deliver him. He imagines his characters similarly: "They'll drop, they'll let themselves drop" (376). Even Watt falls when the door to the train station waiting room, where he is locked for the night, is opened on him; the scene of the waiting room reconstructs the birth process (Büttner 136–39). What distinguishes Murphy's drop, or birth, in the *Fizzles* from these others is that it is so explicitly geographical. The world is a large sexual organ, conceiving him. For Beckett this characterization of the Earth goes far beyond the conventional "mother earth" of *Waiting for Godot* (53), and even beyond the traditional Earth-womb association discussed in Chapter 5, to produce the self-regenerating world that his vision of the life cycle requires. The Earth is female ("her," *First Love* 35), and carries the Beckett protagonist, like a pregnant woman (*From an Abandoned Work* 45). Malone relies on this image of the Earth when he says that he is born out of "the great cunt of existence" (*Malone Dies* 283). Many Beckett characters, moreover, have an active sexual relation with the Earth:

Worm may be in a "hole" in the Earth (*The Unnamable* 359), recalling the town of "Hole" in Molloy country; the names "Worm" and "Mahood" (like "manhood") suggest the male sexual organ; and the Unnamable's movement in his womblike jar seems apposite: "I move my head in and out, in and out" (331). Beckett associates the Earth with a simplified sexual image of the body as womb/vagina, a place where his characters can live and with which, as they wander up and down in it, they interact.

In one place the Unnamable speaks of "topographical and anatomical information" (412): by juxtaposing these terms Beckett brings together two related accounts of the sexual Earth, the schematic and geometrical topographies of Joyce and of Dante. Beckett's schematic journey of enlightenment, to begin with, depends on Dante's.[1] In the *Commedia* Dante's Earth is a sphere containing a double gyre, much like Yeats's picture of the universe, and Beckett's: Hell is the first gyre, narrowing in a spiral to the center of the Earth, where it becomes a second, outward-bound spiral (Freccero, "Dante's Pilgrim in a Gyre" 168). Even if the outward-bound spiral is considered only as an extension of Hell's gyre, Dante's world picture still forms a double gyre, because at the foot of the mount of Purgatory begins the stem of the rose that flowers, as its spiral widens, in Paradise (see Diagram 7.1).[2] Dante's Hell is also like a body, containing "the interior life of the fallen man" (Nohrnberg, "The *Inferno*" 98, and see Rushdie 84); by passing through the nine circles of Hell, Dante imitates a nine-month gestation and is reborn, figuratively, through the narrow passage leading out of the Earth. Dante's pilgrims, like Beckett's, move along the east-west axis in their spiraling journey, reproducing cosmic motion as the classical cosmologists from Aristotle to the Neoplatonists imagined it.[3]

Dante's Earth is sexual in another, more pictorial way. Not only does the hollow of Hell resemble a vagina, but the story of its formation is also one of sexual creation. Hell, this version maintains, was created

1. Rose represents the general critical attitude toward the Beckett-Dante relation when she rejects a parallel "architectural structure," in this case between the *Texts for Nothing* and the *Commedia*. She says that Beckett only echoes Dante ("The Lyrical Structure" 223–24).

2. This diagram of Dante's Earth relies on the more elaborate "Cross section of the Earth" given in Singleton's commentary to the *Inferno*, *The Divine Comedy* 43.

3. Freccero, "Dante's Firm Foot" 252. For Dante's mention of the *Timaeus*, see *Paradiso* iv.49; he rephrases Plato's famous X, the double cycle of the world's creation, in *Paradiso* ii.130ff. For a discussion of Dante and Plato, and of Dante's use of Boethius (a strong Neoplatonic influence), see Freccero, "Dante's Pilgrim in a Gyre" 171–75.

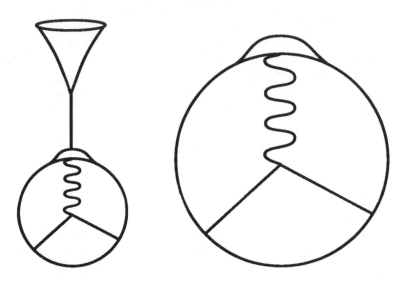

Diagram 7.1

when Satan fell—before then there was no need for it. Satan fell into the globe and so formed the cavity of Hell; the earth he displaced in his entry was forced out in the opposite direction, and created the mount of Purgatory. In Dante's vision, appropriately, Satan is stuck at the end of the narrowing cone of Hell, before the outlet that stretches behind him. His fall is like the sowing of a seed in the earth, or the figurative descent of the Word into Matter; it is redeemed by Jesus when he in turn harrows Hell, the actual Logos entering Matter. In *Malone Dies*, Jesus' descent is "the Easter week-end, spent by Jesus in hell" (280).[4] This sexual penetration or descent is a Christian vision with a good deal of Platonism in it, one that characterizes the Neoplatonist strain in Boethius and Dante and in later Hermeticists like Bruno, and which manifests "the cosmic eroticism" of emanationism and of the hermetic tradition.[5] In the Renaissance, Dante's (and Virgil's) descent into the Earth was considered likewise a reenactment of the descent of Word into Matter, a process called *descensus* (see Thompson 201–3); among the examples of *descensus* given by the twelfth-century Platonist Bernardus Silvestris (*Commentum* 30) is a literal entombment, where one is

4. For a reference in Dante to Jesus as a seed, see *Paradiso*, XXIII.120. Blake draws on this motif for Los's journey into Death, into the vortex. See Mitchell, *Blake's Composite Art* 198.
5. Wetherbee 16. For the influence of Neoplatonism on Boethius, see Klingner 38–67.

immersed in an earthen skirt: Winnie in *Happy Days* is similarly engulfed in a mound of earth, which reaches first to her waist and then to her neck, as though she were reenacting this descent as the play develops.

The association between Hell and Beckett's sexual Earth is explicit, as when Malone describes "the Rock," the Miltonic Eden of his characters' asylum, and then says: "to hell with all this fucking scenery. Where could it have risen anyway, tell me that. Underground perhaps. In a word a little Paradise for those who like their nature sloven" (*Malone Dies* 277). The name for the city of Hole in *Molloy* comes from the German *Hölle*, or hell (cp. *The Smeraldina's Billet Doux* 154). "Anatomy is a whole" (*Enough* 55). This vision of the "cunt of existence" helps explain Beckett's "fuck life" (*Mercier and Camier* 118, *Rockaby* 20);[6] the Earth, a being penetrated by pilgrimage, is a sexual machine combining Logos and Matter. Beckett's geographical self, according to the paradigmatic reading I have advanced, is the World-Mind, micro- and macrocosm, the many subsumed in the One, and this self is sexual. In the Neoplatonist solipsism of emanation and return the Mind creates the particular world, which returns to it. But what then does Beckett's sexual machine produce, if it is itself the All, both the One and the many? It produces itself.

You Rejoyce Me

Dante's topographical scheme becomes central to Beckett's world picture in part because Joyce draws heavily on it, and then bequeaths it to him. While Beckett's idealism, which shapes his quest for union, depends in part on his reading of Proust, his vision of the cycle of being—a journey that includes the return from objectivity—relies on Yeats and Joyce and on the traditions they elaborate. From Yeats, Beckett takes an impersonal, metaphysical construction of the cycle; from Joyce, he receives a lecture on the cycle's sexuality. This information comes chiefly in the "Triv and Quad" chapter of *Finnegans Wake*, where the children's lessons quickly turn into a discussion of where children come from. Joyce's lesson is especially important to Beckett because, as has been remarked, he saw himself as Joyce's pupil; while Beckett's fiction eventually moves away from the baroque ironies of

---

6. "Fuck life" has been called "the exasperated cry" that summarizes "the existential priorities of Beckett's characters" (Zurbrugg, *Beckett and Proust* 50).

Dream and *Watt*, Joyce's conceptual influence emerges more clearly as Beckett's project unfolds.[7]

There are in Beckett's work humorous echoes of Joyce's work. The name "Miss Carridge," for instance—Beckett's character in *Murphy*—replies to Joyce's "Private Carr" of *Ulysses*.[8] Similarly, the word "tundish," which is debated conspicuously in *A Portrait*, crops up in *Murphy* (87), as does "Dear old indelible Dublin" (267), Joyce's Dear Dirty Dublin of the *Wake* (Lady Morgan's celebrated phrase, originally). Beckett's Belacqua is called "an impossible person" in *Ding-Dong* (*More Pricks Than Kicks* 38), just Mulligan's words for Stephen (*Ulysses* 9). These innocent references belong with Beckett's poem "Home Olga" and the *Exagmination* essay as explicit tributes to Joyce, and Joyce does not fail to recognize them:

> I have been reciping om omominous letters and widelysigned petitions full of pieces of pottery about my monumentalness as a thingabolls. . . . Attent! Couch hear! I have becket my vonder-

7. Beckett was not Joyce's secretary, though he did perform readerly services for him. He wrote the poem, "Home Olga," where the first letters in each line spell out "JAMES JOYCE," and "Dante...Bruno.Vico..Joyce" in defense of the *Wake* (at Joyce's request), and participated in the first translation of the "Anna Livia Plurabelle" section from the *Wake* into French.

On the relation of Beckett and Joyce, see Ellmann's biography of Joyce and Bair's biography of Beckett; also Gontarski's "Samuel Beckett, James Joyce's 'Illstarred Punster'" and Gluck's *Beckett and Joyce*.

According to Shenker, Beckett claimed that while Joyce was a master of language, he decided to exploit impotence, but the authenticity of that interview has been put into question (see Gontarski, "Illstarred Punster" 32). Gontarski, however, agrees with the gist of these remarks, and Beckett has repeated to me in 1987 that he had "lost touch with his [Joyce's] later work," and that after his early work he diverged from Joyce's: "He sent me in the opposite direction, but not at first," Beckett said. See also the title of Beckett's fragment, "SUP OF FOUL DRAFT FROM WORK IN REGRESS."

David Hayman's assessment is characteristic: "I would suggest that Beckett, at first influenced by the formal tactics of the *Wake* of which he was more intimately aware than any contemporary writer, was later and ultimately engaged by Joyce's project—the self-annulling, self-perpetuating, self-propelling creation through language of the complete non-statement—the wor(l)d and the human condition as unstillable flux. . . . Beckett's progress toward the minimal evocation, the minimal and most open situation, the rhythmical statement of absence is a development which mirrors and reverses Joyce's creative evolution" (*In the Wake of the Wake* 16–17). Beckett, that is, reverses the Joycean impulse toward complexity because he understands Joyce's lesson, that the wor(l)d is self-unraveling.

8. Cp. Joyce's "Miss Forstowelsy" (*Finnegans Wake* 444.11), from the Danish *mis-forstaaelse*, or "misunderstanding." See Christiani 11. Forster's "Miss Quested" also comes to mind.

bilt hutch in sunsmidnought and at morningrise was encampassed of muchroofs. Rest and bethinkful, with licence, thanks. (*Finnegans Wake* 543.6–13)

In this late passage, full of allusions to Dublin,[9] Joyce thanks his compatriot Beckett for his poetry and begs him to rest. Joyce's "monumentalness as a thingabolls" may refer to Beckett's claim in his essay on Joyce that the *Wake* "is not *about* something; *it is that something itself*" (*Our Exagmination* 14).

Many allusions to Joyce in Beckett's work criticize the master more than they pay homage to him, and, more importantly, help define a meet place for Beckett over and against his immediate ancestor. "To relieve oneself in bed is enjoyable at the time," writes Beckett, "but soon a source of discomfort. Give me a chamber-pot, I said" (*First Love* 30). This passage alludes to Stephen's first real thought in *A Portrait*, "When you wet the bed, first it is warm then it gets cold."[10] The idea behind the allusion, however, seems less than charitable: Joyce relieves himself in bed, as a writer, just as Shem in the *Wake* wallows in his ink-excrement,[11] and while this is fun to begin with, it soon becomes tiresome. Instead Beckett asks for a chamber pot, both Joyce's simpler and unpretentiously musical collection of poems, *Chamber Music*, and Beckett's own dominant metaphor, the pot-head-room. Beckett's problem is that he wants to do what Joyce did, albeit in a very different form. Like Joyce in the *Wake*, Beckett depicts a life cycle characterized by "the beginning again" (*The Unnamable* 413); like Joyce, who uses the impossible geometrical puzzle of "rounding the square" (which Leopold Bloom had tried to solve) to represent the shape of life in the *Wake*, Beckett imagines that his beings travel "round and round this grandiose square" (*Texts for Nothing 8* 115).

9. McHugh notes that Hutchinson was Lord-Mayor of Dublin, and that "Kerwan's mushroom houses" is a line from *Ulysses* (*Annotations* 543). He gives Thomas à Becket as the reference to "becket," though that is probably not the whole story. Christiani refers "becket" to the Danish *bygget* and the Scottish *bigget*, meaning "built," but notes that Samuel Beckett is probably alluded to (209).

Our Exagmination first appeared in 1929, well before *Work in Progress* was completed. For a list of those segments of *Work in Progress* that were published early (1923–32), see Ellmann, *James Joyce* 794–96.

10. See McCarthy 7, for this and four other possible allusions to Joyce's *A Portrait*.

11. See *Finnegans Wake* i.7, especially 176–86: Shem/Joyce, the "tragic jester" (171.15), is "in his inkbattle house" (176.30–31); "chambermade music" (184.4) is mentioned among his dubious accomplishments. It is all a "wetbed confession" (188.1).

Molloy writes that Geulincx, that enemy of the will,

> left me free, on the black boat of Ulysses, to crawl towards the
> East, along the deck. That is a great measure of freedom, for him
> who has not the pioneering spirit. And from the poop, poring
> upon the wave, a sadly rejoicing slave, I follow with my eyes the
> proud and futile wake. Which, as it bears me from no fatherland
> away, bears me onward to no shipwreck. (*Molloy* 51)

Beckett, in other words, is free from artistic ambition because the author
of *Ulysses* holds him captive, because, a re-Joyce-ing slave, he must
follow the futile *Wake*. This passage from *Molloy* also echoes Plotinus,
who is in turn quoting from Homer:

> "Let us fly unto our dear fatherland!" But how shall we fly? How
> escape from here? is the question Ulysses asks himself in that
> allegory which represents him trying to escape from the magic
> sway of Circe or Calypso. (*Enneads* 1.6.8)

Beckett too cannot escape the enchantment of Joyce's *Ulysses*. But
following Joyce leaves Beckett with a Joycean "stain of remorse" (*Texts
for Nothing 12* 133). Moran formulates the problem in a passage that
refers directly to Beckett's relation to Joyce:

> And in writing these lines I know in what danger I am of
> offending him whose favour I know I should court, now more
> than ever. But I write them all the same, and with a firm hand
> weaving inexorably back and forth and devouring my page with
> the indifference of a shuttle. But some I shall relate briefly,
> because that seems to me desirable, and in order to give some
> idea of the methods of my full maturity. . . . And it would not
> surprise me if I deviated, in the pages to follow, from the true and
> exact succession of events. But I do not think even Sisyphus is
> required to scratch himself, or to groan, or to rejoice, as the
> fashion is now, always at the same appointed places. . . . to see
> yourself doing the same thing endlessly over and over again fills
> you with satisfaction. (*Molloy* 133)

Beckett posits that the writing style of his full maturity—as compared
with his early proto-Joycean flashiness—might offend Joyce, but

fancies that it is inevitable, his hand weaving "inexorably back and forth," as inevitable as Joyce's writing, where every syllable is accounted for. His back and forth weaving reinforces the idea that Beckett is a Sisyphus who can only "rejoice, as the fashion is now"—that is, follow Joyce—but is able to introduce some variety in the order with which he repeats the past. "Devouring my page" seems especially apposite to Joyce, who sustains a gastronomic relation with his work in the *Wake*—eating the wafer-Word, micturating the text—though only Beckett could devour with "indifference." Appropriately, "doing the same thing endlessly over and over again" is what Beckett's subjects do in the life cycle: Beckett follows his literary ancestor, Joyce, in the cycle of eternal returns. To reiterate this compulsion, Beckett returns to his rejoicings again and again: Molloy "rejoiced" at the thought of telling (*Molloy* 157), Malone "rejoiced" that he knew what he was to do (*Malone Dies* 224), and the Unnamable is tempted to "rejoice without a cause," but says he "can't rejoice" (*The Unnamable* 353), "rejoice" as one might "at being bereft of speech" (374), though suffering "damps the rejoicings" (376).[12] These too happy bows to the Joycean legacy emphasize the anxiety that accompanies Beckett's compulsion to follow Joyce, and his fear of the master's voice.

Beckett's anxiety is warranted, for several passages in the *Wake* seem to address him directly. Some may address him; others, like the following, did not—it was written before the two met. But Beckett's text responds to Joyce's and shows that he had found himself prefigured in the *Wake*.

> Sam knows miles bettern me how to work the miracle. And I see by his diarrhio he's dropping the stammer out of his silenced bladder since I bonded him off more as friend and as a brother . . . after he was capped out of beurlads scoel for the sin against the past participle and earned the factitation of codding chaplan and being as homely gauche as swift B.A.A. . . . . Illstarred punster, lipstering cowknucks. 'Twas the quadra sent him and Trinity too. And he can cantab as chipper as any oxon ever I mood with, a tiptoe singer! He'll prisckly soon hand tune your Erin's ear for you. (467.18–32)

This passage (from book III, chapter 2) is part of Jaunty Jaun/Shaun's harangue of his naughty brother Sam/Shem, according to some read-

---

12. For other rejoicings see *Murphy* 177, and *Malone Dies* 179.

ings (e.g., Campbell and Robinson 284–86). But "Sam"—and the entire
passage—applies to Beckett as well.[13] Here Joyce seems to review
Beckett's credentials, pretending that Beckett was thrown out of Berlitz
school ("beurlads scoel"; "Beurla" means English in Irish), the school
where Joyce was a master, but affirming that he came from Trinity and
that he could sing well. Beckett would require this defense as one of the
defenders of the faith—one of the twelve who rallied to explain the *Wake*
as Joyce told them to. Beckett was summoned "to read the road roman":
to explain Vico's presence in the *Wake*—to read the novel (Fr. *roman*) in
progress, which is the Vico Road (Vico being Italian). "I bonded him,"
admits Joyce, though as a friend, and he "earned the factitation of
codding chaplan," establishing a connection to the "factification" of the
defending title, *Our Exagmination round his Factification for Incamination of
Work in Progress*. Beckett would have recognized the promising young
author of *Murphy*, "illstarred" because of Murphy's respect for the star
chart, and a "punster" because of his pun in *Murphy*, "In the beginning
was the pun," which refers to the Peter-Rock pun upon which the
Christian Church is founded. Joyce mentions this explicitly on the
following page: "In the beginning was the gest he jousstly says" (468.5;
and see Heath 55–56). A fellow "Areesh" national (467.11), Beckett is
the new Swift; and Joyce alludes, obliquely, to Beckett's 1931 study,
Proust: "Watch the swansway. Take your tiger over it" (465.35–36).
Beckett's study of Proust, of *Swan's Way*, as Joyce puts it, sports an
epigraph from Leopardi, the "tiger" of Joyce's quip. Beckett, Joyce says
admiringly, will soon sing a fine new tune in Ireland's ear. So it would
have seemed to "Sam."

Along with Joyce's swift praise, however, comes a sterner note.
"Fond namer," he cautions (Sam/"Shem" means name), "let me never
see thee blame a kiss for shame a knee!" (468.18–19): let not Joyce see
Beckett, his disciple and student (the one who flunked his "beurlads
scoel"), betray him with a kiss, as at Gethsemane. Let not Beckett try to
imitate the master! "Can you reverse positions?" asks Joyce, with more
than a little hostility.

> I can feel you being corrupted. Recoil. I can see you sprouting
> scruples. Get back. And as he's boiling with water I'll light your

13. Gontarski quotes the passage about the "illstarred punster" in the epigraph to
"Samuel Beckett, James Joyce's 'Illstarred Punster.'"
    Note the Shem-Sam association.

pyre. Turn about, skeezy Sammy, out of metaphor, till we feel
are you still tropeful of popetry. Told you so. . . . Could you
wheedle a staveling encore out of your imitationer's jubalharp,
hey, Mr. Jinglejoys? . . . Or come on, schoolcolours, . . .
Bitrial bay holmgang or betrayal buy jury. (466.7–11, 17–18,
27–29)

Skeezy Sammy, the fake bard with his imitator's harp, could not play
such music as Joyce (though "Jinglejoys" refers simultaneously to James
Joyce himself, ridiculed by Jaunty Jaun). His poetic hopes are
doomed—is he "still tropeful [hopeful] of popetry [poetry]"? He wants
to betray Joyce with his poem about him, "Home Olga": "Bitrial bay
holmgang." Beckett's poem is a threat, the German and Danish word
Holmgang, or duel; "Bitrial" also means duel (Bonheim 135; Christiani
195, 160). Beckett is both applauded as a follower—"You rejoice me!"
(464.36)—and challenged as a mortal antagonist. Joyce's contrary attitude reflects Beckett's supplementary status: he performs a service by
elucidating Joyce's art, but his work—even if it is only a copy—also
questions the self-sufficiency of the original. He is the disturbing aid.
This double bind comes out clearly when Joyce appears to acknowledge
his debt to his debtor:

I have the highest respect of annyone in my oweand smooth way
for that intellectual debtor (Obbligado!) Mushure David R.
Crozier. And we're the closest of chems. Mark my use of you,
cog! Take notice how I yemploy, crib! Be ware as you, I foil,
coppy! (464.1–5)

Joyce respects "anyone in my owe" and promises him a smooth way in
consequence; he and Beckett are "chems" because they are chums with
the same "shem" (or name). But "cog," "crib," and "coppy" are the key
words here: Beckett is the infant writer who cribs from Joyce, the copier
or scribe whose own work is a copy of the original. Three nasty
sentences, finally, dare Beckett to see how ill Joyce uses him: "Mark my
use of you, cog!" sounds like conversation from *Waiting for Godot*.
Beckett is called upon to mark and note (these refer both to money and
to writing), to make something of his enslavement.
    It is clear that Beckett knows Joyce's charge in these pages of the
Wake: Joyce's "our tertius quiddus" (465.18) crops up in *The Unnamable*,
"a tertius gaudens, meaning myself." Here is the fuller passage:

> But perhaps I have been too hasty in opposing these two fomenters
> of fiasco. Is it not the fault of one that I cannot be the other?
> Accomplices therefore. That's the way to reason, warmly. Or is
> one to postulate a tertius gaudens, meaning myself, responsible
> for the double failure? (*The Unnamable* 338)

The Unnamable is talking about Mahood and Worm, or about any of
his self-surrogates, but the echo from the *Wake* suggests a subtext to
Beckett's narrative as well: is he, Beckett, to be responsible for Joyce
too? Perhaps they might be accounted accomplices in failure—for it is
Joyce's fault, he implies, that Beckett could not be a different writer.
Beckett ends up as Joyce's literary offspring, "Shemuel Tulliver, me
grandsourd" (464.13), created in his own image, and burdened with the
debt of his legacy; Beckett understands this charge and, though he fights it,
accepts it. More particularly, Beckett learns from Joyce about the life cycle,
which is found to be a sexual and geometrical topography like Dante's. This
image of life underwrites Beckett's vision of the cycle.

the whome of your eternal geomater

In the passage from the *Wake* (iii.2) just discussed, Jaun introduces Shem
to his "aunt Julia Bride," a relative with whom he wants Shem to have
a sexual relation. The passage draws on the theme of Tristan and Isolde
(Isolde is Tristan's aunt); the scenario also recalls Bloom's fantasy in
Ulysses of introducing Stephen to Molly:

> Be introduced to yes! This is me aunt Julia Bride, your honour,
> dying to have you languish to scandal in her bosky old dell-
> tangle. . . . She has plenty of woom in the smallclothes for the
> bothforus, nephews push! Hatch yourself well! Enjombyour-
> selves thurily! Would you wait biss she buds till you bite on her?
> Embrace her bashfully by almeans at my frank incensive. . . .
> Have a hug! Take her out of poor tuppeny luck before she goes
> off in pure treple licquidance. I'd give three shillings a pullet to
> the canon for the conjugation to shadow you kissing her from me
> liberally all over as if she was a crucifix. It's good for her bilabials,
> you understand. . . . Be offalia. Be hamlet. (465.1–32)

There is in this passage more than a hint that Joyce wants Beckett to
marry his daughter, Lucia: midway Jaun's tone changes, from offering

to share the aunt's womb (she has room for both of us, he says—for both us pashas in her Bosporus) to begging that Shem take pity on her and satisfy her sexual needs. "Have a hug," he says—have a heart. Improve her luck "before she goes off," before she goes entirely crazy: Lucia is Ophelia, the mad daughter, and Beckett is the procrastinating Hamlet, who should be more "like boyrun to sibster" (465.17), like Byron to his beloved sister. ("Licquidance" also suggests Lucia's dancing.) Lucia's deteriorating mental health was linked, for her father, with her failure to find a husband. "Then I knew Samuel Beckett who was half jewish," writes Lucia, "he became my boy friend and he was very much in love with me but I could not marry him as he was too tall for me" (from an autobiography she composed at Beach's request in 1961, now in the Sylvia Beach papers at Princeton, quoted in Fitch 291). Supposedly, Beckett's break with James Joyce, which lasted two years, followed upon his telling Lucia that he came to see her father only. In this passage, which is part of Joyce's lecture, Joyce presents the female sex, "bilabials" and all, in geometrical terms, as a "delltangle"—that is, a triangle in the shape of a delta. This geometrical sex is a "woom," a womb or room in which one can "hatch yourself." By entering this place—Beckett's wombtomb place of objectivity comes to mind—one can remake oneself, hatch as Beckett's protagonists do in his late fiction.

Here, in the context of what seems to be a discussion of Beckett's uneasy succession to Joyce, Joyce lectures his "chem" about the female sex and its role in the rebeginning of life. This lecture alludes to an earlier lesson from the second chapter of book II, "Triv and Quad." The chapter is concerned in general with the details of emanation and incarnation: the Word (or "password," 262.7) is a masculine pilgrim crossing the threshold or bridge into a feminine castle (262.2–12). In this overtly Neoplatonist account of creation,[14] the eternal and upright first number (number 1) mates the feminine void (the round 0) to form all the numbers—from 1 to 10—or "THE PARTICULAR UNIVERSE," as the marginal gloss explains (260.11–13): "Ainsoph,[3] this upright one, with that noughty besighed him zeroine" (261.23–24). The footnote explains "Ainsoph" (Heb. "endlessness" or "eternity") as "groupname for grapejuice," that is, the name we give to the spirit. The problem is

14. For references to Plato in this chapter, see 286.3 and 292.30–31. Brivic discusses the relevance of the *Timaeus* and of Yeats's *A Vision* to Joyce's chapter as "systems of the formation of the mind": "In the *Timaeus*, the orbits of Same and Other are found both in the heavens and in the soul; and Yeats's gyres are images both of history and of psychology" (108, and see also 121–22).

to figure out just where the word enters flesh: the chapter sets out "to find that pint of porter place" (260.5–6), the spiritual point (as "pint" and "porter" imply) where this portage takes place. "Porter" also means door or port, for just as Beckett's pilgrims seek the door or threshold to objectivity and discover that the place of objectivity is where the life cycle regenerates, so Joyce's students learn that the point of portage is the womb.

  The question, as Joyce puts it, is "how, in undivided reawlity draw the line somewhawre" (292.31–32). How, if life is a cycle, can we divide it, find a starting point? Like Yeats before him, Joyce draws the line at the point after the end of life and before its rebeginning, "as a poor soul is between shift and shift ere the death he has lived through becomes the life he is to die into" (293.2–5). "Between shift and shift" is a clever pun, for the place of the dead soul—the half-dead subject, in Beckettian terms—is literally between the shifts, in the female sex. Here Dolph draws for Kev the diagram of the female, with its familiar coordinates, A, L, and P, which stand for ALP or Anna Livia Plurabelle, "aunty annalive" (293.20), the mother figure of the *Wake* (see Diagram 7.2). The double deltas of ALP's sex divide the Platonic double cycle of life: the lower triangle, made of dashes, represents the earthly shadow or mirror image of the Platonic ideal, the upright triangle, and from these two Dolph can deduce the shape of life entire.[15] Joyce introduces the diagram with an allusion to Yeats ("in the lazily eye of his lapis") to show that he has the Yeatsian wheel in mind.[16] Yeats's vision of the head

---

15. This female locus or membrane dividing life's double cycle, the ear's analogue, was already heralded in the *Wake*, and explained in Platonic terms:

> Positing, as above, too males pooles, the one the pictor of the other and the omber the *Skotia* of the one, and looking wantingly around our undistributed middle between males we feel we must waistfully woent a female to focus and on this stage there pleasantly appears the cowrymaid M. whom we shall often meet below who introduces herself upon us at some precise hour which we shall again agree to call absolute zero or the babbling pumpt of platinism. (164.4–11)

The dairy maid is the "zeroine," the middle point between two poles (or "pooles"), two cycles; these cycles shadow or mirror each other: *Skotia* means "dark," and "omber" is both "shadow" and "man" (*hombre*). The liminal place between the cycles is the Platonic bubbling fount, the pump of babble or language.

16. There are several more allusions to Yeats in this context. "One recalls Byzantium. The mystery repeats itself" (294.27–28); "When I'm dreaming back like that I begins to see we're only all telescopes. Or the comeallyoum saunds. Like when I dromed I was in Dairy" (295.10–13); "All's fair on all fours, as my instructor unstrict me. . . . Gyre, O, gyre O, gyrotundo!" (295.21–24).

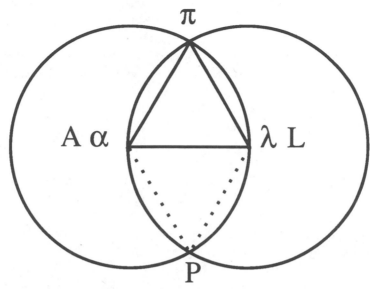

Diagram 7.2.

of the cycle comes to Joyce, and from Joyce it passes on to Beckett.

Dolph's "point of porter" suggests Beckett's place of objectivity because it divides the cycle of life, and because it is the place of the dead. It is also, as Joyce suggests, a place in the head, if one were only pure enough to perceive it:

> an you could peep inside the cerebralised saucepan of this eer illwinded goodfornobody, you would see in his house of thoughtsam (was you, that is, decontaminated enough to look discarnate) what a jetsam litterage of convolvuli of times lost or strayed . . . (292.12–16)

This formulation is much like Beckett's in *Proust* (e.g., 56–57), so it is not impossible that it comes from there (note the reference to Proust— "of times lost or strayed"). If you could look into the head, says Dolph, beyond the ear, you would see the house of thought, littered with language. To do so, however, you would have to be "decontaminated

It is curious that above the window of "Yeates & Son,"-a Dublin shop mentioned in *Ulysses* (166), there is a sign in the shape of a pair of spectacles, which looks like Joyce's double cycle. There is a photograph of the shop and its sign in Tindall 122–23.

enough to look discarnate," that is, in Beckettian terms, a pure subject rid of its material habit.[17] The repetition of "sam" in "thoughtsam" and "jetsam" also hints of Beckett. Dolph's demonstration, then, would appeal to Beckett too, much like the later demonstration already noted. But there is another reason to think that this, too, is a lesson for Beckett. After Dolph and Kev recollect the abstract idea of the female Sex, they lift ALP's hem and, lighting a match, look at the thing itself, "her safety vulve, first of all usquiluteral threeingles" (297.7–27). This is how Dolph/Shem introduces the idea to his slower brother Kev/Shaun:

> Now, *aqua in buccat*. I'll make you to see figuratleavely the whome of your eternal geomater. (296.30–297.1)

Under the figurative fig leaf waits home, the mother's womb: like water into a bucket, Joyce will pour this ancestral knowledge into his vassal, Beckett.

There are several reasons for accepting the connection between Joyce and Beckett that this passage evokes. First, consider the passage itself. The word "geomater" means something like "the geometrical design of the material world-mother": the womb-mother is the earth, a geographical sphere. Joyce refers to Plato's *Timaeus* to secure the Neoplatonic connection: "there's tew tricklesome poinds where our twain of doubling bicirculars," explains Dolph, "mating approxemetely in their suite poi and poi, dunloop into eath the ocher. Lucihere" (295.30–33). Plato's twin strands or loops meet (and mate) in their suite by and by (and π and π, since they are both circles); Wordsworth's "A Slumber Did My Spirit Seal," where the poet's spirit and his beloved Lucy merge into a cosmic vision of the Earth, is certainly called for—"Lucihere," Joyce announces—and Joyce's transposition of "eath the ocher" makes the point nicely. When Beckett expounds in *Malone Dies* on "the looping of the loop," he recalls Joyce's reference to the Platonic loop in this passage.

Another reason one should think that Beckett took Dolph's words to heart is his interest in that bucket. Already in the *Exagmination* essay he quotes from Joyce's *A Portrait*, where "the soul is very like a bucketful of water" (7); he alludes to the children's games chapter on the same page of the essay, and quotes on page 8 from what is now page 282 of

---

17. Of course, Beckett's discussion of the *empêchements* came later, with the van Velde essays, but the idea of the pure, uninhibited subject is explicit in *Proust* (1931).

the *Wake*. In the train station scene in *Watt*, for instance, Mr. Gorman ("in the attitude of a child") suggests that Watt be doused with a bucket, in order to raise him (239). Mr. Nolan suggests the hose, but Gorman insists on the bucket. Nolan (a code name for Bruno of Nola in the *Wake*, as Beckett explains in his essay, page 17) raises the question of which bucket is alluded to:

> What bucket? said Mr. Nolan.
> Bloody well you know what bucket!

All in all the overly conspicuous word "bucket" appears ten times in the passage in *Watt*. What is more, its "handle" is mentioned twice (240), just as Joyce mentions "omething with a handel to it" (*FW* 295.28–29) before his reference to Plato's "dunloop" and the admonition to *buccat*. Another bucket appears in *Malone Dies*:

> For it is not as if he [Macmann] possessed the means of accumulating, in a single day, enough food to keep him alive for three weeks or a month, and what is a month compared to the whole of second childishness, a drop in a bucket. (233)

Together with two references to Joyce—"in a single day," which is the time span of *Ulysses*, and "second childishness," which recalls the *Wake* chapter under discussion—the reader finds both a bucket and Beckett's device of the drop. The connection between birth (the "drop") and the female "whome" is a natural one—like a drop in a bucket.[18]

Beckett's Bicycle

The upshot of Joyce's text is something like this, that Beckett, as Joyce's pupil and follower, should learn from him the geometrical nature of the life cycle and its sexual origin and end. See here, says Joyce: Dante, Wordsworth, and Yeats show that the earth combines geometry and sex, Platonic Form and material substance.[19] Language effects this

18. Mrs. Lambert also deals with a bucket, whose chain and its links (emblems of the chain of generation) are also mentioned (*Malone Dies* 217); in *Murphy* life is a well with two buckets.
19. Joyce already discusses Dante in connection with this geometrical vision of the cycle. The "Oxen of the Sun" chapter in *Ulysses* is about the maturation of the subject in time, which is exemplified in the development of English prose style, the development

combination: it is embedded in the landscape, as HCE's "normative letters"[20] demonstrate, "Howth Castle and Environs." Beckett, in turn, the careful reader, observes that Joyce's drop in the bucket—his lesson— shows the drop or birth of the subject falling into matter, the *descensus* that creates and re-creates the sexual earth, returning the subject to the life cycle. The landscape, he agrees in a telling phrase, is "arses, cunts, and environs" (*The Calmative* 41).[21] The earth is a sexual machine, a "great cunt of existence" (*Malone Dies* 283) that participates in the generative cycle.

Joyce elaborates another idea with his figure of the metaphysical double cycle and its sexual motor. This figure is a "zeroic couplet," the symbol of eternity, "∞" (284.10,11), which he has already used in his scheme of *Ulysses* to represent the hour of Molly's monologue.[22] It is an eternal bi-cycle, a Viconian bicycle, which HCE rides, "cycling (pist!) and recycling (past!)" (*FW* 99.5–6). So in *Finnegans Wake* the Ondt (from Joyce's parable of the Ondt and the Gracehoper) feels exhausted after his labors: "Had he twicycled the sees of the deed and trestraversed their revermer? Was he come to hevre with his engiles or gone to hull with the poop?" (416.30–32). Had he crossed Lethe (the "revermer" of the "deed") in his journey, and is he now at harbor with the angels (the English), or is he in hell with the pope (and with the French at LeHavre)? The Duchess of York, it is reported elsewhere, cycled around Phoenix

---

of the logos in Britain. Bloom sees the red triangle of a Bass beer label, and his mind wonders how "the soul is wafted over regions of cycles of cycles of generations that have lived" (414). He thinks of "metempsychosis" and of "the everlasting bride, harbinger of the daystar, the bride, ever virgin"—his Beatrice—whose veil "floats about her starborn flesh . . . writhing in the skies a mysterious writing till after a myriad metamorphoses of symbol, it blazes, Alpha, a ruby and triangles sign upon the forehead of Taurus" (414). Mulligan appropriately suggests that in contemplating this sexual triangle Bloom is away in a vision as one unborn (416). The connection with Dante is explicit in "Eumaeus," where Stephen—like Bloom "staring and rambling on to himself or some unknown listener somewhere"—speaks of "the impetuosity of Dante and the isosceles triangle" (637). (Bloom's next words, "All are washed in the blood of the sun," seal the connection to the passage from "Oxen.")

For Dante's "gyres," see *Paradiso*, XXVI.120, XXVII, and XXVIII.139.

20. Beckett's phrase from his essay on Joyce.

21. Mahaffey shows that Joyce's figure in the tenth chapter of the *Wake* represents both the front and the rear. She goes on to say that "the diagram is double in yet another way: it represents a 'first cause' that is both material and rational" (38).

22. In the scheme Joyce sent to Carlo Linati in 1920. See Ellmann, *Ulysses on the Liffey*, appendix.

Since the last episode of *Ulysses* originally had eight sentences, it is especially appropriate that Beckett uses the 8 as the alternate figure of eternity.

Park (461.9–10), presumably on her 1897 visit to Dublin, and St. Patrick arrived in Ireland in 432 on a cycle (462.33–35). In "Triv and Quad" Joyce summons the trope:

> Imagine the twelve deaferended dumbbawls of the whowl abovebeugled to be the contonuation through regeneration of the urutteration of the word in pregross. It follows that, if the two antesedents be bissyclitties and the three comeseekwenchers trundletrikes, then, Aysha Lalipat behidden on the footplate . . . (tandem year at lasted length!) . . . (284.18–27)

The twelve authors of *Our Exagmination round his Factification for Incamination of Work in Progress* (with Beckett being the first) carry on his own project to regenerate artistic expression. They proclaim (with bugles, maybe) the progress of the word through its bicyclical course. Joyce then invokes a tandem bicycle, two circles and a female triangle, which Earwigger ("Big Whiggler") rides with his wife Anna Livia pedaling behind him. This is Vico's happy civic order (McHugh)—"this *habby cyclic erdor*" (285.1–2, italics added)—the historical cycle that HCE helps turn.

HCE's and ALP's bicycle is an amusing literalization, but Beckett, who is again addressed here as one of the twelve, sees it as a serious reading of Joyce's key figure of the life cycle. Beckett's protagonists, like Joyce's, move the chain of being and propel the bicycle. Beckett's bicycles have received some attention, especially because Kenner, noting their many appearances in Beckett's fiction (*Samuel Beckett* 117–18), sees in the bicycle and its rider an image of humanity as Descartes invented it, half machine, half spirit.[23] Beckett's bicycle brings together his several concerns. The bicycle wheels represent the recurring cycle of life, a double cycle after Plato's and Joyce's, a literalization of the Yeatsian double gyre, only more locomotive. The triangular center of the machine represents the female sex and "woom," the place of regeneration at the head of the cycle. And the bicycle chain is the Neoplatonic chain of generation that turns the cosmological machine, propelled by the traveling subject.

---

23. But the image of bicycle and rider adds something to the rider, instead of defining the rider. Kenner does not attribute the term to Beckett, but hints to "the skeptical reader" that Beckett confirmed his ideas. See *Samuel Beckett: A Critical Study* 124 n. 1 and 125 n. 2. Beckett told me that it was not his idea.

Molloy connects his bicycle with the idea of generation: "you were green, like so many of your generation" (16). Even the color suggests growth. It is not just a means of transportation but also a vehicle, in the magical sense of the word, for some determining power (like Lady Fortuna, who turns the wheel of generation). Molloy suspects it "to be the vehicle of some malignant agency and perhaps the cause of my recent misfortunes" (59). The narrator of *Texts for Nothing 12*, having discussed in explicit terms the one and the many, and having invoked with "pregnant words" the cycle of life that leads to God or the One (134), suggests the means by which this generation, or degeneration, runs its course: "confess you're not the man you were, you'll end up riding a bicycle" (134–35). Moran too, when he thinks of death, regeneration, birth, and beginning, thinks of a bicycle (140); when he sends his son to get a bicycle he specifies one with a strong carrier, which would serve for them both, much as the Earwigger bicycle serves for both partners. He instructs his son to get this bicycle from the town of Hole—"there are millions of bicycles in Hole!" (141)—that sexual node of the Molloy country. The bicycle, as the magical figure and agent of regeneration, comes from the sex or "hole," recapturing Joyce's equation exactly.

Beckett's bicycle captures Joyce's clever literalization of the cycle from the *Wake*, makes the equation between the bicycle and the female sex, and combines these with Beckett's interest in the generative power of the head of the cycle, the place between the shifts. So when Murphy looks into Endon's eyes—and through them into the formal, chaotic place of objectivity—he sees them as a bicycle. Endon's iris is diminished,

> so like a ballrace between the black and white that these could have started to rotate in opposite directions, or better still the same direction, without causing Murphy the least surprise. (249)

Endon's pupil and white, the Yeatsian poles, are linked by the "spawn-like" iris (249), and so each eye is divided into three parts, dark, light, and neither. Endon's bicycle-eyes are the first instance in Beckett of Plato's circles of Same and Different, recalled more explicitly by the rotating zones of *The Lost Ones*, which Endon's eyes resemble. The circles of Same and Different rotate in opposite directions, and one inside the other, each like an eye, while bicycle wheels rotate in the same direction—hence the narrator's inquiry on this head. How then are the two cycles linked, in this literalization of Beckett's metaphysical system? I have suggested Beckett's chain of being as the obvious answer, and in *Malone Dies* Beckett calls attention to it as the particular power that turns the wheel. It is Easter weekend, when Jesus harrowed hell, and Lemuel, the asylum keeper of Beckett's pilgrims, collects "excursion soups" for the inmates in handled buckets (280). The scene (discussed in Chapter 4) reverses Dante's pilgrimage, from the Miltonic heaven of the asylum to Charon's boat, as the pilgrims ride a "waggonette" through the gates: "A sudden descent, long and steep, sent them plunging towards the sea" (284). (There is water too at the core of Dante's hell, only it is frozen.) Guiding the inmates in their descent is Beckett's Beatrice, or Fortuna: Lady Pedal. "But what matter about Lady Pedal?" asks the narrator dismissively (281). A good deal, certainly, because the pedal turns the wheel of Beckett's subjects, moving, link by link, the chain of Beckett's bicycle.

The Way

In 1981 Beckett composed a one-page fiction provisionally entitled *The Way*.[24] It is in two parts, titled "8" and "∞," respectively; each describes the way or course of travel represented by its title figure: the first, "up from foot to top and thence down another way"; the second, "forth and back across a barren same winding one-way way." This is the bi-cyclical course of Beckett's subject as it wanders up and down, and to and fro in the earth, the way that Beckett's fiction had followed so untiringly.

The first part of *The Way*, "8," begins by describing the course of wandering, "from foot to top." Beckett's fiction too follows the subject's pilgrimage upward, beginning not with emanation but with the return. The top is a particular place, according to "8," distinguished by "thence" in the phrase, "from foot to top and thence on down." It is not like the other points along the way, as the smooth and continuous figure eight might suggest, but, as in Yeats, a special end point from which one returns. The return, Beckett specifies more than once, is "on," a going forward and not a retracing, a one-way journey: "On back down." The chain of being will not reverse direction. As in Yeats's vision, where the subject may linger at Phases 1 and 15 before it continues its recycling, there is freedom at the top and at the foot "to

24. The autograph manuscript, in seven pages (seven consecutive versions), is at Austin, Texas. It is reproduced in Lake, entries 433 and 434, pp. 171–74.

pause or not." "The ways," Beckett writes, referring to the way up and
the way down, "crossed midway more or less": so does the Yeatsian
double gyre, and Beckett's pilgrimage too, with its chiasmic turn,
described as the "equinox" in *Krapp's Last Tape*. That Beckett uses the
past tense ("crossed") to describe what would seem to be an eternal
process suggests that *The Way* is about his own artistic way as much as
it is about the metaphysical journey described in his work. Beckett
reinforces the work's conceptual allusions to the Yeatsian system with
more direct references to Yeats. "Briefly once at the extremes the will set
free," he says; in Yeats's system the "Will," the ego or self, marks one's
position on the wheel, and it is unbound at the poles. Beckett refers to
the midpoint of the ways as "crossways," the title of one of Yeats's
books of poetry (1895). He says that "thorns hemmed the way," a
cryptic phrase unprecedented in the Beckett canon, alluding to Yeats's
Rose, his early symbol of the winding stair of life, the Dantean image.

The second part of *The Way*, "∞," begins: "Forth and back across a
barren same winding one-way way." The way forth and back is
apparently the "same" as the way up and down, though the addition of
"winding" implies that the road itself gyrates. This version stresses the
journey's dominant east-west axis and its attendant geographical and
cosmic aspect: "Low in the west or east the sun standstill." There is
"bedrock underfoot," to underscore the generative ("bed") quality of
the earth. The "ends" of the journey, however, where one may pause,
are "groundless," outside the graphical world; hence the journey's limit
or boundary in space, "unending void": "Through emptiness the beaten
ways as fixed as if enclosed." While the "beaten ways" imply an endless
stream of pilgrims, there are no signs of former travelers' "remains"
along the way, which is in turn "a sign that none before." This cannot
mean that no other subject has traveled the cycle before—it is the
unceasing shuffle of pilgrims, the eternal chain of being, that has
smoothed the path. Instead Beckett proclaims here the uniqueness of his
own vision, that he is the first to travel this artistic path, a way free of
the ruins of literary ancestors. This is emphasized by the phrase that ends
both "8" and "∞": "No one ever before so - [.]" It is a bold claim,
fiercely advanced by Beckett's unprecedented, unfailingly spare, abstract, exacting style. An indisputable claim, then, and Beckett's direct
echoes of Yeats acknowledge its limitations. These echoes also show
that Beckett intends his vision to embrace and use his tradition, to be
unique not by virtue of its originality, but because it is clearsighted and
inclusive, because it balances all, and brings all to mind. For it is

certainly true that Yeats did not have *this* vision—that no one, not Joyce, not Yeats, not Wordsworth, Vico, Dante, or Plato, had ever traveled this way. For only Beckett had said yes to them all.

The Call

In *Proust* Beckett speaks of the enchantment of the object (11), the isolated object celebrated in the van Velde essays: it is the "Idea" imprisoned in matter (59), "the Model, the Idea, the Thing in itself" (69). The object appeals to us from behind its layers of *empêchements*, and we go out to it, then seek it within us. As his project unfolds and develops Beckett recasts this object or Idea—and the union with it that is the goal of the artistic process as he presents it—in metaphysical terms; it is the Platonic unity, the objectivity attainable at the head of the Yeatsian wheel, at the "pint of porter" of the Joycean doubloon. Still he pursues the idea that the object too participates in the quest for unity, that the pilgrim's desire meets in the sepulcher a corresponding need. For in the end the subject participates in the One, the wanderer its own refuge, always "a radius of one from home" (*Company* 60), and if it hears a call then, as Kafka understood, it must come from itself.

Sam says that the weather called to him and to Watt.

> It is so easy to accept, so easy to refuse, when the call is heard, so easy, so easy. But to us, in our windowlessness, in our bloodheat, in our hush, to us who could not hear the wind, nor see the sun, what call could come, from the kind of weather we liked, but a call so faint as to mock acceptance, mock refusal? . . . No, but what is to be wondered at is this, that to us both, disposed to yield, each in his separate soundless unlit warmth, the call should come, and coax us out, as often as it did, as sometimes it did, into the little garden. (*Watt* 152)

The passage is endearing, what with Beckett's gentle humor and his reference to Augustine's call and conversion in the garden (*Confessions* 111). Sam seems to be addressing Augustine as much as Watt, and all three seem to be "disposed to yield." Sam is drawn to a "hole" in the fence made, he speculates, by the weather (*Watt* 160). The call, to complete the syllogism, may come from the threshold, from the sexual point of portage. In the Gnostic version of Neoplatonism, a tradition to which Augustine belongs, the heavenly father calls his child, the emanated particular, to return to him (Sinnige 79). Beckett's subjects hear this call, which helps explain why *The Unnamable* ends by echoing the conclusion of Augustine's confession. But the call of the One is also an artistic calling, the call of the Idea to its all-too-romantic artist, transmuted though it may be in the smithy of metaphysical speculation and classical tradition. If Beckett's characters hear it, so does Beckett; and where they follow he has gone before.

> And if I went on listening to that far whisper, silent long since and which I still hear, I would learn still more. . . . But I will listen no longer, for the time being, to that far whisper, for I do not like it, I fear it. But it is not a sound like the other sounds, that you listen to, when you choose . . . no, but it is a sound which begins to rustle in your head, without your knowing how, or why. It's with your head you hear it. (*Molloy* 40)

A contrary whisper calls Molloy with a vision of unity, the voice of a world collapsing endlessly (40), silent but audible, long gone but present, far off but in his head. "*Whisper in my heart,*" says Augustine (24, 181, cp. 293), quoting *Psalms*. Beckett hears this voice, the voice of his tradition, and his own. So may he be heard. They rustle in his head, all the dead voices, like leaves. Like sand. Like leaves.[25]

> They rustle.
> They murmur.
> They rustle.

They make a noise like wings.

---

25. *Waiting for Godot* 40.

Works Cited

Works by Samuel Beckett

Act without Words II. 1960. *The Collected Shorter Plays*, 47–51.

Afar a bird. Trans. Samuel Beckett. *Fizzles*, 23–27.

All Strange Away. 1976. *Rockaby and Other Short Pieces*, 37–65.

All That Fall. *The Collected Shorter Plays*, 9–39.

Assumption. transition 16–17, 1929. *transition workshop*, ed. Eugene Jolas, 41–44. New York: Vanguard Press, 1949.

A Wet Night. *More Pricks Than Kicks*, 47–84.

Bing. Paris: Minuit, 1966.

...but the clouds.... The Collected Shorter Plays, 255–62.

The Calmative. Trans. Samuel Beckett. *Stories and Texts for Nothing*, 27–46.

Catastrophe. *Ohio Impromptu, Catastrophe, and What Where: Three Plays*.

Closed place. Trans. Samuel Beckett. *Fizzles*, 35–39.

Collected Poems in English and French. New York: Grove, 1977.

The Collected Shorter Plays. Grove, 1984.

Company. Grove, 1980.

"Dante...Bruno.Vico..Joyce." *Our Exagmination round his Factification for Incamination of Work in Progress*, 1929. Reprint. *James Joyce/ "Finnegans Wake": A Symposium*, 3–22. New York: New Directions, 1972.

"Dieppe," *Collected Poems*, 48–49.

Ding-Dong. *More Pricks Than Kicks*, 36–46.

Disjecta: Miscellaneous Writings and a Dramatic Fragment. Ed. Ruby Cohn. Grove, 1984.

Dream of Fair to Middling Women. [Transcript, 1932.] Reading University Library, MS 1227/7/16/8.

Eh Joe. *The Collected Shorter Plays*, 199–207.

Éleuthéria. [1947.] Reading University Archive, MS 1227/7/4/1.

En attendant Godot. Minuit, 1952.

En attendant Godot. Ed. Germaine Brée and Eric Schoenfield. New York: Macmillan Modern French Literature Series, 1963.

The End. Trans. Richard Seaver and Samuel Beckett. *Stories and Texts for Nothing*, 47–72.

Endgame. Grove, 1958.

Enough. *First Love and Other Shorts*, 51–60.

The Expelled. Trans. Richard Seaver and Samuel Beckett. *Stories and Texts for Nothing*, 9–25.

Film, A Film Script. *The Collected Shorter Plays*, 161–74.

Fingal. *More Pricks*, 23–35.

First Love. *First Love and Other Shorts*, 9–36. Grove, 1974.

Fizzles. Grove, 1976.

Footfalls. *The Collected Shorter Plays*, 237–43.

For to end yet again. Trans. Samuel Beckett. *Fizzles*, 53–61.

From an Abandoned Work. *First Love and Other Shorts*, 37–49.

Ghost Trio. *The Collected Shorter Plays*, 245–54.

Happy Days. Grove, 1961.

He is barehead. Trans. Samuel Beckett. *Fizzles*, 5–15.

"Home Olga." 1934. *Collected Poems*.

Horn came always. Trans. Samuel Beckett. *Fizzles*, 17–22.

How It Is. Grove, 1964.

I gave up before birth. Trans. Samuel Beckett. *Fizzles*, 29–33.

Ill Seen Ill Said. Grove, 1964.

Imagination Dead Imagine. 1966. *First Love and Other Shorts*, 61–66.

"Intercessions by Denis Devlin." *Disjecta*, 91–94.

Krapp's Last Tape and Other Dramatic Pieces. Grove, 1958.

"La peinture des van Velde ou le Monde et le Pantalon." *Disjecta*, 118–32.

Le Dépeupleur. Minuit, 1970.

Lessness. *New Statesman*, 1 May 1970, 632.

The Lost Ones. Trans. Samuel Beckett. Grove, 1972.

Love and Lethe. *More Pricks*, 85–100.

"Malacoda." *Collected Poems*, 26.

Malone Dies. Trans. Samuel Beckett. *Three Novels*. Grove, 1965.

Mercier and Camier. Trans. Samuel Beckett. Grove, 1970.

Molloy. Trans. Patrick Bowles and Samuel Beckett. *Three Novels*. Grove, 1965.

More Pricks Than Kicks. Grove, 1972.

Murphy. Grove, 1957.

Neither. *As the Story Was Told: Uncollected and Late Prose*. London: John Calder, 1990.

Not I. *First Love and Other Shorts*, 73–87.

Ohio Impromptu, Catastrophe, and What Where: Three Plays. Grove, 1984.

Old earth. Trans. Samuel Beckett. *Fizzles*, 41–44.

"On Murphy." *Disjecta*, 113.

"On Way to *Comment c'est*." Reading University Library, No. Acc 1655.

"Peintres de l'empêchement." *Disjecta*, 133–37.

Ping. *First Love and Other Shorts*, 67–72.

Play. *The Collected Shorter Plays*, 145–60.

Poems in English. London: Calder and Boyars, 1961.

"Preliminary to *Textes pour rien*." Reading University Library, No. Acc 1656.

Premier Amour. Minuit, 1970.

Proust. Grove, 1957.

Rockaby and Other Short Pieces. Grove, 1981.

The Smeraldina's Billet Doux. *More Pricks*, 152–57.

Still. *Fizzles*, 45–51.

Stirrings Still. Reading University Library, Recent Acquisitions, No. 40.
Stories and Texts for Nothing. Grove, 1967.
SUP OF FOUL DRAFT FROM WORK IN REGRESS. Houghton Library, Harvard University, MS Thr 70.2(1).
Three Dialogues. *Disjecta*, 138–45.
The Unnamable. Trans. Samuel Beckett. *Three Novels*. Grove, 1965.
Waiting for Godot. Trans. Samuel Beckett. Grove, 1954.
Walking Out. *More Pricks Than Kicks*, 101–13.
Watt. Grove, 1953.
Watt. Minuit, 1968.
The Way. *No Symbols Where None Intended: A Catalogue of Books, Manuscripts, and Other Material Relating to Samuel Beckett in the Collections of the Humanities Research Center*, ed. Carlton Lake, 173. Austin, Tex.: Humanities Research Center, University of Texas, 1984.
What a Misfortune. *More Pricks*, 114–51.
What Where. *Ohio Impromptu, Catastrophe, and What Where: Three Plays*, 37–59.
Worstward Ho. Grove, 1983.

Related Beckett Materials Cited

Letter to Georges Duthuit, 3 September 1949. Reading University Library, Recent Acquisitions.
Notebook. [1987.] Reading University Library, Recent Acquisitions, Nos. 33 and 34.
Proust, Marcel. *A la recherche du temps perdu*. 15 vols. [Originally 16 vols.] Paris: Gallimard, Editions de la Nouvelle revue française, 1925–29. Beckett's copy, with holograph annotations. Reading University Library.

General Works

Abbott, H. Porter. *The Fiction of Samuel Beckett: Form and Effect*. Berkeley and Los Angeles: University of California Press, 1973.
Abrams, M. H. *Natural Supernaturalism: Tradition and Revolution in Romantic Literature*. New York: W. W. Norton, 1971.
———. "Structure and Style in the Greater Romantic Lyric." *Romanticism and Consciousness*, ed. Harold Bloom, 201–29. New York: W. W. Norton, 1970.
Acheson, James. "Murphy's Metaphysics." *Journal of Beckett Studies*, no. 5 (Autumn 1979).
Acheson, James, and Kateryna Arthur, eds. *Beckett's Later Fiction and Drama: Texts for Company*. New York: St. Martin's Press, 1987.
Albright, Daniel. *Representation and the Imagination*. Chicago: University of Chicago Press, 1977.
Andreasen, Esben. "Form and Philosophy in Samuel Beckett." *Extracta* 2 (1969): 11–16.
Armstrong, Gordon S. *Samuel Beckett, W. B. Yeats, and Jack Yeats*. Lewisburg, Pa.: Bucknell University Press, 1990.

Attridge, Derek. *Peculiar Language: Literature as Difference from the Renaissance to James Joyce.* Ithaca, N.Y.: Cornell University Press, 1988.

Auden, W. H. *Collected Poems.* Ed. Edward Mendelson. New York: Random House, 1976.

Augustine. *Confessions.* Trans. R. S. Pine-Coffin. New York: Penguin, 1961.

Bair, Deirdre. *Samuel Beckett: A Biography.* New York: Harcourt Brace Jovanovich, 1978.

Barnard, G. C. *Samuel Beckett: A New Approach.* New York: Dodd, Mead & Co., 1970.

Barnes, Djuna. *Nightwood.* 1936. New York: New Directions, 1946.

Bate, Walter Jackson. *Samuel Johnson.* Harcourt Brace Jovanovich, 1977.

Baudrillard, Jean. *Simulations.* New York: Semiotext(e), 1983.

Beckett, Samuel, Georges Duthuit, and Jacques Putman. *Bram van Velde.* New York: Grove, 1960.

Beckett, Samuel, et al. *James Joyce/ "Finnegans Wake": A Symposium.* [*Our Exagmination*] New York: New Directions, 1972.

Bercovitch, Sacvan. *The American Jeremiad.* Madison: University of Wisconsin Press, 1978.

The Holy Bible. Authorized King James Version. New York: Oxford University Press, 1971.

The Holy Bible. Old and New Testaments. Oxford, 1895.

Bishop, John. *Joyce's Book of the Dark, "Finnegans Wake."* Madison: University of Wisconsin Press, 1986.

Blake, William. *The Complete Poetry and Prose of William Blake.* Ed. David Erdman. New York: Anchor Books, 1982.

Bloom, Harold. "The Internalization of Quest-Romance." *Romanticism and Consciousness*, ed. Harold Bloom. New York: W. W. Norton, 1970.

———. *Yeats.* New York: Oxford University Press, 1970.

Boethius, Anicius Manlius Severinus. *The Consolation of Philosophy.* Trans. Richard Green. New York: Bobbs-Merrill, 1962.

Bonheim, Helmut. *A Lexicon of the German in "Finnegans Wake."* Berkeley and Los Angeles: University of California Press, 1967.

Booth, Wayne C. *A Rhetoric of Irony.* Chicago: University of Chicago Press, 1974.

Brater, Enoch. *Beyond Minimalism: Beckett's Late Style in the Theater.* New York: Oxford University Press, 1987.

———. "Voyelles, Cromlechs, and the Special (W)rites of *Worstward Ho.*" *Beckett's Later Fiction and Drama*, ed. James Acheson and Kateryna Arthur. New York: St. Martin's Press, 1987.

Breuer, Horst. *Samuel Beckett: Lernpsychologie und liebliche Determination.* Munich: Wilhelm Fintz, 1972.

Brienza, Susan D. *Samuel Beckett's New Worlds: Styles in Metafiction.* Norman: University of Oklahoma Press, 1987.

Brivic, Sheldon. *Joyce the Creator.* Madison: University of Wisconsin Press, 1985.

Brontë, Charlotte. *Villette.* 1853. New York: Penguin, 1979.

Bunyan, John. *The Pilgrim's Progress.* New York: Penguin, 1965.

Burton, Robert. *The Anatomy of Melancholy: What it is, with all the kinds, causes, symptomes, prognostickes and severall cures of it.* 1932. Ed. Holbrook Jackson. Reprint. New York: Vintage, 1977.

Büttner, Gottfried. *Samuel Beckett's Novel Watt.* Trans. Joseph Dolan. Philadelphia: University of Pennsylvania Press, 1984.

Calder, John. "Embarrassing Mr Beckett." *As No Other Dare Fail,* ed. John Calder, 11–14. London: Riverrun Press, 1986.

Cameron, Sharon. *Lyric Time: Dickinson and the Limits of Genre.* Baltimore: Johns Hopkins University Press, 1979.

Campanella, Tommaso. *The City of the Sun: A Poetical Dialogue.* Trans. Daniel J. Donno. Berkeley and Los Angeles: University of California Press, 1981.

Campbell, Joseph, and Henry Morton Robinson. *A Skeleton Key to "Finnegans Wake."* New York: Penguin, 1944.

Carroll, Lewis. *Through the Looking-Glass and What Alice Found There.* New York: Random House, 1946.

Céline, Louis-Ferdinand. *Journey to the End of Night.* Trans. Ralph Manheim. New York: New Directions, 1983.

Chambers, Ross. "Beckett, homme des situations limites." *Cahiers de la Compagnie Renaud Barrault,* no. 44 (1963): 37–62.

Champigny, Robert. "Adventures of the First Person." *Samuel Beckett Now,* ed. Melvin J. Friedman, 119–28. Chicago: University of Chicago Press, 1970.

Christiani, Dounia Bunis. *Scandinavian Elements of "Finnegans Wake."* Evanston, Ill.: Northwestern University Press, 1965.

Coe, Richard N. *Samuel Beckett.* London: Oliver and Boyd, 1964.

Cohn, Ruby. *From Desire to Godot: Pocket Theater of Postwar Paris.* Berkeley and Los Angeles: University of California Press, 1987.

———. *Samuel Beckett: The Comic Gamut.* New Brunswick, N.J.: Rutgers University Press, 1962.

———. "Samuel Beckett, Self-translator." *PMLA* 76, no. 5 (December 1961): 613–21.

Coleridge, Samuel Taylor. *Collected Works.* Bollingen Series. Princeton, N.J.: Princeton University Press, 1972.

Colum, Mary, and Padraic Colum. *Our Friend James Joyce.* New York: Doubleday, 1958.

Connor, Steven. *Samuel Beckett: Repetition, Theory, and Text.* Oxford: Basil Blackwell, 1988.

Cortázar, Julio. *Hopscotch.* 1963. Trans. Gregory Rabassa. New York: Avon, 1966.

———. *62: A Model Kit.* 1968. Trans. Gregory Rabassa. New York: Avon, 1972.

Cunningham, Valentine. *British Writers of the Thirties.* New York: Oxford University Press, 1988.

Dante. *The Divine Comedy.* 3 vols. Trans. Charles S. Singleton. Princeton, N.J.: Princeton University Press, 1970.

de Man, Paul. *Allegories of Reading: Figural Language in Rousseau, Nietzsche, Rilke, and Proust.* New Haven, Conn.: Yale University Press, 1979.

———. "Intentional Structure of the Romantic Image." *Romanticism and Consciousness,* ed. Harold Bloom. 65–77. New York: W. W. Norton, 1970.

Derrida, Jacques. *Dissemination.* Trans. Barbara Johnson. Chicago: University of Chicago Press, 1981.

———. "White Mythology: Metaphor in the Text of Philosophy." Trans. F.C.T. Moore. *New Literary History* 6 (1974): 5–74.

Descartes, René. *The Philosophical Works of Descartes.* Trans. Elizabeth Haldane and G.R.T. Ross. 2 vols. 1911. Reprint. Cambridge: Cambridge University Press, 1970.

Dickinson, Emily. *The Poems.* 3 vols. Ed. Thomas H. Johnson. Cambridge: Harvard University Press, 1955.

Dobrez, L.A.C. *The Existential and Its Exits: Literary and Philosophical Perspectives on the Works of Beckett, Ionesco, Genet, and Pinter.* New York: St. Martin's Press, 1986.

Driver, Tom. "Beckett by the Madeleine." *Columbia University Forum* 4 (Summer 1961): 21–25.

Duthuit, Georges. *Derrière le miroir.* February 1952.

Eliade, Mircea. *Myths, Dreams, and Mysteries.* 1957. Trans. Philip Mairet. New York: Harper & Row, 1960.

Eliot, T. S. *The Complete Poems and Plays, 1909–1950.* New York: Harcourt, Brace and Company, 1952.

Ellmann, Richard. *Golden Codgers: Biographical Speculations.* New York: Oxford University Press, 1973.

―――. *James Joyce.* New York: Oxford University Press, 1959; rev. ed., 1982.

―――. *Ulysses on the Liffey.* New York: Oxford University Press, 1972.

―――. "W. B. Yeats's Second Puberty." Washington, D.C.: Library of Congress, 1985.

Esslin, Martin. "Samuel Beckett—Infinity, Eternity." *Beckett at Eighty/ Beckett in Context,* ed. Enoch Brater. New York: Oxford University Press, 1986.

―――. *The Theatre of the Absurd.* New York: Penguin, 1961.

Federman, Raymond. *Journey to Chaos: Samuel Beckett's Early Fiction.* Berkeley and Los Angeles: University of California Press, 1965.

Finneran, Richard J. *Editing Yeats's Poems.* London: Macmillan, 1983.

Fish, Stanley. *Self-consuming Artifacts.* Berkeley and Los Angeles: University of California Press, 1972.

Fitch, Noel Riley. *Sylvia Beach and the Lost Generation: A History of Literary Paris in the Twenties and Thirties.* New York: W. W. Norton, 1983.

Flaubert, Gustave. *Bouvard and Pécuchet.* Trans. A. J. Krailsheimer. New York: Penguin, 1976.

Fletcher, John. *The Novels of Samuel Beckett.* 2d ed. New York: Barnes and Noble, 1970.

Freccero, John. "Dante's Firm Foot and the Journey Without a Guide." *The Harvard Theological Review* 52 (1959): 245–81.

―――. "Dante's Pilgrim in a Gyre." *PMLA* 76, no. 3 (June 1961): 168–81.

Friedman, Melvin J. "Introduction." *Samuel Beckett Now,* ed. Melvin J. Friedman. Chicago: University of Chicago Press, 1970; 2d ed., 1975.

Frye, Northrop. *Anatomy of Criticism: Four Essays.* Princeton, N.J.: Princeton University Press, 1957.

―――. "The Top of the Tower." *William Butler Yeats,* ed. Patrick J. Keane. New York: McGraw-Hill, 1973.

Girard, René. *Deceit, Desire, and the Novel: Self and Other in Literary Structure.* 1961. Trans. Yvonne Freccero. Baltimore: Johns Hopkins University Press, 1965.

Gluck, Barbara Reich. *Beckett and Joyce: Friendship and Fiction.* Lewisburg, Pa.: Bucknell University Press, 1979.

Godwin, William. *Caleb Williams.* New York: W. W. Norton, 1977.

Goethe, Johann Wolfgang von. *Elective Affinities.* Trans. Elizabeth Mayer and Louise Bogan. South Bend, Ind.: Gateway Editions, 1963.

Gontarski, S. E. "Crapp's First Tape: Beckett's Manuscript Revisions of *Krapp's Last Tape.*" *Journal of Modern Literature* 6, no. 1 (February 1977): 61–68.

―――. *The Intent of Undoing in Samuel Beckett's Dramatic Texts.* Bloomington: Indiana University Press, 1985.

―――. "Molloy and the Reiterated Novel." *As No Other Dare Fail,* ed. John Calder, 57–65. London: Riverrun Press, 1986.

———. "Samuel Beckett and Intrinsic Form." *Perspectives on Contemporary Literature* 5 (1979): 3–9.

———. "Samuel Beckett, James Joyce's 'Illstarred Punster.'" *The Seventh of Joyce*, ed. Bernard Benstock, 29–36. Bloomington: Indiana University Press, 1982.

Guggenheim, Peggy. *Confessions of an Art Addict.* London: André Deutsch, 1960.

Guicharnaud, Jacques. *Modern French Theatre from Giraudoux to Genet.* New Haven, Conn.: Yale University Press, 1967.

Hahm, David E. *The Origins of Stoic Cosmology.* Columbus: Ohio State University Press, 1977.

Harrington, John P. *The Irish Beckett.* Syracuse: Syracuse University Press, 1991.

Harvey, Lawrence E. "A Poet's Initiation." *Samuel Beckett Now*, ed. Melvin J. Friedman. Chicago: University of Chicago Press, 1975.

———. *Samuel Beckett: Poet and Critic.* Princeton, N.J.: Princeton University Press, 1970.

Hayman, David. "*Molloy* or the Quest for Meaninglessness: A Global Interpretation." *Samuel Beckett Now*, ed. M. J. Friedman. Chicago: University of Chicago Press, 1975.

———. "Some Writers in the Wake of the *Wake*." *In the Wake of the "Wake,"* 3–38. Madison: University of Wisconsin Press, 1978.

Heath, Stephen. "Ambiviolences: Notes for Reading Joyce." *Post-Structuralist Joyce*, ed. Derek Attridge and Daniel Ferrer, 31–68. Cambridge: Cambridge University Press, 1984.

Hegel, G.W.F. *The Phenomenology of Mind.* Trans. J. B. Baillie. New York: Harper & Row, 1967.

Heidegger, Martin. *On the Way to Language.* 1959. Trans. Peter D. Hertz. New York: Harper & Row, 1982.

Henning, Sylvie Debevec. *Beckett's Critical Complicity: Carnival, Contestation, and Tradition.* Lexington: University Press of Kentucky, 1988.

———. "The Guffaw of the Abderite: *Murphy* and the Democritan Universe." *Journal of Beckett Studies*, no. 10 (Spring 1985): 5–20.

Hesla, David H. *The Shape of Chaos: An Interpretation of the Art of Samuel Beckett.* Minneapolis: University of Minnesota Press, 1971.

Hewitt, Nicholas. *The Golden Age of Louis-Ferdinand Céline.* Lemington Spa, Eng.: Berg Publishers, 1987.

Hobson, Harold. "Samuel Beckett, Dramatist of the Year." *International Theatre Annual*, no. 1, 153–55. London: John Calder, 1956.

Hoffman, Frederick J. *Samuel Beckett: The Language of Self.* Carbondale: Southern Illinois University Press, 1962.

Hollander, John. *The Untuning of the Sky: Ideas of Music in English Poetry, 1500–1700.* New York: W. W. Norton, 1970.

Hughes, Peter. "From Allusion to Implosion. Vico. Michelet. Joyce, Beckett." *Vico and Joyce*, ed. Donald Phillip Verene, 83–99. Albany: State University of New York Press, 1987.

Hull, Eleanor. *A Textbook of Irish Literature*, part 1. Dublin: M. H. Gill & Son, 1910.

Huysmans, Joris-Karl. *Against Nature.* Trans. Robert Baldick. New York: Penguin, 1959.

Jenkins, Alan. "A Lifelong Fidelity to Failure." *Times Literary Supplement*, 14 November 1986, 1281.

Jolas, Eugene, ed. *transition workshop.* New York: Vanguard Press, 1949.

Jones, Anthony. "The French Murphy: From 'Rare Bird' to '*cancre*.'" *Journal of Beckett Studies*, no. 6 (Autumn 1980).

Joyce, James. *Dubliners. The Portable James Joyce.* New York: Viking, 1947.
———. *Finnegans Wake,* New York: Penguin, 1976.
———. *Letters.* Vol. 1. Ed. Stuart Gilbert. New York: Viking, 1957.
———. *A Portrait of the Artist as a Young Man.* New York: Penguin, 1964.
———. *Ulysses.* New York: Random House, 1961.
Juliet, Charles, and Jacques Putman. *Bram van Velde.* Paris: Maeght, 1975.
Jung, C. G. *Analytical Psychology, Its Theory and Practice.* New York: Pantheon, 1968.
———. *Dreams.* Trans. R.F.C. Hull. Bollingen Series. Princeton, N.J.: Princeton University Press, 1974.
Kafka, Franz. *The Complete Stories.* Ed. Nahum N. Glatzer. New York: Schocken, 1971.
Kandinsky, Wassily. *Concerning the Spiritual in Art.* Trans. M.T.H. Sadler. New York: Dover Publications, 1977.
Kaufmann, Walter. *Existentialism from Dostoevsky to Sartre.* Cleveland: World Publishing Co., 1956.
Keane, Patrick J. *Yeats's Interactions with Tradition.* Columbia: University of Missouri Press, 1987.
Kennedy, Sighle. *Murphy's Bed: A Study of Real Sources and Sur-real Associations in Samuel Beckett's First Novel.* Lewisburg, Pa.: Bucknell University Press, 1971.
Kenner, Hugh. *Samuel Beckett: A Critical Study.* Berkeley and Los Angeles: University of California Press, 1968.
———. *The Stoic Comedians.* Berkeley and Los Angeles: University of California Press, 1962.
Kern, Edith. *Existential Thought and Fictional Technique: Kierkegaard, Sartre, Beckett.* New Haven, Conn.: Yale University Press, 1970.
———. "Structure in Beckett's Theatre." *Yale French Studies* 46 (1971): 17–27.
Kirkpatrick, Diane. "Generative Systems in Visual Art." *Generative Literature and Generative Art,* ed. David Leach, 17–24. Fredericton, N.B., Canada: York Press, 1983.
Klingner, Friedrich. *De Boethii Consolatione Philosophiae.* 2d ed. Zurich: Weidmann, 1966.
Knowlson, James, and John Pilling. *Frescoes of the Skull: The Later Prose and Drama of Samuel Beckett.* New York: Grove, 1980.
Kristeva, Julia. *Desire in Language: A Semiotic Approach to Literature and Art.* 1977. Trans. Thomas Gora, Alice Jardine, and Leon S. Roudiez. Ed. Roudiez. New York: Columbia University Press, 1980.
Kroll, Jeri L. "Belacqua as Artist and Lover: 'What a Misfortune.'" *Journal of Beckett Studies,* no. 2 (Summer 1977).
Lake, Carlton, ed. *No Symbols Where None Intended: A Catalogue of Books, Manuscripts, and Other Material Relating to Samuel Beckett in the Collections of the Humanities Research Center.* Austin, Tex.: Humanities Research Center, University of Texas, 1984.
Langbaum, Robert. *The Mysteries of Identity: A Theme in Modern Literature.* 1977. Chicago: University of Chicago Press, 1982.
———. *The Poetry of Experience: The Dramatic Monologue in Modern Literary Tradition.* 1957. New York: W. W. Norton, 1971.
Langer, Susanne. *Feeling and Form: A Theory of Art.* New York: Charles Scribner's Sons, 1953.
Leach, David. "Parallel Methods in Writing and Visual Arts." *Generative Literature*

and Generative Art, ed. David Leach, 11–16. Fredericton, N.B., Canada: York Press, 1983.

Leighton, Angela. "Lost Leader and Witty Prophet." *Times Literary Supplement*, 16 September 1988, 1025.

Lewis, Wyndham. *Snooty Baronet*. 1932. Ed. Bernard Lafourcade. New York: Black Sparrow, 1984.

Lloyd, A. C. *The Anatomy of Neoplatonism*. Oxford: Clarendon Press, 1990.

Lodge, David. "Some Ping Understood." *Encounter* 30 (February 1968): 85–89.

Louzoun, Myriam. "Fin de partie de Samuel Beckett: Effacement du monde et dynamisme formel." *Les Voies de la création théatrale*, ed. Bablet, Denis, and Jean Jacquot, vol. 5, 377–445. Paris: Centre National de la Recherche Scientifique, 1977.

Lovejoy, Arthur Oncken. "The Dialectic of Bruno and Spinoza." *Philosophy*, vol. 1, 141–74. Berkeley and Los Angeles: University of California Press, 1904.

Mahaffey, Vicki. *Reauthorizing Joyce*. Cambridge: Cambridge University Press, 1988.

Mallarmé, Stéphane. *Selected Poetry and Prose*. Ed. Mary Ann Caws. New York: New Directions, 1982.

McCarthy, Patrick A., ed. *Critical Essays on Samuel Beckett*. Boston: G. K. Hall, 1986.

McHale, Brian. *Postmodernist Fiction*. New York: Methuen, 1987.

McHugh, Roland. *Annotations to Finnegans Wake*. Baltimore: Johns Hopkins University Press, 1980.

Mercier, Vivian. *Beckett/Beckett*. New York: Oxford University Press, 1971.

Miller, J. Hillis. *The Linguistic Moment*. Princeton, N.J.: Princeton University Press, 1985.

Milton, John. *Paradise Lost*. Ed. Alastair Fowler. New York: Longman, 1971.

Mitchell, W.J.T. *Blake's Composite Art*. Princeton, N.J.: Princeton University Press, 1978.

———. *Iconology: Image, Text, Ideology*. Chicago: University of Chicago Press, 1986.

———. "Spatial Form in Literature: Toward a General Theory." *Critical Inquiry* 6, no. 3 (Spring 1980): 539–67.

Morrison, Kristin. *Canters and Chronicles: The Use of Narrative in the Plays of Samuel Beckett and Harold Pinter*. Chicago: University of Chicago Press, 1983.

Morrissette, Bruce. "Generative Techniques in Robbe-Grillet and Ricardon." *Generative Literature and Generative Art*, ed. David Leach, 25–34. Fredericton, N.B., Canada: York Press, 1983.

Murrin, Michael. *The Allegorical Epic: Essays in Its Rise and Decline*. Chicago: University of Chicago Press, 1980.

Neumann, Erich. *The Great Mother: An Analysis of the Archetype*. Trans. Ralph Manheim. New York: Bollingen Edition, Pantheon, 1955.

Nietzsche, Friedrich. *The Birth of Tragedy*. Trans. Francis Golffing. Garden City, N.Y.: Doubleday, 1956.

Nohrnberg, James. *The Analogy of the Faerie Queene*. Princeton, N.J.: Princeton University Press, 1976.

———. "The Inferno." *Homer to Brecht*, ed. Michael Seidel and Edward Mendelson. New Haven, Conn.: Yale University Press, 1977.

O'Brien, Eoin. *The Beckett Country: Samuel Beckett's Ireland*. Dublin: Black Cat Press, 1986.

O'Brien, Flann. *The Third Policeman*. New York: New American Library, 1967.

O'Hara, J. D. "Jung and the Narratives of 'Molloy.'" *Journal of Beckett Studies*, no. 7 (Spring 1982).

Ortega y Gasset, José. "The Dehumanization of Art." *Literary Modernism*, ed. Irving Howe, 83–96. New York: Fawcett Publications, 1967.

Ovid. *Metamorphoses*. Trans. Mary M. Innes. New York: Penguin, 1955.

Pascal, Blaise. *Pensées*. Trans. A. J. Krailsheimer. New York: Penguin, 1966.

Pearce, Richard. "From Joyce to Beckett: The Tale That Wags the Telling." *The Seventh of Joyce*, ed. Bernard Benstock, 44–49. Bloomington: Indiana University Press, 1982.

Peter, John. *Vladimir's Carrot: Modern Drama and the Modern Imagination*. Chicago: University of Chicago Press, 1987.

Picon, Gaëtan. "Sur Bram van Velde." *Bram van Velde*, 7–14. Paris: Archives de l'art contemporain 12, 1970.

Pilling, John. "Beckett's 'Proust.'" *Journal of Beckett Studies* (Winter 1976).

―――. *Samuel Beckett*. London: Routledge and Kegan Paul, 1976.

Plato. *The Dialogues of Plato*. 2 vols. Trans. B. Jowett. New York: Random House, 1892; repr., 1937.

Plotinus. [Plotinos.] *Complete Works*. Ed. and trans. Kenneth Sylvan Guthrie. London: George Bell and Sons, 1918.

―――. *Select Works of Plotinus*. Trans. Thomas Taylor. London: George Bell and Sons, 1909.

Poulet, Georges. "The Metamorphoses of the Circle." *Twentieth-Century Views of Dante*, ed. John Freccero, 151–69. Englewood Cliffs, N.J.: Prentice-Hall, 1965.

Proust, Marcel. *A la recherche du temps perdu*. [See under Works by Samuel Beckett, "Related Materials."]

Putman, Jacques. "Bram van Velde." *L'Oeil*, no. 65 (May 1960): 44–49.

―――. *Catalogue raisonné de l'oeuvre du peintre*. Turin: Edizioni d'Arte Fratelli Pozzo, 1961.

―――. "Introduction." *Bram van Velde*. Edizioni d'Arte. Turin: Fratelli, n.d.

Pynchon, Thomas. *Gravity's Rainbow*. New York: Viking, 1973.

Rabinovitz, Rubin. *The Development of Samuel Beckett's Fiction*. Champaign: University of Illinois Press, 1984.

Read, David. "Artistic Theory in the Work of Samuel Beckett." *Journal of Beckett Studies*, no. 8 (Autumn 1982).

Reiss, Timothy J. *The Uncertainty of Analysis: Problems in Truth, Meaning, and Culture*. Ithaca, N.Y.: Cornell University Press, 1988.

Richardson, Samuel. *Clarissa, or the History of a Young Lady*. 1748. Ed. John Angus Barrell. New York: Modern Library, 1950.

Ricoeur, Paul. *The Rule of Metaphor*. Toronto: University of Toronto Press, 1977.

Rimbaud, Jean-Nicholas-Arthur. *Complete Works, Selected Letters*. Trans. Wallace Fowlie. Chicago: University of Chicago Press, 1966.

Robbe-Grillet, Alain. "Samuel Beckett, or 'Presence' in the Theatre." *For a New Novel: Essays on Fiction*, trans. Richard Howard. New York: Grove, 1965.

Robinson, Michael. *The Long Sonata of the Dead: A Study of Samuel Beckett*. New York: Grove, 1969.

Rorty, Richard. *Philosophy and the Mirror of Nature*. Princeton, N.J.: Princeton University Press, 1979.

Rose, Marilyn Gaddis. "The Irish Memories of Beckett's Voice." *Journal of Modern Literature* 2, no. 1 (September 1971): 127–32.

————. "The Lyrical Structure of Beckett's *Texts for Nothing.*" *Novel* 4, no. 3 (Spring 1971): 223–30.

Rosen, Steven J. *Samuel Beckett and the Pessimistic Tradition.* New Brunswick, N.J.: Rutgers University Press, 1976.

Rothenberg, John. "A Form of Tension in Beckett's Fiction." *Degré Second: Studies in French Literature* 6 (July 1982): 157–76.

Rousseau, Jean-Jacques. *The Confessions.* Trans. J. M. Cohen. New York: Penguin, 1953.

Rushdie, Salman. *Grimus.* 1975. New York: Penguin, 1991.

Sambursky, Shmuel. *The Concept of Place in Late Neoplatonism.* Jerusalem: Israel Academy of Sciences and Humanities, 1982.

Sartre, Jean-Paul. *Saint Genet: Actor and Martyr.* 1952. Trans. Bernard Frechtman. New York: Pantheon Books, 1963.

Schneider, Alan. "On Directing *Film.*" *Film,* by Samuel Beckett. New York: Grove, 1969.

Schneider, Pierre. *L'Express,* 25 November 1968.

Scholes, Robert, and Robert Kellogg. *The Nature of Narrative.* New York: Oxford University Press, 1966.

Schurman, Susan. *The Solipsistic Novels of Samuel Beckett.* Cologne: Pahl-Rugenstein, 1987.

Seidel, Michael. *Epic Geography: James Joyce's "Ulysses."* Princeton, N.J.: Princeton University Press, 1976.

Sen, Supti. *Samuel Beckett: His Mind and Art.* Calcutta: Firma K. L. Mukhopadhyay, 1970.

Shakespeare, William. *The Complete Works.* Ed. John Dover Wilson. Cambridge: Cambridge University Press, 1921.

Shenker, Israel. "Moody Man of Letters." *New York Times,* 6 May 1956, sec. 2, pp. x, 1, 3.

Shipley, Joseph T. *Dictionary of Word Origins.* New York: Philosophical Library, 1945.

Silvestris, Bernardus. *Commentum super sex libros Aenidos Vergilii.* Lincoln: University of Nebraska Press, 1977.

Sinnige, Th. G. "Gnostic Influences in the Early Works of Plotinus and in Augustine." *Plotinus amid Gnostics and Christians,* ed. D. T. Runia, 73–97. Amsterdam: Free University Press, 1984.

Skeat, Walter W. *A Concise Etymological Dictionary of the English Language.* 1882. New York: Perigee Books, 1980.

Sorabji, Richard. *Matter, Space, and Motion: Theories in Antiquity and Their Sequel.* Ithaca, N.Y.: Cornell University Press, 1988.

States, Bert O. *The Shape of Paradox: An Essay on "Waiting for Godot."* Berkeley and Los Angeles: University of California Press, 1978.

Stempel, Daniel. "History Electrified into Anagogy: A Reading of *Waiting for Godot.*" *Contemporary Literature* 17, no. 2 (Spring 1976): 263–78.

Stevens, Wallace. *The Collected Poems of Wallace Stevens.* New York: Vintage, 1982.

Swift, Jonathan. *Gulliver's Travels.* 1726. New York: Penguin, 1982.

Tanner, Michael. "Organizing the Self and the World." *Times Literary Supplement,* 16 May 1986, 520.

Thackeray, W. M. *Vanity Fair.* New York: Airmont Publishing Co., 1962.

Thompson, David. "Dante and Bernard Silvestris." *Viatorl* (1970): 201–8.

Tindall, William York. *The Joyce Country.* 1960. New York: Schocken, 1972.

Trezise, Thomas. *Into the Breach: Samuel Beckett and the Ends of Literature*. Princeton, N.J.: Princeton University Press, 1990.

Unamuno, Miguel de. *Ficciones: Four Stories and a Play*. Trans. Anthony Kerrigan. Princeton, N.J.: Princeton University Press, 1976.

Unseld, Siegfried. "To the Utmost." *As No Other Dare Fail*, 91–95. London: Riverrun Press, 1986.

Vickers, Brian, ed. *Occult and Scientific Mentalities in the Renaissance*. Cambridge: Cambridge University Press, 1984.

Vico, Giambattista. *The Autobiography of Giambattista Vico*. Trans. and ed. Max Harold Fisch and Thomas Goddard Bergin. Ithaca, N.Y.: Cornell University Press, 1944.

Weiskel, Thomas. *The Romantic Sublime*. Baltimore: Johns Hopkins University Press, 1986.

Westman, Robert S. "Nature, Art, and Psyche: Jung, Pauli, and the Kepler–Fludd Polemic." *Occult and Scientific Mentalities in the Renaissance*, ed. Brian Vickers, 177–229. Cambridge: Cambridge University Press, 1984.

Wetherbee, Winthrop, ed. *Platonism and Poetry in the Twelfth Century: The Literary Influence of the School of Chartres*. Princeton, N.J.: Princeton University Press, 1972.

Whittaker, Thomas. *The Neo-Platonists: A Study in the History of Hellenism*. 2d ed. Cambridge: Cambridge University Press, 1918.

Williams, Raymond. *Drama from Ibsen to Brecht*. New York: Penguin, 1968.

Wittgenstein, Ludwig. *The Blue and Brown Books: Preliminary Studies for the "Philosophical Investigations."* New York: Harper & Row, 1965.

———. *Philosophical Investigations*. 3d ed. Trans. G.E.M. Anscombe. New York: Macmillan Co., 1958.

———. *Tractatus Logo-Philosophicus*. Trans. C. K. Ogden. 1922. Rev. ed., 1955. Reprint. London: Routledge and Kegan Paul, 1986.

Wolosky, Shira. "The Negative Way Negated: Samuel Beckett's *Texts for Nothing*." *New Literary History* 22, no. 1 (Winter 1991), 213–30.

Worth, Katharine, ed. *Beckett the Shape Changer: A Symposium*. London: Routledge, 1975.

Yates, Frances A. *Giordano Bruno and the Hermetic Tradition*. Chicago: University of Chicago Press, 1964.

Yeats, William Butler. *Essays and Introductions*. New York: Collier, 1968.

———. *Explorations*. New York: Collier, 1962.

———. *The Letters of W. B. Yeats*. New York: Macmillan Co., 1955.

———. *The Poems*. Ed. Richard J. Finneran. New York: Macmillan, 1983.

———. *A Vision*. New York: Collier, 1966.

Zurbrugg, Nicholas. *Beckett and Proust*. Gerrards Cross, Buckinghamshire: Colin Smythe, 1988.

———. "*Ill Seen Ill Said* and the Sense of an Ending." *Beckett's Later Fiction and Drama: Texts for Company*, ed. James Acheson and Kateryna Arthur, 145–59. New York: St. Martin's Press, 1987.

Index

Beckett, Samuel, et al., *Our Exagmination round his Factification for Incamination of Work in Progress*, 194, 195 n. 9, 198, 207

being, absence and, 7; body and, 183–84; difference and, 34, 39, 44, 61, 84, 90, 128–29; double, 128–29; formless, 159; "Non-Newtonian," 92; is one, 156; perception and, 70, 79, 89, 161, 171, 185; perpetual, 139–40; serial, 149–50, 155–56; triple, 152

Bercovitch, Sacvan, 77 n. 20

Berkeley, George, 66 n. 3, 70, 125

Bishop, John, 142 n. 29

Blake, William, 9, 61, 123, 127, 136, 192 n. 4; *Jerusalem*, 21, 134 n. 17

Bloom, Harold, 8 n. 4, 9, 132 n. 14

Boethius, Anicius Manlius Severinus, 50, 123, 152–53 n. 36, 167, 191 n. 3; *The Consolation of Philosophy*, 153 n. 36; and Neoplatonism, 192

Bonheim, Helmut, 199

Booth, Wayne C., 7–8

boundary, 47, 93, 96, 174–75, 183, 210

Brater, Enoch, 15, 138 n. 23, 183 n. 20

Breuer, Horst, 182 n. 19

Brienza, Susan D., 177 n. 17